Coming Out of War

Coming Out of War

Poetry, Grieving, and the Culture of the World Wars

Janis P. Stout

THE UNIVERSITY OF ALABAMA PRESS

Tuscaloosa

Typeface: Minion

∞

The paper on which this book is printed meets the minimum requirements of American
National Standard for Information Sciences—Permanence of Paper for Printed Library
Materials, ANSI Z39.48-1984.

Library of Congress Cataloging-in-Publication Data

Stout, Janis P.
Coming out of war : poetry, grieving, and the culture of the world wars / Janis P. Stout.
p. cm.
Includes bibliographical references (p.) and index.
ISBN 0-8173-1472-5 (alk. paper)
1. English poetry—20th century—History and criticism. 2. World War, 1914–1918—English-
speaking countries—Literature and the war. 3. World War, 1939–1945—English-speaking
countries—Literature and the war. 4. Music—Great Britain—20th century—History and
criticism. 5. Music—United States—20th century—History and criticism. 6. American
poetry—20th century—History and criticism. 7. War poetry, American—History and
criticism. 8. War poetry, English—History and criticism. 9. World War, 1914–1918—Music
and the war. 10. World War, 1939–1945—Music and the war. 11. Loss (Psychology) in
literature. 12. Grief in literature. I. Title.
PR605.W65S76 2005
821′.9109358—dc22

2004030748

to my grandchildren, and to everyone's grandchildren,
in the hope that they will live in a better world

It is possible for people to come out of war and learn peace.
—Maxine Hong Kingston, NPR interview, September 24, 2003

I am waiting for the Grapes of Wrath to be stored.
—Lawrence Ferlinghetti, "I Am Waiting"

Contents

Illustrations

Preface

If World War II is widely conceived by Americans as "the good war," World War I has been known by the more elevated but less benign designation it was given before world wars had to be given numbers, "the Great War." Together, these two linked calamities—along with various comparatively lesser wars that were waged almost continuously between them as well as afterward—defined the twentieth century as a century of war. Together, the two world wars spawned an enormous and persisting culture of grief, as grieving for the dead and maimed permeated the lives of thousands, even millions of people in Europe, the United States, and Asia. That grieving has been expressed in both popular and high-art cultural products: paintings, popular songs, art music, monuments and cemeteries, literature.

Many of these expressions of grief have also been arguments for an end to the fighting, whether an end to a specific war or an end to war, period. Somewhat paradoxically, then, if the twentieth century was a century of war, it was also—to a lesser degree, to be sure—a century of opposition to war. Often that opposition was driven by the determination of artists and writers to convey a clearer understanding of the appalling nature of modern warfare than is communicated in official and officially sanctioned rhetoric. The persistence of this cultural work of grieving and crying out against war has been the impetus of this book.

David Cannadine, in his article "Death and Grief in Modern Britain," writes that in England after World War I "the abiding sense of loss throughout the land was as real as it was unassuageable"; the war left a "shocking legacy of grief and bereavement of unprecedented ubiquity" (201, 231). In America as in Britain, a profusion of monuments and observances—the Cenotaph unveiled in London on Armistice Day 1920, national monuments to the unknown dead in both nations, American cemeteries for the war dead in Europe, the wearing of poppies, all these and more—testified to the profound grieving that settled over survivors and to the sense that a collective ordeal of enormous magnitude had been endured.[1] In England, this culture of grieving peaked during the interwar years; even with sixty thousand civilians killed in air raids, British war losses in World War II were far less than in World War I (Cannadine 233).[2] In the United States, the extent of the grieving was greatly magnified by the nation's involvement and consequent losses in the Second World War, which greatly exceeded those of the First—one reason why the preponderance of the poetry considered here shifts from British to American as we move chronologically from the First to the Second World War.

In retrospect, the world wars have frequently come to be regarded as having been more like "different episodes of the same conflict" than two separate wars (Cannadine 233). Philip Beidler observes that the "one-war view of nearly a century of mass geopolitical conflict" is "now accepted sufficiently to have become a historians' commonplace" (173). The continuity between the two wars is demonstrated, as Cannadine points out, by the fact that in England public opinion did not favor construction of new war monuments on any grand scale. The dates 1939–1945 were added to 1914–1918 on the Cenotaph, and at most local memorials the names of World War II dead were "merely tagged on" to the earlier list. Even so, the Great War retains its particular hold on the attention of historians and literary scholars, as well as many general readers, as probably the single most significant shaping event of the twentieth century. It was a break point in time. Edmond Taylor, in his now forty-year-old history of the changes in ruling power structures that occurred in the course of the war and its immediate aftermath, *The Fall of the Dynasties,* states magisterially, "Looking back from the vantage point of the present we see clearly today that the outbreak of World War I ushered in a twentieth-century 'Time of Troubles' . . . from which our civilization has by no means yet emerged" (16). That was in 1963. In the early years of the twenty-first century we still have not emerged. The very land itself over which those vast, doomed armies struggled on the Western Front—only one of the great fronts of the war, but the usual focus of discussion among British and American writers—still bears its scars and yields up shells from bombardments that took place more than eighty years ago. Nation-states that were rearranged, combined, or split apart by the Treaty of Versailles still puzzle over—and contest—their boundaries.

In retrospect, it seems inevitable that the arbitrariness and vindictive spirit that characterized the Versailles peace (referred to in John Dos Passos's novel *1919* as the fake peace) would have led to renewed war. Robert McNamara, secretary of defense under Presidents Kennedy and Johnson, who led in the expansion of the Vietnam conflict but later came to regret his role, writes succinctly that "the Allies at Versailles helped sow the seeds of their own devastation at Germany's hands in the Second World War" (*Wilson's Ghost* 62). The so-called interwar years of 1919 to 1939 were not truly years between wars, either in Europe or in Asia. The eruption of World War II, when Hitler's armies invaded Poland on September 1, 1939, and England and France two days later declared war, was not so much a new beginning as the culminating explosion in a series of linked repercussions of the earlier one. What began with World War I flowed through the Spanish Civil War and the Japanese invasion of China into World War II and on through Korea and Vietnam, the Gulf War and Kosovo, and now into Afghanistan, Iraq, and whatever comes next. It was not solely the Versailles Peace Treaty, of course, that so thoroughly dismantled the twentieth-century world and shaped the future. The Great War itself—in the bitterness of its hatreds, the newness of its weaponry, and the way technology so utterly outran both the military and the civil, humane thinking needed for its control and direction—set off shock waves throughout European civilization and beyond. In much the same way, casualties of previously unimaginable dimensions sent shock waves of grieving and dislocation through families and ultimately the full range of social institutions and structures.

In a book that challenges virtually all received understandings of World War I, *The Pity of War*, Niall Ferguson deplores the fact that "it is not from historians that the majority of modern readers gain their impressions of the First World War" but from literature (xxxi). While agreeing with Ferguson's call to inform our collective memory through searching historical study, I would argue that literature and other cultural products offer an indispensable means of gaining impressions of war, especially if we make a distinction between impressions and knowledge. They also, I would insist, contribute to knowledge; a secondary reason for reading literature of war—or for listening to the music of war or for looking at paintings of war—may indeed be to gain information. Historian Roger Beaumont points to knowledge of a particular kind when he states that "writers of fiction and artists have seemed more effective in capturing the randomness and chaos of war than historians, social scientists, and military memoirists" (29).[3]

But the primary reasons we turn to this literature have to do with values intrinsic to art as a form of meaning-making and meaning-expression. Not only are such cultural products ends in themselves, they are also means to the end of gaining insight into how the war was experienced and perceived by specific human beings. By examining a number of such expressions, we may begin to understand the cultural response more generally and begin to see the patterns of a history of cultural response and meaning-making. Our experiencing of such texts and works of art may also help us formulate our own feelings about these complex and painful episodes. It is interesting that while fretting about readers' inclination toward literary versions of the war rather than historians' versions, Ferguson nevertheless takes as his title an echo of a poet's words. It was Wilfred Owen, often regarded as the major poet of the Great War, who famously declared that the purpose of his writing was to communicate the pity of war.

The two world wars yielded a spate of such cultural products: novels, memoirs, films, and compelling works of visual and plastic art and of music, as well as poetry. My subject here is the cultural response to the two world wars primarily as expressed in British and American poetry. I am interested in the scope of that response, its persistence, its varied nature, and ultimately its significance for the future. Although I also, at some points, give attention to music and visual art of the world wars, it is the poetry that is of greatest interest here because it is poetry, I believe, that has most fully caught and expressed the emotional and moral intensity of the cultural response.

The poetry of the two world wars—if we include in that body, as I believe we must, poetry addressing the full range of the wars' experiences and concerns, not combat alone—is of enormous abundance and richness. My purpose here, in part, is to establish this abundance and rich array of concerns, ethical intentions, styles, and rhetorical modes more fully than they have yet been conveyed in existing critical discussions. Most of the poetry I discuss—indeed, most of the poetry that emerged from the two world wars—is antimilitary in impulse. And most of *that* reflects an antiwar impetus. The two are not necessarily the same. "Antimilitary" indicates a dislike of the culture of military organizations. "Antiwar"—a term that often taxes our definitional abilities, with its variance from narrow to general meaning—designates a powerful distaste for and opposition to either a specific war or more sweepingly, war in general. Being antiwar does not necessarily mean being pacifist, any more than opponents of, say, the 2003 war in Iraq are necessarily pacifists. Indeed, genuine pacifism is a conviction held by very few. The three terms—antimilitary, antiwar, and pacifist—form a rough continuum, with pacifist texts (or persons) at a far extreme. Texts or persons expressing zest for war's supposed heroic values lie beyond this continuum, at the far opposite from pacifism. They are, so to speak, off the scale. We rarely find such celebrations of heroism in war in twentieth-century poetry.

At times the chapters that follow summarize, complement, or extend existing understandings of this enormous body of literature and the larger culture of grieving for the wars. At other points, however, I argue that existing understandings have been inadequate or distorted. In particular, I debate the notion that the term "war poetry" applies only to verse reflecting battlefield experience and its corollary notion that war poetry is written only by men. Such narrow views have often been challenged, yet incredibly enough, still seem to persist. As recently as 2003, Lorrie Goldensohn's otherwise admirable study *Dismantling Glory* identified war poetry almost totally with soldier poetry. Excluding a "poetry of meditation" from the genre she recognized as war poetry because of its "lyric altitude" above the dailiness and specificity of combat experience (97), Goldensohn reinscribed the validation of direct experience that has traditionally excluded women's voices from the canon of war writing. I also challenge the perhaps equally egregious misconception that while World War I was a literary war and produced a great volume of fine poetry, World War II did not. The noted historian Frank Vandi-ver has written that poetry of World War I is "one of the great strains in the war's literary legacy" (Hannah xvi). I would say that poetry has also been one of the great strains in the literary legacy of the Second World War, despite the increased prominence of novels and film.

Just as the two catastrophes commonly designated World War I and World War II are not separable but locked together in a complex pattern of reaction and reprisal, so also the poetry of the two wars merged and spread, sweeping up texts of foreboding and of reflection produced be-tween and long after the years of the conflicts themselves. We might well ask, what *is* the literature "of" this or that war, anyway? Does the phrase refer only to what is produced during the war? or include also the texts about it? the texts reflecting it in more indirect ways—say, by pon-dering the morality or the personal and social costs of a war, as well as describing the experience itself? Is a poem written in 1950 that talks about, say, Bataan, a World War II poem or a Korean War poem? My answer is, all of the above. The scope of this book, then, takes in British and American poetry written about war or reflecting, in imagery and themes, the concerns existing during the years that define World War I and World War II, but also texts that look back on one or both or, during the 1930s, anticipate, with foreboding, the renewal of war.

In limiting myself almost exclusively to American and British poetry, I am by no means denying the richness of German, French, Italian, Rus-sian, and other verse that emerged from the two world wars. One must affix limits, however, or the book becomes a library and never gets writ-ten. Moreover, I have long felt reluctant to write about any text that I could not, with confidence, read in its original language, along with critical commentary. Sadly, that limits me to English. I can only hope that comparatist scholars will continue to demonstrate the commonali-ties, connections, and distinctions that exist among the various lan-guages' bodies of twentieth-century war poetry and that they may find this present effort useful as they do so.

Despite my recognition of the need for limits, I do occasionally move beyond poetry to visual and musical arts. Primarily this is for compara-tive purposes but also because all art forms *together*—sometimes liter-ally together, as in musical settings of poems—constitute the abundant, complex, and intensely emotional cultural response to war. It is not only the nature of that response but also the devastating fact of its failure to move beyond emotion to preventive social action that engages me here.

The scholarship relating to war literature in the twentieth century is extraordinarily rich. I am building here on predecessors such as Jeffrey Walsh's *American War Literature* (1982), Eric J. Leed's *No Man's Land* (1979), and Paul Fussell's literary/historical studies of the world wars. These latter, especially his well-known *Great War and Modern Memory* (1975), are standards in the field. Though I often differ with Fussell, as well as others, I recognize that I might never have begun this work if his prior studies had not compelled my interest and stimulated my thinking.

Because of this abundance of attention to twentieth-century war writing, scholars sometimes regard the field as being saturated. Cannadine, for example, in his 1981 analysis of grief and mourning in modern Britain and their connection with war, asserted that the poetry of the First World War had by then been "so thoroughly analyzed" that it needed no further comment (202). But the three books Cannadine cited as evidence for his claim illustrate why I reject it. Jon Silkin's otherwise valuable 1981 anthology includes only three poems by women, only one American, none British. Hilda D. Spear's 1979 study *Remembering We Forget* also adopts so narrow a definition of the subject that it ignores the existence of women poets of the war. The third of the three books offered by Cannadine as evidence that Great War poetry had already been sufficiently analyzed, J. H. Johnston's 1964 *English Poetry of the First World War,* not only restricts itself to "soldier poets," ignoring poetry by women and other noncombatants, but does so as a story of failure. While conceding that the war poets (again, all of them male) achieved "a directness almost unprecedented in verse" (13), he finds them deficient in that they failed to escape the limitations both of realism and of the lyric form so as to achieve the distance and balance of epic. The "generally negative character" of their verse, Johnston complains, "contrasts directly with the positive, affirmative character of epic battle literature, with its proud sense of past glories and its total commitment to the imperatives of heroic action" (11). But of course that was the point. Blind to the antiwar purpose of most of the World War I poets, Johnston regards as failure what I celebrate as success.

In recent years there have been a number of excellent studies of specific topics within the wide field of war writing. These include such books as Nosheen Khan's *Women's Poetry of the First World War* (1988), Claire M. Tylee's *The Great War and Women's Consciousness* (1990), Susan Schweik's *A Gulf So Deeply Cut* (1991), Philip K. Jason's *Fourteen Landing Zones* (1991), Margaret Higonnet's volumes on women writers of the Great War, and Steven Trout's *Memorial Fictions* (2002). While I differ with Tylee, Khan, and Higonnet, for example, at specific points, I recognize the value of their work and the extent to which I rely on it. Such focused studies—and the list could be greatly extended—forgo developing an overview of the field in favor of examining intensively a small number of selected texts or arguing a pointed thesis. The depth that such a method affords is obvious and of great importance as scholars, collectively, seek to develop a body of criticism that enhances our understanding of such complex and culturally important texts. But focus comes with a price. Even Margot Norris's important *Writing War in the Twentieth Century* (2000), which ranges from the trenches of the Western Front to the disputed body counts of the Gulf War, proceeds primarily through the method of intensive examination of a small number of specific landmark texts. One gets little sense of the large outlines of the writing of war in the twentieth century.

Excellent work has also been done on the products of popular culture, especially popular music and movies of the World War II era—for example, Philip Beidler's *The Good War's Greatest Hits* (1998), Frank E. Huggett's *Goodnight Sweetheart* (1979), and Brian Murdoch's *Fighting Songs and Warring Words* (1990), a study primarily of the vernacular outpourings of British soldiers.

Coming Out of War differs from these and other studies of twentieth-century war literature in its combination of the methods of survey with those of focused critical discussion. In the belief that understanding can be enhanced by placing scrutiny of specific texts within the context of a more sweeping overview, I seek to provide both a history of cultural response to world war in American and British poetry and a consideration of the complexity and power of selected individual works. Though the effort to give a sense of large patterns—indeed, to establish something approaching a taxonomy of twentieth-century war poetry—means including a great many texts, I do not attempt (even if I could achieve) true comprehensiveness. Readers who find themselves objecting to the omission of favorite or otherwise important texts are asked to remember that comprehensiveness is not, after all, a cardinal critical virtue. Even so, I do seek to offer a large overview that will establish a sense both of the extent of the canon and of the range of forms, subject matter, and rhetorical modes that characterize it. I mean by this an experiential and affective sense, as well as an intellectual one. It is partly for that reason that I quote rather extensively. At every point I seek to refute the critical commonplace that identifies a single mode as being characteristic of World War I poetry or World War II poetry. In the poetry that came out of both wars, the range of responses is impressive and important.

Paul Fussell has already provided influential overviews of literary responses in English to the two wars in separate volumes on each. Why, then, do I undertake to provide another? In part for the purpose of treating poetry, aside from other forms of literature, more fully and in the context of both world wars together, rather than separately. Further, because at several points I challenge his interpretations. Foremost of these, perhaps, is his muting of the voices of women. As I hope to make clear in several of the chapters that follow, women have written abundantly and well about war, its griefs, and the moral issues it raises. I challenge, too, Fussell's disparaging judgment that World War II did not produce any significant body of poetry of distinction. I trust that my discussions of a great range of Second World War poetry, as well as readers' own experiencing of that poetry in quoted passages, will convince them that a great deal of very fine poetry came out of the Second war. Moreover, I disagree with Fussell's assertion that what World War II poetry there was followed a single characteristic mode. "Such as they were," he writes, the poets of the later war roused themselves from silence only to the point of producing "laconic notations." [4] As I demonstrate in chapters 8, 9, and 10, the poetry of World War II went greatly beyond mere "notations" and was only occasionally "laconic."

In surveying the landscape of twentieth-century war poetry and other manifestations of the antiwar culture of grieving, and in identifying the sectors and features of that vast terrain, I move in a generally chronological order. As my chapter titles indicate, however, the structure of what follows is also analytical. Chapters 1 through 4 consider the poetry (as well as some music and art) of the First World War: the traditional martial verse that continued into the early months of the conflict; the harsh and passionately antimilitary and antiwar expressions usually regarded as its characteristic mode; the abundance, range, and moral emphasis of poetry by women; and the retrospective poetry and music that demonstrate the persistence of the war in the minds not only of those who lived through it but also a succeeding generation. Chapter 5 shows the depth of alarm in the 1930s about the prospect of another world war, with emphasis on Louis MacNeice's underappreciated major work "Autumn Journal." Chapters 6 through 9 turn to the poetry and music of World War II: expressions of patriotic support for the war effort; the hard-edged poetry that is often regarded as the war's single defining mode; poetry of grieving and moral meditation; and the music and poetry of the last half of the century demonstrating a persistence of concern with the war. The concluding chapter proposes Benjamin Britten's memorialization of the two world wars in *War Requiem* as the consummate pacifist work of the century.

~

I was driving home one day around the apron of the southernmost peak of New Mexico's Sangre de Cristos, near Santa Fe, listening to our local NPR station in the way one listens while driving and enjoying a fine day, when I heard a beautifully quiet voice speak the most heartening sentence I had heard in years. It was the novelist Maxine Hong Kingston, and what she said that day is quoted as the first epigraph to this book and echoed in its title: "It is possible for people to come out of war and learn peace." At first I thought of the phrase "coming out of war" in the sense of emerging from *a* war at its end—as, for example, in 1918 humanity came out of World War I. But then I thought of it in the larger and more visionary sense of coming *out of war* altogether, of putting war behind us. Only then, with the aid of Maxine Hong Kingston's words, did I fully understand what it was that had so engaged my emotions as I worked on this book.

A question implicit throughout, and addressed explicitly at the end of the last chapter, is why a vision such as Kingston's has not been fulfilled, despite the eloquence of poems such as those discussed here and the grieving of millions of people. I realize there is probably no answer to that question. But my hope is that by pondering the poetry that came out of World War I and World War II, we can indeed *come out of* war, in the larger sense, and learn peace.

Acknowledgments

First, I acknowledge and thank the many scholars whose work has preceded my own. Among the many persons who have contributed to this volume in more direct ways, I especially thank my colleague Alan Houtchens at Texas A&M University, with whom I team-taught a course in the twentieth-century poetry and music of war and with whom I collaborated in writing two articles on material examined in that course. Alan first brought to my attention some of the musical texts discussed here, and he contributed to the early stages of my writing in numerous discussions. Without our joint work, I would not have gone on to write this book. Many thanks go to the staff of Evans Library, Texas A&M University, especially Kristen Smith and Carolina De Leon, who found and supplied the materials I needed for this project even when my appetite for books, books, and more books must have seemed insatiable. To my dear friend and fellow scholar Mary McLean, who read the entire manuscript in a late draft and made numerous valuable suggestions, is due the credit for much of whatever merit the final product may have but none of the blame for its deficiencies. A small group of friends at La Mesa Presbyterian Church in Albuquerque, who met for several weeks to read and discuss some of the poems considered here, both encouraged me and sharpened my thinking through interaction with their own. Afterward, George O'Neil, a member of that group, kept expressing his fascination with what he called the poetic way of thinking and its power to change the world. George's words kept me focused on the question I address at the end. Thanks, too, to my best bud Beth Alvarez for her virtual listening (via email) to my laments and enthusiasms as the project went forward.

I acknowledge with gratitude the permission granted by the editors of the *Choral Review* to use parts of my article with Professor Houtchens, "'The dreadful winnowing-fan': Rhetoric of War in Edward Elgar's *The Spirit of England*," published in April 2004, and I thank the following museums for permission to use photographs of artwork in their collections: the Imperial War Museum, London, for John Nash's *Over the Top* and Paul Nash's *The Menin Road;* the British Museum, London, for Otto Dix's *Wounded Man Fleeing (Battle of the Somme, 1916);* the Courtauld Institute of Art, London, for photographs of Frederick Derwent Wood's *Machine Gun Corps Memorial* and Charles Sargeant Jagger's *Recumbent Figure, Royal Artillery Memorial;* the Tate Gallery, London, for Paul Nash's *Totes Meer;* the National Gallery of Canada, Ottawa, for Paul Nash's *Void.* Also I thank Koen Blomme, Roeselare, Belgium, for photographs of Käthe Kollwitz's *Memorial to the Fallen.*

Coming Out of War

1

Aspirations to Heroism
The Old That Passed Away

... men and women who still thought of war in terms of heroic
pageantry.
　　　　　　　　　　　　　—Philip Gibbs, *Realities of War* (1920)

We had vague childish memories of the Boer War, and from these and
from a general diffusion of Kiplingesque sentiments, we managed to
infuse into war a decided element of adventurous romance.
　　　　　　　　　　　　　—Herbert Read, *The Innocent Eye* (1947)

A study of literary and artistic representations of World War I is also,
necessarily, a study of the origins of modernism. The linkage has been
made so often and so persuasively that it has become virtually a commonplace.[1] Paul Fussell states ringingly in *The Great War and Modern Memory*
that "there seems to be one dominating form of modern understanding; that it is essentially ironic; and that it originates largely in the application of mind and memory to the events of the Great War" (35).
Barbara Tuchman writes more succinctly in *The Guns of August* that
among the various results of the war was "one dominant one transcend-
ing all others: disillusion" (440). Disillusion and irony: the characteristic
tones of modernism. And we owe their prevalence largely to the war. In
Sandra M. Gilbert's words, the First World War "fostered characteristically modernist irony in young men" ("Soldier's Heart" 201). Trudi Tate
concludes that the terms "modernism" and "war writing" were virtually
interchangeable at the time and that "modernism after 1914 begins to
look like a peculiar but significant form of war writing" (3). Samuel
Hynes, in *A War Imagined,* moves his frame of reference a decade later
than Tate's to find that "during the later years of the Twenties, war writing and Modernist writing interpenetrated each other" (458). Together,
these various comments capture the standard view of the Great War's

causal relation to modernism. It is a view that I do not contest though I do seek to amplify and refine it.

Modernism had, in fact, many beginning points. The modernist way of seeing, with all that it implies, can be (and certainly has been) traced, for example, to the paintings of Paul Cézanne in the late 1880s. Joyce Medina makes such an argument in her *Cézanne and Modernism,* citing the position taken by British art critics Clive Bell and Roger Fry as early as 1913 (Medina 1–3). Sandra M. Gilbert and Susan Gubar, in the first two volumes of *No Man's Land,* trace *both* the Great War *and* modernism to an unsettlement of gender relations in the years leading up to the war, and Hynes points to prewar "blasts" of modernism in the avant-garde movements of futurism and vorticism.[2] What seems clear is that the modern implements of war and the horrors of their use were *one,* even if not the only, great wellspring of modernism as it continued in the twenties and beyond. The war served as a great dividing line in human conceptions of the world and in the language in which such conceptions were expressed. As James Hannah, an anthologist of Great War writings, puts it, the war "murdered romanticism" and "established a very real boundary between the old ways of seeing and a modernity best characterized by its attitudes of irony and skepticism" (xvii–xviii). That sense of fundamental change—a boundary or dividing line or break point—was widespread and profound at the time and has persisted to our own day.

Some commentators go beyond identifying modernism's origins with the war and propose that it was born specifically at the Battle of the Somme, fought from July to November 1916. Even Samuel Hynes, whose challenge of what he calls "the Myth of the [Great] War" entails debating the notion that the war gave rise to modernism, says that a "new realism" emerged at the Somme (120). Fussell narrows the point of origin to a single day, writing that on the first day of that immense battle, July 1, 1916, the "innocent [British] army fully attained the knowledge of good and evil" (*Great War* 29). Such a statement is, of course, a great (and certainly, as Fussell proposes it, a deliberate) hyperbole. To date so complex a cultural change, let alone the ultimate moral awareness of a people, from one historic episode, distilled in one day, is to exaggerate its singularity. But as hyperboles go, it is a plausible one.

The sequence of suicidal engagements known collectively by the name of the river along which it was fought, the Somme, was a disaster of enormous dimensions for both sides. On only the first day of the assault, July 1, Britain alone suffered 60,000 casualties, including 19,000 dead. By its end in November, the Battle of the Somme would generate more than 500,000 Allied and about 600,000 German casualties—more than a million men dead or wounded in slightly less than five months. And to no outcome. The assembled armies still occupied the same basic positions they had before, and the war went on. Earlier that same year, 1916, casualties in the Battle of Verdun had been almost a million (540,000 French, 430,000 German), as a result of which Germany succeeded in advancing four miles in six months. Little wonder the thinking of a generation should become characterized by disillusionment and irony! Greater lessons in futility and the ugliness to which modern technology could be turned can scarcely be imagined.

Even before Verdun and the Somme, however, the Great War had already provided horrors enough to account for the epochal change in worldview, and thus in art, that is associated with modernism. Widespread use of the fully automatic machine gun and massive artillery like the Germans' so-called Big Bertha had made war a matter of mass killing and maiming. Zeppelins, airplanes, and submarines struck new terror into the souls of a generation. Flamethrowers were introduced. Poison gas, probably the most noted and apparently, to soldiers, the most unnerving of the war's innovations, was first used by Germany in October 1914 at the First Battle of Ypres, was used again by Germany in April 1915 at the Second Battle of Ypres, and then was used by Britain in fighting near Loos on September 15, 1915. The form used at these battles was chlorine gas. Soon phosgene and mustard gases were developed, as well as more exotic variations. Though never a very practical weapon, being too uncontrollable (at Loos, the chlorine gas used by the British blew back into their own lines), it was a terrifying one, causing hideous deaths, debilities, and nightmares. These are graphically described by Wilfred Owen in one of the best-known poems of the war, "Dulce et Decorum Est." It also made troops more vulnerable to other forms of attack by producing helplessness, panic, and disorientation. And then, at the Somme, tanks were used for the first time—by the British.

The conditions of the trenches themselves, which had been extended to previously unimagined dimensions, were a new kind of warfare—

filthy, vermin-infested, muddy, or standing in water from the incessant rains, stinking from natural functions and from bodies and body parts that lay necessarily unburied or reemerged from the earth with new bombardments. Prolonged entrenchment entailed a nearness of death and decay succinctly conveyed in Cannadine's summary observation, "The combat zone might remain littered for weeks with bodies" while "new trenches might be dug through them; parapets might be made of them" (204; also quoted by Gilbert, "'Rats' Alley'" 186). These conditions, or some ameliorated version of them, were communicated with such readiness that people back home became aware of the filthiness, misery, and impersonality being experienced by the troops.[3]

Colonialism and nationalistic fervor, feeding a congeries of ancient ethnic hostilities and geopolitical resentments, had borne a bitter fruit. Total casualties of the war among military personnel are estimated at more than 10 million dead, plus some 3 million missing and presumed dead, with a far larger number wounded or psychologically crippled. Civilian casualties have been estimated at an additional 5 million dead from injuries, famine, and illness spread by the war. These numbers do not include (except when they occasionally overlap) the 15 to 25 million deaths in the flu epidemic of 1917–20. But how many of those should also be attributed to the movement of people caused by the war? The extent of the Great War's havoc—even setting aside that of the Second World War and wars in between—becomes incalculable.[4]

A sea change in literary and artistic content, vision, and style occurred, impelling us all—not the avant-garde alone—into the modernist mentality. Interestingly, leaders among the so-called high modernists— W. B. Yeats, T. S. Eliot, Ezra Pound—regarded the poets of the war such as Wilfred Owen and Siegfried Sassoon as excessively emotional and therefore alien to the spirit of hard-edged modernist writing. Yeats famously excluded the "trench poets" from *The Oxford Book of Modern Verse.* In Margot Norris's judgment, the result of this exclusion of Owen, Sassoon, and others from the canon of modernism was that "the poetry of the Great War skipped a generation, leaving little trace of itself on the literature of World War II" (37). Had not Yeats ousted these writers from the canon of modernism, Norris argues, the poetry of the late war "might have (in 1936) rhetorically served as remembering, warning, and prophecy of the mass violence of the imminent Second World War" (37).[5] Many other readers and critics, however, have identified a decisive turn in the writing and art that came out of the later years of the Great War, after the Somme. Charles Harrison, in a study of modernism in English painting, judges that the most successful artists of the period 1900 to 1939 were those whose work was "most thoroughly modified by the experience" of the war (121). Richard Cork, in *A Bitter Truth: Avant-Garde Art and the Great War* (1994), insistently points out the change in paintings of 1916 and after, in which stark horror is increasingly evident.[6] Music, with its greater abstractness, did not reflect the change so immediately or perhaps so clearly, although the rhetoric of twentieth-century art music relating to war can be understood by its rejection of conventions of martial music that had prevailed before World War I. (Primary among these were regular rhythms suitable for marching; emphasis on drums and brass instruments, or sometimes bagpipes, because of their audibility for signaling troop movements; and the use of intervals that could be played by brass instruments lacking valves—that is, the intervals we associate with fanfares.) Although long-established conventions in the arts persisted in officially sanctioned popular usage, they were displaced in what has been recognized as high art by an idiom conveying disruption, indeterminacy, and bitterness.

The change from traditional martial verse to a poetry of irony, disillusionment, and bitterness was abrupt and emphatic. But to better understand what was new about the new war poetry, we first need a clearer understanding of the old and its persistence into the early years of the Great War

Before July 1, 1916, the poetry of war had largely continued along the traditional lines laid down by centuries of patriotic martial verse.[7] It was often hortatory or given to praise of glorious deeds. Its rhetoric drew on ancient Greek and Roman ideas of manly honor, courage, and individual achievement and on Medieval conceptions of knightly chivalry. Its trappings were often archaic, linking present conflicts with mythical or historic events so distant as to be readily glorified in an elevated language of lances, banners, and trumpets, duty and manly honor. It is scarcely incidental that the Latin root of the English word "virtue," *virtus,* meant not only moral excellence or goodness but "manliness, manhood, virility; strength; valor, gallantry" (Traupman 446). As Fussell has so influentially indicated in *The Great War and Modern Memory* (22), the vocabulary of ennoblement and abstraction that served these ends readily covered up the gritty actualities. Its appeal can be explained in part by the prevalence, in the years leading up to the war, of a sense of need to break out of bourgeois stasis and stagnation of the imagination—a sense that produced a widespread language of smashing and fighting in journalism and social commentary.[8]

The Battle of the Somme made the old kind of war poetry "difficult to sustain" (Martin 33). Before, war poetry drew on long-established tropes to convey a sense of glorious masculine achievement, courage, and valor; it celebrated ideals of patriotism, of fighting for love of country. Afterward, the poetry of war imbibed a quality of irony, bitterness, and brutality that radically altered the arts and critical thinking. These are, of course, broad outlines, and in much of what follows I challenge the notion that twentieth-century poetry of war can be so neatly categorized, as if it all followed a single pattern. Just as we now discern multiple modernisms, not just the "high modernism" of complexity and irony that was once taken to be the sole and defining type, so must we recognize that the poetry that emerged from the Great War was more various in its sensibility and rhetoric, and in the aspects of the totality of war which it addressed, than the ironic and disillusioned "trench poetry" alone. But as broad outlines go, they are sufficient.

Traditional war poetry tended to have a clear, readily grasped meaning. After all, if a writer's purpose, whether conscious or not, is to evoke a specific action—to call men to arms or to a mental readiness to take up arms—it can scarcely be useful to leave readers in a state of uncertainty. They need to know right away what to do and how to feel about it. The message such poetry conveyed was linked to an equally clear, black-and-white vision of good and evil. God is on our side, it proclaimed.[9] Assuming a hierarchical social framework, it was disproportionately interested in the experience of officers and tended to depict common soldiers as quaint (as in Rudyard Kipling's dialect poems of barracks life in India) or boyish (in English verse, with the idealizing use of the word "lad"). This emphasis on youth or boyishness is implicated in the depiction of warfare as a kind of game—a peculiar variant of the heroic idiom that became widespread in the early poetry of the Great War. The usefulness of such a conception for propaganda purposes is readily apparent. Conceiving of enlistment in war as joining a vast game or contest being played out by two sides or teams effaces its mortal consequences. The battlefield becomes an enlarged playing field, perhaps an extension of school. "Lads" might go off to war with a jaunty attitude. Indeed, on a few occasions British soldiers actually did kick footballs—in American parlance, soccer balls—ahead of them in assaults. The trope of sport is surprisingly prevalent—surprising, that is, to twenty-first-century eyes; contemporary readers were accustomed to such language through the "propagating" of images of war as a game by British newspapers in the decade or two leading up to the conflict (Wilkinson 29). Just how prevalent is demonstrated by Willa Cather's invocation of the metaphor in her Pulitzer Prize–winning novel *One of Ours*, excoriated by male reviewers of its day for naïveté, as if she did not understand just what it was she was writing about. When the deluded central character of the novel is leaving shore on a troop ship "going over," he and his fellows look like "a crowd of American boys going to a football game somewhere" (222). The line catches not one but two of the most common tropes of Great War conventional verse: the rendering of men as boys and of the grim business of war as sport.

Metrically, traditional war poetry, like traditional music paying tribute to war heroes or calling men to valor, evoked the heavy, regular cadence of parade marching.[10] Rhythmic regularity—obviously an appropriate vehicle for clarity of meaning—conveys a tone that Fussell calls "thoroughly resolute" (*Great War* 58). Such a metrical effect (though in fact an inventively varied one) is heard in Thomas Hardy's 1914 poem "Men Who March Away":

> What of the faith and fire within us
> > Men who march away
> > Ere the barn-cocks say
> > Night is growing gray,
> Leaving all that here can win us;
> What of the faith and fire within us
> > Men who march away? (538)

Hardy's lines also illustrate another major strand in the idealizing tendencies of traditional war poetry in English: the loving depiction of a rustic England left behind, glancingly seen here in the reference to "barn-cocks."

The onset of war in August 1914 evoked an outpouring of poetry in England that (like Hardy's "Men Who March Away") initially followed the conventional course of virtuous patriotism and solemn commitment to a great cause—the traditional ideals of martial verse.[11] Reading these poems now, aware of what came afterward, we can scarcely give credence to the writers' hopes for heroic deeds, their assurance that they were furthering a righteous cause, their sacralization of sacrifice (a mentality that has been persuasively traced to the pervasive Christianity of British culture), their general air of cleanness.[12] All this would change as, appalled by the waste, inhumanity, and sheer brutality of the war, poets turned away from the rhetoric of heroism to expressions of resentment and disgust and depictions of physically revolting, psychologically disabling, or pitiable experiences—the "rats' alley" sensibility captured in the poetry of T. S. Eliot.[13] The cadences of poetry of the late war and the years that followed became typically the slower, more muffled ones of despair or the disrupted, irregular rhythms that express resistance to the coercive uniformities of militarism. The broken meters of modernism's war poetry convey confusion and disorder, disconnection from accepted truisms, or utter futility—not the stirring calls to duty and individual valor issued earlier. Generally speaking, heroic marching cadences in poetry persisted only in uninformed or unskilled doggerel or in ironic mockery of military rhetoric.

The cultural work of the twentieth century turned more to memorializing, grieving, and deploring war, rather than affirming and glorifying it. To be sure, in its most public and institutionalized expressions—cemeteries and government-sanctioned commemorative art—this cultural work of remembrance has often adopted a mode of monumentality and traditionalism.[14] The clashing incongruousness of the archaic mode still sometimes persisting alongside the markers of modernism is evident in the contrast between two Great War memorials at Hyde Park Corner in London: Frederick Derwent Wood's *Machine Gun Corps Memorial*, with its classical nudity and sword, and Charles Sargeant Jagger's figure of the dead soldier on the nearby *Royal Artillery Memorial*, with

1. Frederick Derwent Wood, *Machine Gun Corps
Memorial,* Hyde Park Corner, London. Photograph
courtesy of the Conway Library, Courtauld Institute
of Art, London.

its realistic Great War boots and helmet (see figs. 1 and 2). Jagger's figure
of the dead soldier fully acknowledges the devastation of the war and
participates in the culture of grieving. The "royal fellowship" asserted in
the large inscription just below the figure is a fellowship of death. In its
more personal and literary expressions, as in this sculpted figure, the
effort to memorialize and understand the linked disasters of the two
world wars has usually been carried on in ways that defy monumentality
and tradition, invoking, instead, bitterness and grief.

~

The two World War I poets most famously identified with traditional
martial verse and its characteristic sentiments are Rudyard Kipling

2. Charles Sargeant Jagger, *Recumbent Figure, Royal Artillery Memorial*, 1921–25, Hyde Park Corner, London. Photograph courtesy of the Conway Library, Courtauld Institute of Art, London.

(1865–1936) and Rupert Brooke (1887–1915). Kipling brought to his writing about the Great War a set of attitudes and practices he had long utilized in verse about military life, the attitudes and practices that have inescapably identified him as the poet of empire. In 1896, for example, in "Hymn before Action," he had solemnized England's imminent entry into the Boer War in a language of duty and sacrifice linked to confidence that God was on England's side.

> E'en now their vanguard gathers,
>   E'en now we face the fray—
> As Thou didst help our fathers,
>   Help Thou our host to-day.

Fulfilled of signs and wonders,
    In life, in death made clear—
Jehovah of the Thunders,
    Lord God of Battles, hear! (324)

During World War I he continued in much the same vein, publishing a number of poems extolling the nobility of serving one's country in battle.

At the very outbreak of the war, Kipling joined this tone of reverential patriotism to a rhetoric that has remained a convention of public discourse about war generally, exhorting his countrymen in "'For All We Have and Are'" to think of the enemy in dehumanized terms. Calling the Germans "crazed and driven" instigators, he uttered, with astonishing aplomb, a line that would become synonymous with mindless jingoism: "The Hun is at the gate!" (*Rudyard Kipling's Verse* 328). The English he characterized by the virtues of "silent fortitude," "patience," and "strength," calling on his countrymen to face "iron sacrifice" for the sake of the nation:

There is but one task for all—
One life for each to give.
What stands if Freedom fall?
Who dies if England live? (329)

It would perhaps become more difficult for Kipling's audience to share the chauvinistic spirit of that last ringing line after the long lists of the dead began to appear in daily newspapers. As Hilda Spear puts it, the sentiment he expressed would "wear thin" (29).[15] One of the peculiarities of the poem is an image of a "sword / Unsheathed and uncontrolled" that becomes magically transformed into a knitting needle, as the sword "once more . . . knits mankind." But at the moment of its publication in the *Times* on September 2, 1914 (Harbord 5442), "'For All We Have and Are'" caught the spirit of the country. Eby observes that this "widely reprinted poem set the tone for the home front yellow press during the next four years" (171).

Toward the end of 1915, Kipling was still confidently invoking such flourishes as trumpets and such tropes as playing the game. In the rollicking lines of "A Song in Storm," he called on England's soldiers to persevere, assuring them that nature itself, presumably at God's behest, favored their cause: "Be well assured that on our side / The abiding oceans fight."[16] The concluding stanza presents a virtual compendium of the conventions of traditional war poetry—a rhetoric of duty and sacrifice, the mantra of nationalism, the language of game or sport, and a regularity of meter that in itself conveys ideas of duty and military determination:

> Be well assured, though in our power
>   Is nothing left to give
> But chance and place to meet the hour,
>   And leave to strive to live,
> Till these dissolve our Order holds,
>   Our Service binds us here.
> Then welcome Fate's discourtesy
>   Whereby it is made clear
>   How in all time of our distress,
>   As in our triumph too,
>   The game is more than the player of the game,
>   And the ship is more than the crew! (147)

In 1916, in "The Question,"[17] Kipling challenged Americans to imagine how guilty they were going to feel when they had to face the fact that their safety had been purchased by the valor of others:

> Brethren, how shall it fare with me
>   When the war is laid aside,
> If it be proven that I am he
>   For whom a world has died? (326)

Literature was being explicitly enlisted in the service of recruitment into the war. More than two decades later, in February 1939, W. H. Auden would write that Time "worships language and forgives / Everyone by whom it lives" and on grounds of "this strange excuse / Pardoned Kipling and his views" (*Collected Poetry* 50).[18] We can only assume that Kipling's service as spokesperson for imperialism, war, and national authority in poems such as these was at least part of what Auden was thinking of.

In a way, it seems unfair to hold Kipling up as an example of hollow jingoism. In 1915 he suffered the loss of a son (missing and supposed dead) whom he grieved deeply, and after the war he produced many solemn, moving, and terse epitaphs for military cemeteries. James Bentley judges some of Kipling's epitaphs to have been "vicious" (9), citing as an example "Unknown Female Corpse":

Headless, lacking foot and hand,
Horrible I come to land.
I beseech all women's sons
Know I was a mother once. (Kipling 389)

Another of the epitaphs, however—"If any question why we died / Tell them, because our fathers lied (388)—is singled out by Adam Gopnik as "the best poem Kipling ever wrote about war and its consequences" and as evidence that Kipling "learned" (85). Even so, Kipling remains identified with a jingoism that was soon to become, for most writers and readers, a thing of the past.

Rupert Brooke was still in his twenties when the war broke out—indeed, he never lived to be thirty—but was already well established among the Georgian poets.[19] He became a focal point of Britain's national sentiment about her soldiers abroad when he quickly enlisted. After serving briefly in Belgium, where he was present at the retreat from Antwerp, he was attached to the Royal Naval Division for the campaign in the Dardanelles but died on shipboard on the way, of blood poisoning apparently from an insect bite. Yet as David Perkins points out, despite the tragic quality of this story of untimely death, the war was for Brooke "a mode of redemption." Shifting his center of interest from his earlier aestheticism mixed with socialism and spasmodic bouts of emotional confusion, he took the war as his own "supreme cause" (Perkins 211–12), making it a vehicle for the expression of love of country.

It is difficult now to understand the elation with which Brooke and others like him greeted what was to be civilization's nightmare. Yet as scholars such as Samuel Hynes and Glen Wilkinson rightly remind us, Brooke was a member of a generation that for two decades had been reading newspaper and periodical discussions of the necessity and benefit of periodic wars as a cleansing or renewing agent for a moribund society. If such an attitude seems more than a little incredible from our perspective, the reason is that we cannot rid ourselves of our awareness of subsequent history. For Brooke and other Edwardians who "shouted and cheered for war" in 1914 (Wilkinson 34), there could be no such awareness. Casting the struggle as one between youth and all that would dash its hopes for nobility or cause it ennui—a different vision of enmity between the young and the old than would characterize writings of the later war—Brooke exulted in the opportunity for newness of life that he saw before him. It was the long-awaited chance to rid himself of the lingering fin de siècle sentiment of exhaustion and indifference. His feelings were only one conspicuous instance of what Eric Leed calls a widespread "euphoria of August" that extended beyond England to Germany and France as well.[20]

Brooke is now best known for the "1914 Sonnets," a group of five sonnets published in a transitory literary journal in December 1914, four months after the beginning of the war. Probably the most famous of the group is number 5, "The Soldier," with its familiar opening "If I should die, think only this of me: / That there's some corner of a foreign field / That is for ever England" (Brooke 316). Brooke did die, of course, early in the war—as Gilbert and Gubar point out, "before disillusionment could set in" (*Sexchanges* 265). Beloved for its tone of reverent patriotism toward an idealized England and perhaps for its reassuring assumption that dead soldiers would find their deaths worthwhile, "The Soldier" was read in the pulpit by the dean of Saint Paul's on Easter Sunday, 1915 (Martin 32; Giddings 37, et al.). This "plug," in Eby's words, made the "superciliously nationalistic" poem "an instant success" (230, 233). Gavin Ewart, writing not only after the Great War but after World War II as well, and therefore less intoxicated with glory than the good dean, says bluntly that Brooke "died in an imperialist war, and such a poem glorified it" (Ewart, Introduction 11). But glorifying it, along with glorifying England, was, after all, the point.

The language of Brooke's war sonnets is a distinctive and moving blend of martial convention with a gentle directness in expressing love of daily pleasures. A little more of the former and they would become bombast; a little more of the latter and they would scarcely be war poems at all. Yet the conventions that in lesser hands could become specious, indeed deceptive, are fully in evidence here. "Dawn was theirs, / And sunset"—the magical times of day that, with the entrenchment

that came to define the Western Front in 1915, would become ironically the most dangerous times (because of the routine of "stand-to," a
twice-daily ritual of mounting the firing step, weapon in hand, on alert
for an assault). Here, these magical times are simply moving. But the
prettiness of Brooke's syntactic inversion is the kind of poetic device
that would soon be rejected by poets intent on stating a more brutal
truth. Bugles and kings, capitalized abstractions such as Love and Pain,
the assertion of certainty that the dying hero will carry on beyond
death, substitutions such as "sweet wine of youth" for young men's
blackened blood: these are the tropes of the "1914 Sonnets."

Perhaps most shocking to present readers and most poignant in its
ignorance of what was to come (Ewart terms it "unthinking") is the
opening of the first of the five sonnets:

> Now, God be thanked Who has matched us with His hour,
>   And caught our youth, and wakened us from sleeping,
> With hand made sure, clear eye, and sharpened power,
>   To turn, as swimmers into cleanness leaping,
> Glad from a world grown old and cold and weary. . . . (Brooke 312)

God would be called on in many ways in the years of slaughter ahead,
but seldom in thanks.[21] Brooke was by no means the only British writer
to employ a language of cleansing when speaking of the war; Hynes
points out that such established spokespersons for the arts as Edmund
Gosse and Selwyn Image also spoke of the newly launched war as a
"sovereign disinfectant" or a "cleansing purge" (12–15). Since the war effort would soon become mired in the filth of the trenches, a rhetoric
of cleansing appears in retrospect particularly ironic. Yet Brooke, who
would not know any of that, announced confidently,

> Honour has come back, as a king, to earth,
>   And paid his subjects with a royal wage;
> And Nobleness walks in our ways again;
>   And we have come into our heritage. (314)

"It is this basic insincerity and lack of depth," one critic has complained,
"that make his poetry ultimately disappointing" (Moeyes 467). But the

charge of insincerity, if it means conscious dissembling, is questionable. Adrian Caesar is on sounder ground in calling Brooke's war sonnets "now infamous" for their "expression of a discredited, imperialist chauvinism" (1).

A similar gap of irony interposes itself between us and the early-war enthusiasm of American painter Childe Hassam's *Allies Day, May 1917,* conveying in its bright, sunny scene and large, festively waving flags of England, the United States, and France the elation that prevailed in that month following the American declaration of war. And we could find many other examples; Rupert Brooke was not alone in striking the note of heroism. John Freeman (1880–1929), a prolific poet and the author of two postwar books of criticism, could also celebrate, in 1914, an England "happy . . . in the brave that die" (in a poem called "Happy Is England Now"). For him, in that year of the war's beginning, the prospect of "a great people moving towards the deep / Of an unguessed and unfeared future" was "wonderful" (Freeman 152–53). In "The Stars in Their Courses," dated August 1914, the rousing of military courage in this "magnificent" though "cruel" and "disastrous" war struck Freeman as a process making England—à la Brooke's swimmers—"clean again" (Freeman 144–47, cited by Perkins 271). Even Wilfred Owen, so soon to recoil into bitter pathos, wrote of the war in 1915, in "An Imperial Elegy," "This is the Path of Glory."

The tone of noble sacrifice and assurance of the worthwhileness of the war struck by Brooke, Freeman, and (here) Owen reaches a kind of apotheosis, though with a gloomy foreboding, in John McCrae's "In Flanders Fields." McCrae (1872–1918), who quickly volunteered when the war broke out, had been going to war and writing poems about it since 1899, when he enlisted for service in the Boer War. "In Flanders Fields" was published in *Punch* on December 6, 1915, long after it had become obvious that the Great War had settled into an unprecedented mode of grinding meanness, paralleling the settling into the trenches.[22] The familiar poem (which once, many people could recite) bears witness to the immortality of the dead and our obligation to continue in their cause:

> "In Flanders fields the poppies blow
> Between the crosses, row on row
>   That mark our place; and in the sky

> The larks, still bravely singing, fly
> Scarce heard amid the guns below.
>
> We are the Dead. Short days ago
> We lived, felt dawn, saw sunset glow,
>   Loved and were loved, and now we lie
>   In Flanders fields.
>
> Take up our quarrel with the foe:
> To you from failing hands we throw
>   The torch; be yours to hold it high.
>   If ye break faith with us who die
> We shall not sleep, though poppies grow
>   In Flanders fields.

McCrae's first two stanzas reflect the growing melancholy verging on despair that increasingly characterized the times. A strong elegiac tone conveyed in the slow pace and long *o* sounds emerges in the image of lines of crosses "row on row"—a quiet interrupted by the clash of singing larks and booming guns so loud the birds above are "scarce heard." In the second mournful stanza the imagined speakers (signaled by the quotation mark at the beginning) identify themselves as "the Dead" and quickly recall the pleasures of life now denied them, including the glow of dawn and sunset, the two ironically emblematic times of the daily cycle. One could almost think this was a poem designed to rouse one's sense of the waste of war. But not so. At the third stanza, in an emphatic change of rhetorical direction (or "turn"), the dead exhort their listeners to hold high the "torch" (another archaic symbol) now passed to them and continue the war effort, because otherwise their sleep in death, despite the narcotic poppies that famously grew in Flanders, will not be an easy or satisfied one.

After all, then, the war is seen not only as a cause to grieve but also as an incentive to heroism. This latent ambiguity or discontinuity in a poem so familiar that one might easily think it not ambiguous at all would be emphasized by Charles Ives when he set the poem to music in early 1917.[23] In McCrae's lines the disjuncture between the pathos of the first two stanzas and the last stanza's call to fight on is resolved with the speakers' implied expectation that if the war is fought on to victory their "sleep" will be a sound one, undisturbed by misgivings. In Ives's musical setting, the contrast remains essentially unresolved, as the dissonant chords of the music itself are unresolved. The piece ends uneasily with a subdued drum roll sounded by the piano.

Ives composed "In Flanders Fields" in the early spring of 1917; it was first performed at a luncheon for insurance agents at the Waldorf Astoria Hotel in New York less than two weeks after the U.S. entered the war on April 6, 1917.[24] One can only suppose that the listeners on that occasion were at least as puzzled by the music as listeners are today. The song problematizes McCrae's seemingly simple verses through a combination of Ives's characteristically complex techniques, to the point that the composer's intention becomes radically uncertain. Preexistent melodies such as the Civil War tune "The Battle Cry of Freedom" are quoted in ways that create tension. "Taps" and "Reveille" are alluded to simultaneously at one point, putting in question whether Ives was affirming the sentiments of the originals or quoting them for purposes of irony. McCrae's minimal ambiguities are heightened by dissonances, ominously thudding bass patterns, and musical discontinuities that accentuate the sense of mournfulness and alarm latent in his lines. At "loved and were loved," clashing piano chords seem to cry out in bitter protest. Yet the injunction to "take up our quarrel" brings on an echo of "La Marseillaise" and a fanfare figure, conveying patriotic and militaristic fervor. These quandaries are never reconciled or brought to a sense of closure; we remain uncertain of the composer's intent. McCrae would surely have been surprised at what Ives made of his words.

Ives seems to have shared the national war fervor of the early days of America's entry into the Great War despite misgivings about the morality of making war. He may even have felt that the moral fervor he associated with the early days of the Civil War (of which he had heard much from his father) had been restored (Feder 283). But within a year he would be seeking to propose peace and a vision of a world democracy designed to prevent the exploitation of the lower classes that he saw as being involved in war efforts. There is evidence, then, that even well before armistice his attitude toward the war was at least ambivalent.

The combination of pathos with determination to fight on seen in McCrae's "In Flanders Fields" also characterizes, though with a less

clashing effect, Alan Seeger's "Rendezvous," another of the most familiar poems of the war. Seeger (1888–1916), a Harvard graduate who went
to the French Foreign Legion in 1914, has been styled by David Perkins
"the only American poet of significant promise who was killed in the
war" (270). His poem, implying what Hannah calls "a certain romance
at the thought of death's oblivion" (358), begins pathetically with "I have
a rendezvous with Death" and ends with an assertion of the soldier's
honor in carrying out his sworn duty: "And I to my pledged word am
true, / I shall not fail that rendezvous." To what, though, is the soldier
"true"? On first reading it might seem to be his duty to fight on, despite the expectation of death. The poem does not really say that, however, but something rather different—that the soldier's face is set toward
death, as if in his swearing in, he had taken an oath to die. He won't fail
to be true to his oath because he can't; death will meet him at the appointed (though not foreknown) time. Unlike McCrae's "In Flanders
Field," though almost as popular and at first glance similar in sentiment,
Seeger's poem does not actually affirm the cause for which the soldier
has taken this oath. Indeed, the war is not mentioned at all except in
images of its traces on the landscape, the "scarred slope of battered hill."
We know it is a war poem primarily because we know the context; we
know that Seeger died in the war.

～

By 1915 the sense of cleansing renewal through participation in the
war felt by Brooke and others only the previous autumn had faded.
By mid-1916 the heroic tone in poetry would come near to vanishing altogether. It was continued, after a fashion, in a subgenre often identified
with the now notorious but then quite popular woman poet Jessie Pope
(1868–1941), a writer commonly and accurately labeled "jingoistic." In
Khan's words (28), she "could seize upon any situation in order to celebrate British pluck." The kind of verse associated with Pope—calling on
England's men to play the game, to do their duty and enlist—is now essentially despised, largely because of the bitterness with which Wilfred
Owen would single it out as part and parcel of the authority system that
sent young men off to die.

Pope herself was not so inconsiderable in her poetic skills as her
reputation would indicate, but the mode of poetry—or more accurately,
doggerel verse—she wrote seems in retrospect keenly distasteful. Her in-

sistent calls to arms were designed to goad an increasingly reluctant male populace into military service and were also, in some few instances, directed toward the women of England whose work was needed to free up men for the trenches. Khan may see Pope's notice of women's war work (for example, in "War Girls") as "vibrantly celebrat[ing]" their pluck and the importance of their contribution (71), but her relentless dogtrot versification and formulaic sentiments are, to me, anything but "vibrant." Gilbert and Gubar, in *Sexchanges,* describe it as "smug" (263).

The most frequently quoted of Jessie Pope's poems is the truly despicable "The Call," which dichotomizes the young men of England as either eager to get into the fray or cowards:

> Who's for the trench—
> > Are you, my laddie?
> Who'll follow French—
> > Will you, my laddie?
> Who's fretting to begin,
> Who's going out to win?
> And who wants to save his skin—
> > Do you, my laddie? (38)

And two more stanzas in the same vein. Faced with what is now the almost total eradication of Pope's verses, except for this and perhaps one or two other occasionally cited examples, we might wonder whether her name has been unfairly blackened. But if one takes the trouble to locate copies of her three volumes of popular war poems, one finds that the plucky "Call" and "Socks" (the latter probably her best poem, with its evocation of a daily female occupation, knitting, combined with worry for the combatants) are characteristic. "St. George and the Dragon," for instance, cited by Tylee for its "medieval commonplaces" (56), encourages England's "gallant St. Georges today" to go fight the "dragon" of Germany. Pope's hearty call to the trenches contrasts starkly with Herbert Read's memory of those same trenches as "that mess . . . in which I cowered" (*CP* 158). We might contrast with Read's sense that "we gave in vain" (*CP* 152)—an increasingly prevalent sentiment following the armistice—Pope's tone of "crashing cynicism about wounds and disablement" (Williams 197), expressed, for instance, in "The One-Legged

Soldier Man": "Another leg they'll find him / For the one he left behind him."

The callow optimism in these verses by Pope was equaled, perhaps,
only by George M. Cohan's rousing song "Over There," phenomenally
popular in the United States with the nation's entry into the conflict in
April 1917. Cohan's patriotic song provides another example of traditional war rhetoric (direct and simple in its appeal, aimed toward the
call of duty, with an optimistic confidence in victory) rendered the more
martial in tone by its catchy melodic approximation of a bugle call. The
song both captured and purveyed a brash sense that Americans were going to "play the hero and bring the war to a swift conclusion" (Bergreen
151).[25] So popular was "Over There" that it could be echoed, in full confidence of being recognized, by Charles Ives in his 1917 art song "Tom
Sails Away." It was parodied to drastically different effect by E. E. Cummings: "things are going rather kaka / over there, over there" (231).

~

The poems of Laurence Binyon (1869–1943) are a very different matter. Though rarely mentioned today even in literary histories, Binyon
was one of the most thoroughly competent of the poetic voices of aspiration to heroism. A resident scholar of Chinese and Japanese art at the
British Museum, he was an important figure in the world of both poetry
and the visual arts in London.

Three of Binyon's war poems that were published in the *Times* (a rich
storehouse of poems throughout the war) in August and September
1914—"The Fourth of August" on August 11, "To Women" on August 20,
and "For the Fallen" on September 21—were set to music by Edward Elgar in a triptych called *The Spirit of England*.[26] Fussell calls the last of
these "uncanny" in its "prescience" of what was to come (*Great War* 56).
So great was its impact on readers that at least three composers quickly
began choral settings of it.[27] Elgar, inveterate celebrant of British imperial majesty, began composing his setting of "For the Fallen" within a
month of its publication. In this majestic choral work, words and music come together in a consummate example of the romantic rhetoric
of war—a rhetoric of "noble generalizations and national pieties" that,
as Perkins observes, "the war at first heightened" (271). "To Women"
and "For the Fallen" were given their first performance on May 3, 1916,
with the king and queen in attendance, and the complete work in three

movements premiered on October 4, 1917. It is widely considered one of Elgar's "profoundest, most inward, and most deeply imagined choral works" (Hatcher 196).[28]

Not only are the aesthetic qualities of Binyon's poems and Elgar's music of interest, but also their rhetoric. Clearly, both poetry and music function here as a language of persuasion. Does the attempted persuasion vitiate their "purely" aesthetic dimension? Betty Bennett, editor of *British War Poetry in the Age of Romanticism, 1793–1815*, regards the relationship between aesthetics and rhetoric this way: "The quality of the war verses varies greatly, ranging from plainly nationalistic songs, which embody rhetorical effect *rather than intrinsic poetic merit*, to the most seriously intended works of art with their metaphoric use of the war experience" (1; emphasis added). Such an opposition would seem to assume that one can never have both, but only one at a time, either poetic merit or rhetorical effect, and further, that the "war experience" becomes part of a "seriously intended" work of art only when it is invoked metaphorically, not when it occupies the literal center of the poet's attention. Yet in the case of *The Spirit of England*, which most certainly conveys rhetorical intent, the music remains overwhelmingly beautiful even to someone like myself who resists the message.

The first of the three Binyon poems in order of publication and the one that comes first in *The Spirit of England*, though it was the last of the three that Elgar actually set to music, is the inspirational patriotic poem "The Fourth of August." The poem begins, in the first and second of its seven stanzas:

> Now in thy splendour go before us,
> Spirit of England, ardent-eyed,
> Enkindle this dear earth that bore us,
> In the hour of peril purified.
>
> The cares we hugged drop out of vision.
> Our hearts with deeper thoughts dilate.
> We step from days of sour division
> Into the grandeur of our fate.

At this early point in the war, only a week after Britain entered the conflict and nine days after the publication of Kipling's "For All We Have and Are," Binyon seems to have shared the impulse of the thousands of young men who flocked to volunteer.[29] Adopting a first-person plural representing the people of England generally, he speaks of "our" commitment to a "living cause" for which the "glorious dead" have given their lives in the past. The Spirit of England, apostrophized as a kind of nation-goddess of glorious "splendour," leads her people into a state of "grandeur" (more bluntly called war) that Binyon confidently asserts will redeem them from the pettiness of the ordinary—the redemption Rupert Brooke also envisioned. Claiming for this gloriously personified England a kind of mystical oneness with the eternal order of things ("for her immortal stars are burning"), Binyon demonizes the enemy as a "vampire" serving a "creed of blood and iron." Language that dehumanizes the enemy either as a monster or as an animal is, of course, a standard rhetorical trope in wartime.[30] Binyon's language is more generally, however, one that might have served Paul Fussell as a source for his list (in *The Great War and Modern Memory*) of stilted elevated terms that would later be avoided in the war poetry associated with modernism; "ardent," "peril," and "fate" in fact appear on Fussell's list.

Writing in 1914, Binyon could not yet know that his vision of "splendour" would turn out to be an ordeal of filth and horror. The mentality of irony and skepticism that makes it hard for us to credit that vision had not yet emerged. But when Binyon apostrophizes the earth itself, in the last stanza, to "awaken / Purged by this dreadful winnowing-fan" he is invoking a devotion to the life of the earth widely felt by the people of England, and when he closes by addressing the "Soul of divinely suffering man," he is using a trope that would become a regular convention of World War I poetry: the soldier as Christ. Herbert Read, for example, would write in "My Company," "My men, my modern Christs / your bloody agony confronts the world" (*CP* 39). Isaac Rosenburg, in "Dead Man's Dump," likens the barbed wire to a "crowns of thorns" (Giddings 93). And in G. A. Studdert Kennedy's poem of overt protest, "My Peace I Leave with You," millions "come to Golgotha / To suffer and to die . . . asking, Why?" (Bentley 71).[31] Binyon's poem moves from a vision of nationalistic and military glory to one of suffering and trial.

When Elgar set "The Fourth of August" to music, he employed a musical language he had already used in a number of patriotic pieces such as the *Pomp and Circumstance Marches* (1901–7) and the *Coronation Ode* (1902)—that is, a musical language very conservative for the time. Even so, today's listener can still be moved by the sense it conveys of what Elgar himself identified as "courage and hope." This sense is conveyed primarily through the broad strokes he paints with the orchestra, the generally rising melodic line, and an angelically soaring solo soprano voice.

In Binyon's "To Women," the second of the three poems in order of publication and the second movement of *The Spirit of England*, the poetic language is again one of "splendour" and "sacrifice," a terminology readily yielding itself to use for recruiting purposes and one to which Elgar responded by echoing the courage/hope motif of the first movement.[32] The unironic sincerity with which Binyon employed such language marks the poem as belonging to an expiring tradition, as do his invocations of "marching drums" and "lance and sword." Despite this anachronistic imagery, "To Women" demonstrates not only the prescience Fussell observes but also prescience of another kind—a forward-looking grasp of the fact that the scope of experience considered in war poetry goes well beyond the battlefield alone, to include the deprivations, griefs, and shattered lives of those at home, many of them women and some of whom also recorded their feelings about the war in poetry. Indeed, since modern war is total war and airplanes and rockets have so greatly extended the range of attack, the extent of the battlefield is no longer definable. Civilians as well as armies are bombed, and civilians, many of them women, would die during the Great War from accidents in munitions plants.[33] Binyon's vision does not include these possibilities, but does embrace those who are casualties of war indirectly. In the closing words of the poem—"to bleed, / To bear, to break, but not to fail!"—he echoes the ringing last line of Tennyson's "Ulysses," "To strive, to seek, to find, and not to fail!" That is, he appropriates a masculine poetic to a feminized (by the title), or essentially a universalizing, purpose. There can scarcely be a better indication of his conservative nature as a poet than this appropriation of the deceased poet laureate's archaically inspirational lines—but with a difference.

The conservative and elegiac qualities of Binyon's poem are, once again, well if rather obviously captured in Elgar's music. A comment that Elgar made in a letter written in 1917, relating to "The Fourth of August," that the subject called for a "simple and straightforward" treatment (J. Moore, *Letters of a Lifetime* 307), could have been applied to "To

Women" as well. Elgar was not given to estimating the musical sensibility of his audience very highly; his composition of several blatantly propagandistic war songs demonstrates that fact clearly enough.

The last of the three Binyon poems used by Elgar in *The Spirit of England* was the one that had initially launched him on his project, "For the Fallen." John Hatcher, in his authoritative book on Binyon, has pointed out that many features of this poem, too, now read like stilted gestures, falsified by what the war became. Among these Hatcher mentions the poet's faith that casualties really were "fallen in the cause of the free," the notion that conscription could be regarded as "thrill[ing] . . . drums" or that death in the trenches could possibly be "august and royal," the belief that soldiers in the circumstances they actually faced were "staunch"—when in fact as Fussell points out (*Great War* 47) they were often bolstered with stiff shots of rum before an assault—or that it made any difference whether, as Binyon claims, they died "with their faces to the foe" (193). Despite the tiredness of the traditional form and language, however, Hatcher is correct in judging that Binyon's adoption of the mode of elegy here and in "To Women," rather than the tone of inspiration that prevails in "The Fourth of August," gives this poem a degree of foreknowledge of what his generation of poets would come to reckon with. Even so, for all its solemn grief, "For the Fallen" is also a poem of pride in the heroism of England's soldiers lost in the early weeks of what was expected to be a brief war. It is "with proud thanksgiving," Binyon writes, that England mourns her (idealized) dead, who went into battle unafraid and with a youthful joyousness; their death, he claims, was one of "glory." Moreover, by dying young they were spared the indignities of growing old: "They shall grow not old, as we that are left grow old: / Age shall not weary them, nor the years condemn." It is an idea familiar from A. E. Housman's "To an Athlete Dying Young," written two decades earlier and built on the "sporting metaphor" so "potent" in British culture, which would permeate martial verse of the early part of the war (Bentley 7).

In snippets such as these, Binyon's "For the Fallen" is easy to mock; the brittleness of its optimistic assurances is only too obvious now. Binyon struck here a note of heroic grief and moral certainty that in lesser hands could and often did sound glib. Always a profoundly conservative versifier, he produced lines of a sweeping rhythmic flow that carries

one irresistibly into solemn and elevated emotions. It is the kind of poetry that unites nations in moments of crisis. And it did unite England,
in the sense that numerous readers came across the poem in the newspaper and, as if in unison, were moved by it. The tenderness of its language, its personification of England as a grieving mother, and the assurance of remembrance in its final line—"To the end, to the end, they
remain"—were deeply reassuring. Elgar's setting, with its dense late Romantic style, underscores this solemnity and the poem's emphasis on
grieving rather than glory. "For the Fallen" has continued to be quoted
on auspicious occasions and reprinted, in whole or in part, for its note
of solemnity and assurance, though Binyon's own reputation has lapsed
into obscurity.

Binyon and Elgar, with their "vocabulary of late Romanticism" (Hatcher
197) were well suited for collaboration. Binyon once labeled himself "a
belated Victorian" (Hatcher 281)—a term equally appropriate to the
imperial-minded Elgar.[34] Neither of them participating in the advent of
modernism, they can both best be described as Georgian. The Georgians
were, in a specific sense, a small and now little-read group of poets who
appeared in Edward Marsh's anthologies *Georgian Poetry,* the first of
which appeared in 1912. But the term is sometimes used in a more general sense as referring to late nineteenth- and early twentieth-century
artists of "the amiable aspect of things" and a belated romanticism
(Perkins 206). The Georgian temperament was the essentially conservative sensibility expressed in the "noble generalizations and national
pieties" of patriotic fervor that the war fostered in its first two years
(Perkins 271). Neither of these belated Victorians could foresee the great
transformation in literary perceptions of warfare that lay ahead.

The power of Elgar, in particular, to evoke archaic and seemingly rejected emotions is conveyed in a story involving Siegfried Sassoon, one
of the most respected of the *new* poets of the war. In his diary entry for
June 30, 1921, Sassoon recalled that the same date five years earlier had
been "the night before the Somme attack started" and that on the previous night (June 29) he had been out cutting wire and had been driven
back by shelling (*Diaries* 73). Oddly enough, at the start of that same
day's diary entry, June 30, 1921, he had written, "I've given up thinking
about the War." Yet that very evening he "pull[ed] out" his "war notebooks" and began to read entries from 1916—while sitting "with some

Elgar music in my head" (73). Elgar, the Georgian patriot, seems to have carried him back to thinking about the war despite his insistence to the contrary.

It is a useful parable of the inner conflicts experienced by literary survivors of the war. Poets might write in a new, hard-hitting style, yet still enjoy listening to the music of Elgar, with its echoes of largely bygone sentiments. They might, as did Sassoon, come to disbelieve and reject the aims of the war—indeed, to hate the war and protest against its continuance—and yet go back to the front to fight for reasons of loyalty to their fellow soldiers. The generalizations we make about them nearly a century later are far neater than their experience at the time. Binyon, for example, I have classified as a voice of stale conservatism, albeit an honorable and skilled one. Yet in his poems written in 1914 he already envisioned, dimly but more accurately than Kipling or Brooke, the extent of the war's devastation and the burden of grieving that would descend on survivors.

2

The New War Poetry
The Soldier Poets

Let us be frank for once:
Such foisted platitudes
cannot console sick hearts.
                    —Herbert Read, "Auguries of Life and Death"

War had been a subject for poetry, but never like this.
                    —Robert Giddings, *The War Poets*

By mid-1916 it would have been impossible for any rational soldier poet, a veteran, say, of Gallipoli or of the First and Second Battles of Ypres or of the early months of the Battle of Verdun, to have thanked God for matching him with that hour, as Rupert Brooke did in the first of his 1914 sonnets.[1] By then, the war in which they were fighting had proved to have very little to do with glory, and the "foisted platitudes" of traditional patriotic verse were exposed as nothing but pretty verbiage (Read, *CP* 50). In the mature poetry of these soldier poets, or as they are often called trench poets, there is little of such verbiage, but instead a great deal of resentment against it. This chapter traces that change to disillusion and resentment, primarily as it occurs in the poetry of Siegfried Sassoon and Wilfred Owen, the two figures commonly taken as the defining examples of the trench poet. In doing so, I provisionally adopt a version of the conceptual framework that Nosheen Khan refers to as the "received opinion" of the history of World War I poetry, which she characterizes as holding that there was a "steady progression from illusion to disillusion, from vision to reality" (35). Rather than a steady progression, I see it as a swerve.[2] Certainly, however, I endorse Khan's view that this standard version of literary history is an oversimplification, since in fact "various attitudes" existed and were expressed in verse "alongside one another." Women poets in particular, such as Lady Margaret Sackville, were "writing and publishing protest poetry before such was conceived of by Sassoon and Owen" (Khan 31).

Changes in sensibility are never clean-cut or clearly delineated, and a rigid schematic inevitably abstracts from a reality clotted with exceptions and contradictions. Even so, the generally accepted view that with the Battle of the Somme in mid-1916 war poetry abruptly became both more brutally factual and less guided by grand illusions proves to be a useful approximation, fitting the general outlines of the considerable body of memorable poetry that came out of the war.

One corollary of the premise that poetry changed in the course of the war from an expression of martial aspiration and the glory of sacrifice to one of disillusionment is that the change came about because of the trench poets' direct experience on the war's horrific front lines and that out of this experience they produced "the essential work of the Great War" (Hannah 358). But that corollary is one it is important to resist. By labeling only the soldier poets "essential," it implies a narrow definition of war poetry as poetry of the battlefield, to the exclusion of poetry written out of other experiences and concerns of wartime. Admirable as is David Perkins's brief summary of the history of the change in poetic sensibility that occurred during the war, he falls into the fallacy of such a definition when he writes, for example, that the change was one of a difference "between the poets who merely read about the fighting and those who actually did it" (272). That is, as James Campbell writes, Perkins betrays "combat gnosticism," Campbell's term for an "ideology [that] has served . . . to limit severely the canon of texts that mainstream First World War criticism has seen as legitimate war writing" (203). To be sure, direct experience is valuable, and accuracy and vividness are important attributes of writing that reports firsthand witness, but war is a far larger, more multidimensional social calamity than is encompassed in battlefield experience alone, and the kinds of experiences and causes for reflection it brings are of many sorts.[3] Women poets (the group in whose behalf Khan challenges the "received opinion" and whose work I consider in the next chapter) wrote, for the most part, a poetry of emotional and moral reflection on the war. Their writings often reflected direct experience too: an experience of absence, loss, and grieving.

The poets who have traditionally been recognized as the major voices of World War I—a judgment that is in itself largely a function of selective memorializing—wrote out of experience of the battlefield. It is a group that includes Richard Aldington (1892–1962), noted imagist; Edmund Blunden (1896–1974), quiet celebrant of the English countryside who served at the Somme and Ypres and wrote some horrific verse about what he saw; Robert Graves (1895–1985), an accomplished and influential poet best known for his memoir *Goodbye to All That*; Ivor Gurney (1890–1937), musician as well as poet, whose mental disturbance after 1918 sometimes caused him to believe the war was ongoing (Giddings 183); Isaac Rosenberg (1890–1918), a visual artist before he was a poet, killed in action in the last year of the war; Charles Sorley (1892–1915), killed at the Battle of Loos; Siegfried Sassoon (1886–1967), who enlisted on August 3, 1914, but by 1917 lodged a protest against the war on pacifist grounds, even while continuing to serve out of loyalty to his troops; and Wilfred Owen (1893–1918), often regarded as the chief of the war poets, killed in action a week before armistice. All of these and others wrote about the war from the perspective of combat.

At the time, however, the phrase "soldier poets" was not used with reference to the poets considered here, but for the various contributors to two volumes of verse published in 1916 and 1917 by "Erskine Macdonald" (pseudonym for Galloway Kyle): *Songs of the Fighting Men* by "the Soldier Poets" and *More Songs by the Fighting Men*. The "soldier poets" whose verses were collected in these popularly acclaimed volumes gave "perhaps an occasional gesture at the undesirability of War in the abstract" but for the most part "endorse[d] an unquestioning acceptance of the necessity for continued prosecution of *this* war and of all the sacrifices entailed" (Norgate 517). There is a certain irony, then, in my use of the term for the title of this chapter. We can feel confident that Wilfred Owen noted the irony of the phrase, as well; he owned a copy of *More Songs* given to him by one of the contributing poets (Norgate 519).

The swerve from heroic aspiration to the bitter disillusionment that characterizes poetry of the later war years can be seen in process, at the very moment of turning, in a poem by Siegfried Sassoon, "To Victory." Here, not yet as embittered as he was to become, Sassoon wishes he could regain a sense of war as pageantry. Written in 1915, before the Somme and long before Sassoon undertook overt protest against the war, the poem cries for a return of "lustre," "colours that were my joy," and "banners," all now lost in a great weariness of "the greys and

browns and the leafless ash" (*War Poems* 21). For Sassoon, something
had already changed. It is not entirely clear whether the lost but remembered "colours" and "banners" are, as they first appear, the trappings of
military zest or perhaps the colorful beauties of an English spring. But
one feels that whichever is the literal and which the figurative meaning—
and the two seem to shift—he is referring to both: both his English
home before the eruption of the war and his own vision of war itself
before weariness and disillusion set in. Clearly, the "streaming / Banners
of dawn and sundown after rain" would seem to be the colors of *other*
dawns and sunsets than those seen by the men in the trenches. (Dawn
and sunset brought "stand-to," when, even if no assault were known to
be in process, troops had to move up onto the firing step and peer over
the top, exposing themselves to fire.) Phrases such as "young-limbed"
inevitably refer to soldiers, despite serving grammatically as modifiers
of remembered "copses"—that is, woods. But the word "copses" necessarily evokes "corpses," the present condition of many of the "young-
limbed" soldiers. And "banners of dawn," for all their attachment to
memories of home ("colours that were my joy"), call to mind the "banners" and "colours" to which enlistees rallied.

In this poem Sassoon seems already aware of his own participation
in a midwar shift in sensibility. Yet its style is not by any means that of
his later exposés of war's horrors or his attacks on warmongering. When
he showed "To Victory" to Robert Graves in manuscript in November
1915, when the two had just met, Graves observed that he "would soon
change his style." The word "victory," for that matter, would soon become either an impossible or else a deeply ironic one. For his part, Sassoon judged Graves's poetry at the time too "realistic" (Graves 175). Sassoon's opinions, as well as his style, would soon change.

Elsewhere in 1915, Jessie Pope might summon the pluck to hope that
"he'll come out on top, somehow" ("Socks"), but Edward Thomas was
already fixated on thoughts of how the war "began / To turn young
men to dung" ("Gone, Gone Again," Giddings 62).[4] It was in October of
that year that Charles Sorley was shot in the head and his stringent
war poems, exhorting his readers not to say "soft things," were found
in his field kit (Giddings 29, 55). Wilfred Owen, in 1915, envisioned a
path of glory extending across Europe, but this was before he left his
work as language tutor and enlisted (in the same month in which Sorley
was killed). When he reached the trenches, his poetry would drastically

change. Herbert Read's change of tone had come earlier. In January 1915, when he enlisted, he already regarded the war as "a conflict between rival imperial powers which would bring destruction to the peoples engaged"—a turn from his "completely unreal" idea of the war in 1914 (*Innocent Eye* 150). Even in 1915, before either Owen or Sassoon, Read began publishing poems in a starkly imagist manner that were critical of the war (*Innocent Eye* 151).

The long-lived Read would write in *Annals of Innocence and Experience* (1940) that he had "discovered" himself and his style by the end of the war and was no longer subject to "acquired mannerisms" (102). How clearly he had realized his voice is evident in "The Refugees," where his compassion toward the "mute figures with bowed heads" who "travel along the road" is all the more compelling for being rendered in tersely direct statement (*CP* 37). Often and rightly grouped with the imagists, Read might equally well be likened to American poet John Crowe Ransom, especially in his poems that operate through sharply phrased plain statement. Yet at times Read's voice was intensified beyond *either* the acerbic observational tone of Ransom's variety of early modernism *or* the reliance on image associated with, say, H. D. or Aldington. In "The Happy Warrior," a poem of overt rebellion against the rhetoric of traditional war poetry, it takes on an almost savage sarcasm as he parodies Wordsworth's "Character of the Happy Warrior":

> His wild heart beats with painful sobs
> his strain'd hands clench an ice-cold rifle
> his aching jaws grip a hot parch'd tongue
> his wide eyes search unconsciously.
>
> He cannot shriek
>
> Bloody saliva
> dribbles down his shapeless jacket.
>
> I saw him stab
> and stab again
> a well-killed Boche.
>
> This is the happy warrior,
> this is he . . . (*CP* 35)

The ellipses shown here are how the poem ends. In Wordsworth's lines, however, the phrase goes on: "This is the happy warrior, / This is he whom every man in arms / Would wish to be." Hardly.

This early stream of disillusionment and protest became a flood after the brutal spectacle of the Somme. In the following year, 1917, Edward Thomas would be killed at Arras, and Sassoon would write his poem "The General":

> "Good-morning, good-morning!" the General said
> When we met him last week on our way to the line.
> Now the soldiers he smiled at are most of 'em dead,
> And we're cursing his staff for incompetent swine.
> "He's a cheery old card," grunted Harry to Jack
> As they slogged up to Arras with rifle and pack.
>
> But he did for them both by his plan of attack.(*War Poems* 78)

The plain monosyllables and the anglicized accentuation of the French place-name, the way Harry and Jack would have said it, are characteristic of Sassoon's direct style by this point in the war. It was in that same year, 1917, that events occurred that Ernest Hemingway would write of in his 1929 novel about the Italian front, *A Farewell to Arms,* giving definitive statement to the rejection of the high-minded abstractions of the early war: "Abstract words such as glory, honor, courage, or hallow were obscene" (185). These were the abstractions of traditional war poetry. With that rejection, poetry became increasingly centered on graphic visual images of a brutality and ugliness that would formerly have been left discreetly unnoticed, concealed behind the "abstract words."

~

Parallel developments were occurring in the visual arts, as painters such as Paul Nash abandoned the heroic mode of traditional military paintings in favor of grimly reportorial and expressionist depictions of ugliness, devastation, and inhumanity. Nash joined the British army in August 1914, in the rush of enthusiasm that carried so many volunteers into service, but remained in England on Home Guard duty until he was sent to Belgium in February 1917. From early March until May 25, when he suffered a broken rib in a fall, he was in the lines as an infantryman in the deadly Ypres Salient. (A protrusion of the trench line into German lines in Flanders about four miles deep and nine miles wide at its base, the salient exposed men to fire from three sides.) On October 31, 1917, Nash returned to Belgium for slightly over a month, this time as one of the artists employed by the British Ministry of Information for the purpose of documenting the war as seen through painterly eyes. "It was the intention," Charles Harrison writes, "that priority should be accorded to eye-witness over imaginative reconstruction" (120).[5] But Nash had begun making sketches of the battlefield during his first tour at the front, working mostly in white chalk on brown paper during "periods off duty behind the front line" (Causey 67) while his memories of what he had seen were fresh. The paintings he produced in 1918 and 1919 were made from these numerous sketches done during both his initial service at the front and his later weeks there as official artist (a status also held by his brother John Nash).

Although the time Paul Nash spent at the front was fairly brief, experience provided dramatic changes in his apprehension of the war. During his first stint at Ypres, the descriptions he sent home in letters convey an interest in color and mass, a weirdly jarring sensibility of the picturesque. When he returned, in time to witness the debacle in the mud at Passchendaele (the Third Battle of Ypres), his "earlier enthusiasm" for the scenery of war had yielded, Harrison writes, to "a deep disgust" (138). Now the sunrise and sunset struck him as "blasphemous." He labeled himself "a messenger who will bring back word from the men who are fighting to those who want the war to go on for ever . . . a bitter truth, and may it burn their lousy souls" (quoted by Harrison 139 and Cork 137). He had been, he said, "jolted" by his war experience into a new and more powerful way of painting (Causey 73).

The "bitter truth" Nash referred to is the message of the war paintings he completed in the year after armistice. These have been called "quite simply, the most impressive paintings and graphic works made by any British artist during the conflict" (Cork 196). Nash's *Void* (1918)—termed by Causey (77) "a statement of hopelessness"—and his well-known *Menin Road* (1919) convey his anger at the desecration of the natural world and show the war's cruelty to the men lost in this tortured landscape (see figs. 3 and 5). *We Are Making a New World* (1918), a painting of bizarre and tormented landscape without living figures, conveys

3. Paul Nash, *Void*, 1918. Courtesy of the National Gallery of Canada, Ottawa; transfer from the Canadian War Memorials, 1921.

Nash's anger and his powerful antiwar message in its sarcastic title as well as the canvas itself.[6] The novelist Arnold Bennett observed that Nash's "dead . . . landscapes" showed "little figures of men creeping devotedly and tragically over the waste" (quoted by Causey 71). Similarly, a painting by his brother John Nash, *Over the Top* (also 1918), though done in a very different style, also conveys the misery and futility of the soldiers who doggedly walk on, past the bodies of their newly killed comrades, in a blank waste of snow and into a fog, or perhaps the smoke of enemy fire (see fig. 4).

These bleak paintings by the Nashes provide an especially useful gloss for the poetry coming out of the war by 1916 and '17, but they were by no means unique. Paintings conveying disillusionment, discouragement, and loss of identity were being produced in Axis countries as well—for example, by the Austrian Albin Egger-Lienz and the German Ludwig Meidner. Although heartening or anti-German propaganda painting continued in England through 1916 and into 1917,[7] such mournful can-

4. John Nash, *Over the Top*, 1918. Courtesy of the Imperial War Museum, London.

vases as Charles Sims's *Clio and the Children*, showing the Muse despairing over a blood-stained parchment while children watch attentively, and George Clausen's *Youth Mourning*, painted after his daughter's fiancé was killed in the war, appeared in 1915 and 1916. The year of the Somme also produced Christopher Nevinson's *La Patrie*, among the bleakest of all paintings of the war, depicting wounded French soldiers dying in agony on the floor of an abandoned warehouse—an explicit memory of the artist's from his service with the Red Cross. It was also in 1916 that Mark Gertler painted *Merry-Go-Round*, in which a carousel with starkly unadorned horses on which gleeful soldiers ride in circles serves, in Cork's words, as "a metaphor for the military machine transforming everyone caught up in its diabolic motion" (131, 137). Gertler's *Merry-Go-Round* was so disturbing in its exposure of society's captivation by the war machine that the artist's friends advised him not to exhibit it, lest he become the target of retaliation or government repression. D. H. Lawrence called it "horrible and terrifying," and pacifist leader Ottoline Morrell said that "one might as well think of liking a machine-gun" (Cork 137). But even with such an abundance of visual art capturing the horror and disillusionment of the war, the work of Paul and John Nash remains especially memorable.

⌒

Paul Nash's title *We Are Making a New World* could well be used for Wilfred Owen's personal accounts of the devastation to the natural scene he encountered while in combat in early 1917. Owen went into the line at Betancourt, on the Somme, on January 9. Less than a month later, in a letter to his mother dated February 4, he emphasized not so much the danger he had recently experienced (about which, after all, he could not give any specifics, due to censorship) as the "universal pervasion of *Ugliness*" (his own capitalization and underscoring) and the "hideous landscapes . . . everything unnatural, broken, blasted" (*Collected Letters* 482). Significantly, Owen noted the incongruity between this ugliness and traditional heroic war poetry: "unburiable bodies sit outside the dug-outs all day, all night, the most execrable sights on earth. In poetry we call them the most glorious." He acknowledged, then mocked as inadequate, his aunt's "shrewd" observation that a prevailing tone of "distaste" underlay his accounts (482–83).

Writing poetry that was "direct, critical, even brutal in its assertiveness" (Hannah 358), the trench poets insistently turned their attention to the ruination of the earth itself, along with the brutalization of the soldiers and the appalling horror of their experiences. The new physical world of stripped, broken trees and cratered earth, the result of artillery bombardment and dense rifle or machine-gun fire, became an apt equivalent of the human dismemberment and degradation they witnessed. Herbert Read, adapting the name of an actual place near Ypres, Polygonwald (or the Polygon Wood), called this ruined world "Polygonveld," a phrase meaning more or less geometric-figure world.[8] The term evokes in his readers' visual imaginations the expanse of earth Read and others actually saw from the trenches, a devitalized landscape of jumbled angles and lines—the kind of landscape we see in Paul Nash's sketches and paintings, with their defoliated, sticklike twisted trees, such as *The Menin Road* (see fig. 5). The Battle of Polygon Wood, in which the wood was taken from the German army in September 1917, was in fact a sector of the Battle of Menin Road.

In Read's "Kneeshaw Goes to War" Polygonveld is "a ghastly desola-

5. Paul Nash, *The Menin Road*, 1919. Courtesy of the Imperial War Museum, London.

tion"; the earth is "scarr'd and broken / By torrents of plunging shells; / Then wash'd and sodden with autumnal rains" until it becomes "a viscous ooze." Kneeshaw watches as the man marching by his side sinks into this ooze up to his neck beyond all efforts to dig him out, until, in one of the most horrific moments in all the poetry of the war, an officer shoots him in the head. Read's tersely blunt statement leaves the details to the reader's reluctant imagination: "Not a neat job—the revolver / Was too close" (*CP* 31–32). Edmund Blunden, constantly remembering his beloved English countryside, imagined the Ancre's "battered bank" uttering a "wounded moan" and lamented "a whole sweet countryside amuck with murder" ("The Ancre at Hamel" and "Third Ypres," *Selected Poems* 50, 33). Ever the gentleman farmer in his leanings, Blunden developed a farming metaphor to viciously ironic effect in "Rural Economy," where spring plowing and planting are changed from rituals of life to rituals of death. The battlefield has been "raked and ploughed with a will" by a combination "sower"/ "ploughman"—that is, artillery shells. Sowing seeds of iron and body parts into the earth, this planter is growing a harvest of death (40). Ivor Gurney, who would soon go mad, drew his primary poetic imagery from the contrast between "unravaged nature" and the "havoc" wreaked on it by the war (Perkins 273). Even the red poppy of Isaac Rosenberg's celebrated "Break of Day in the

Trenches"—which Perkins considers one of his three or four best works (286) and Fussell calls, without qualification, "the most sophisticated poem of the war" (*Great War* 55)—draws much of its power as an image from the contrast between its natural vitality and the "white dust" of the "torn" battlefield that settles over it.

In poems such as Rosenberg's marvel of compressed complexity, the conventions of war poetry that prevailed at the start of the Great War— the language of patriotic pieties and such techniques as insistent marching meter and predictable rhymes—have been thoroughly subverted. "Break of Day in the Trenches" is, indeed, an excellent example of the utter change in war poetry simply because it is not so startling an example as some, with their brutally graphic depictions of wounds and of the decaying dead, their stark imagism, and their bitterness. Written in June 1916, Rosenberg's poem is quieter, subtler. Here it is in its entirety:

> The darkness crumbles away.
> It is the same old druid Time as ever,
> Only a live thing leaps my hand,
> A queer sardonic rat,
> As I pull the parapet's poppy
> To stick behind my ear.
> Droll rat, they would shoot you if they knew
> Your cosmopolitan sympathies.
> Now you have touched this English hand
> You will do the same to a German
> Soon, no doubt, if it be your pleasure
> To cross the sleeping green between.
> It seems you inwardly grin as you pass
> Strong eyes, fine limbs, haughty athletes,
> Less chanced than you for life,
> Bonds to the whims of murder,
> Sprawled in the bowels of the earth,
> The torn fields of France.
> What do you see in our eyes
> At the shrieking iron and flame
> Hurled through still heavens?
> What quaver—what heart aghast?

Poppies whose roots are in man's veins
Drop, and are ever dropping;
But mine in my ear is safe—
Just a little white with the dust. (Giddings 67–68)

The poet's tone of ironic humor, seen in the labeling of the rat as "cosmopolitan" because it willingly infests German as well as British trenches and consumes German as well as British dead, comes close to breaking only when he allows himself to think, momentarily, of the inner state of the soldiers in their trenches. With the urgent rhetorical questions of lines 19 through 22 and in the words "shrieking," "quaver," and "aghast," he becomes almost distraught, then pulls back to his hard-won note of factual reportage tinged with determination to maintain distance, as he makes his minimalist statement about the poppies and the dust whitening one he has tucked behind his ear.[9] In addition to this delicately contained irony, we might note the poem's cuttingly precise, yet odd diction (the verb "crumbles," the adjective "droll") and a subtle associativeness that quietly elevates details to the status of symbol (through the parallel established between the "sardonic" and "droll" rat and the droll or perhaps sardonic speaker as he places a flower behind his ear at morning stand-to). Resonant throughout is the suggestion of blood in the image of poppies that "drop, and are ever dropping"—both, of course, being red.

How can so odd a poem be seen as indicative of a general trend? What about its antic spirit demonstrates a new kind of war poetry? One can find an exception to almost any of the following, but in general the new kind of war poetry was characterized by:

Irony, as seen in Rosenberg's ironic tone, in Read's allusion to Wordsworth, in Blunden's paralleling of an artillery barrage with a farmer's planting. Irony became the dominant mode in soldier poetry as it persistently voiced a perception of difference between expectation and reality. People in great numbers, both those exposed to battlefield experience and those not, came to see themselves as having been duped by a rhetoric of jingoistic patriotism and of sentimental aspiration to noble sacrifice for a glorious cause.

Bluntness of visual details, in a growing emphasis on immediate,

unprettified facts, a determination to show the truth of war for
what it was. In part, this was linked with the sense of having been
duped. The new war poets seemed to say, "You, Society, you old
men who wield the power, you deceived us into thinking we
should go into this thing; now let us tell you how it really is."
(The hostility in this imagined but implicit statement was sometimes also directed at women who both in fact and in government
propaganda urged men to enlist.) And so we are treated to such
details as the "lean green flies upon the red flesh madding" in Blunden's "Third Ypres" (1917) or the "brains splattered on / A stretcher-
bearer's face" and the wagon wheel grazing the face of a just-dead
soldier in Rosenberg's "Dead Man's Dump" (also 1917)—harsh
realities carrying the weight of the poets' statements in their mere
presentation (Giddings 122, 94). As Hemingway would write in
A Farewell to Arms, abstractions stopped carrying much weight.

A reluctance to use marching rhythms, the heavy four-beat meter
approximating the footfalls of parading soldiers that had been
characteristic of martial music and the older military poetry. These
were rarely heard after the midpoint of the war. Any regular meter
tended to be disrupted if not entirely abandoned, unless used with
irony or by a naive versifier.

Ambiguity and disorder. Meaning became less and less clear, even
as the war itself yielded to disordered mayhem.

Sadness and misery, an emphasis on what Owen called "the pity
of war." In the face of devastating losses and griefs, a resistant refusal to see glory became the predominant attitude.

Ruined landscapes of pollarded (stripped and broken) trees and
"torn fields" (as in Rosenberg's "Break of Day in the Trenches")
appear both in poetry and in visual art. As Fussell has classically
observed in *The Great War and Modern Memory* (52), dawn and
evening became even more insistent as emblematic settings but
with the "cruel reversal" of a new reason: stand-to. The symbol of
dawn, as a stock poetic image, changed from a time of glorious
beauty, redemption, and new beginnings to one of summons to the
day's first stand-to on the firing step, with its associated danger
and heightened tension. Birds, too, became more frequently recurrent, but with a pointedly ironic association: as emblems of a

wished-for or perhaps illusory freedom, in contrast to men pinned down in the muck of their trenches.

∾

Siegfried Sassoon and Wilfred Owen provide examples of all these attributes of the sea change in war poetry, but in different ways. Sassoon was less technically innovative than Owen or, say, Read or Rosenberg. Both Sassoon and Owen tended to persist in the use of regular meters and forms, but Owen did so with a rapidly increasing suppleness of rhythm and near-rhyme, or pararhyme. Yet both demonstrate the swerve or lurch that occurred midwar, as they became increasingly critical of its continuance, Sassoon characteristically in anger, Owen in bitter pathos. Not only are they the two most famous of the trench poets, but they knew each other. Sassoon, the elder and more established, had a powerful, probably determinant, influence on Owen. Together, they provide an interesting and important story of poetic influence, and together demonstrate the variousness of World War I poetry, even after the Somme and even if we consider, for now, only the male poets who were for so long singled out as if they were the only poets of the war.

A member of the country gentry, educated at Cambridge (though he left without taking a degree), Sassoon was almost twenty-eight when he enlisted at the start of the war. He was awarded the Military Cross in June 1916. After being hospitalized for trench fever and again for measles, he served on the Somme for more than a month in 1917 before being sent back to England with a shoulder wound. On July 30, 1917, he publicly declared his protest against the war in a statement read in the House of Commons. Through the efforts of Robert Graves he was brought before a medical board in Liverpool which, largely as an official dodge to avoid the controversy of a court-martial, ordered that he be sent to Craiglockhart War Hospital, where he was treated for shell shock and "antiwar complex" by the famous anthropologist and psychiatrist W. H. R. Rivers. Ruled once again fit for service, he returned to active duty in December 1917. In July 1918 he was again wounded and sent home.

Sassoon's poems provide one of the most instructive of all histories of the change in both the style and the substance of war poetry. Read in chronological order by date of composition (to the extent it is known), as they are arranged in Rupert Hart-Davis's compilation *The War Poems of Siegfried Sassoon* (1983), they tell a story of bitter awakening. It is for these verse satires on the cruelty of war that Sassoon has been best known, though he was also a prolific author of fictionalized memoirs after the war.

As we have already noted, Sassoon did not always write in the style for which he became known. In mid-1915, after about nine months in the military, he could still speak of the army as "the happy legion" and address his fellow soldiers in elevating and generalizing terms as "my comrades and my brothers" ("Absolution" 15). In December 1915 he would employ such archaic language as "laurell'd head" in a poem called "To My Brother" and refer to death as "victory," a conventional notion indeed. But at that same time (that is, according to Hart-Davis, between November 1915 and March 1916) he was writing what he himself called his "first front-line poem," "The Redeemer," a relatively realistic sketch of a laden trench laborer with an assertion of the trope of the soldier as Christ. He would not write what he regarded as his first really "outspoken" war poem, "In the Pink" (rejected for publication by the *Westminster* for likely bad effect on recruiting) until February 1916, but by then he had already begun using the war as a vehicle for questioning God, a theme that would become more insistent in his verse as hostilities wore on. "The Prince of Wounds," which he dated December 27, 1915 (printed from manuscript in *War Poems*), employs the trope of the soldier as Christ skeptically:

Have we the strength to strive alone
Who can no longer worship Christ?
Is He a God of wood and stone,
While those who served him writhe and moan,
On warfare's altar sacrificed? (*War Poems* 19)

Although it is not at all clear that Sassoon showed this unpublished poem to Owen when they met a year and a half later, one wonders if its image of sacrifice on "warfare's altar" might have triggered Owen's "Parable of the Old Man and the Young," written in July 1918 and retelling the story of Abraham and Isaac with a twist.

The idea of sacrificial suffering emblematized in Christ would have been entirely familiar to both poets, of course, from the pervasive influence of Christianity's valuation of sacrifice and physical pain. They and their contemporaries, whether Christian or not, would have grown up steeped in the "Christian inheritance" of sexual repression and what Adrian Caesar charges, in *Taking It Like a Man*, was a very real strain of spiritualized sadomasochism. Caesar forcefully argues that in this respect the contrast regularly drawn between the poetry of Sassoon and Owen, on the one hand, and that of Brooke, on the other, was in fact a continuity, in that all three shared the impulse to see the sufferings of the soldier in terms of the sufferings of Christ and to find meaning in pain. The kind of meaning they found and the tone in which they conveyed it in their verse differed, of course, enormously. Sassoon would return to the trope of the soldier as Christ in "Golgotha" (March 1916), but then abandon it in favor of more graphic presentations of the dead, wounded, and wearied. The role of religion in his poetry became increasingly satiric. One of the most biting expressions of such a view, a cry for an end to the war called "Christ and the Soldier" (August 1916), he later came to regard as "contrived" (*War Poems* 47), but his poems written late in the war frequently imply an abandonment of religion, as if godliness and warfare had come to seem mutually exclusive.

Sassoon himself recognized that he wrote the best poetry of his life from mid-1916 until 1918. After the war, in 1921, he recorded his dissatisfaction with the poetry he was then producing and exclaimed, "If only that feeling and fluency would return, as it did in May 1916!" (*Diaries* 35). Beginning in mid-1916, his poetry confronted such socially unacceptable topics as soldiers' willingness to sustain a wound or even amputation if it meant being invalided home ("The One-Legged Man," August 1916, and "A Ballad," October 1916) and the mystifications and misrepresentations in official rhetoric ("The Hero," also August 1916). Perhaps the best known of his poems pointing out the falsification inherent in public rhetoric is "'They,'" which he dated October 31, 1916. A "Bishop" intones his certainty that when the "boys" return from war they won't "be the same," because they will have participated in a heroic struggle. But the veterans' transformations are seen more realistically by the "boys" themselves:

> "We're none of us the same!" the boys reply.
> "For George lost both his legs; and Bill's stone blind;

Poor Jim's shot through the lungs and like to die;
And Bert's gone syphilitic: you'll not find
A chap who's served that hasn't found *some* change."
And the Bishop said: "The ways of God are strange." (*War Poems* 57)

Any number of observers of the returning troops found that "they had not come back the same men" (Leed 187), but not necessarily in the way Sassoon's bishop seems to mean. His specious elevated diction is punctured by the boys' colloquial language, just as the vagueness of his high-flown rhetoric is punctured by their bluntness in translating his prediction of "changes": "stone blind" and "syphilitic." Besides contrasting the elevated and the common in language, the poem implies contrasts between the old and the new consciousness, the presumably aged and the nominally young, the influential and the victimized, the upper class and the lower. Sassoon's attacks on the proponents of war were becoming more direct and sweeping as his statement of the soldiers' misery grew blunter.

In the fall of 1916, while on medical leave in England, Sassoon became acquainted with prominent pacifists such as Bertrand Russell and Lady Ottoline Morrell. In his own words, he then began to write poems that would unsettle public complacency. He had already written, earlier that year, the long poem "A Night Attack," which though it dwells on the stench of the dead and the casual hatred of the British soldiers for the "bloody Bosche" (*War Poems* 42), yet counters that hatred with the equal pathos of German casualties. Such harshness and such refusal to enter into routine demonizing of the enemy would characterize his war poems from that time on. His anger is apparent in the noted "'Blighters'" (February 4, 1917), with its vision of a tank crushing its way through rows of theater-going civilians. Here, like Hemingway, he cites facts and names of places as a kind of sacralizing mantra, but unlike Hemingway adds commentary to his citations:

I'd like to see a Tank come down the stalls,
Lurching to ragtime tunes, or "Home, sweet Home",
And there'd be no more jokes in Music-halls
To mock the riddled corpses round Bapaume. (*War Poems* 68)

Much of Sassoon's anger was directed at those who fomented war at a safe distance. In April 1917, while hospitalized, he wrote (in "To the War-mongers") of being "back again from hell" while accusingly recognizing "For you our battles shine / With triumph half-divine" (77). In a similar vein, in a poem written at Craiglockhart and published in the *Cambridge Magazine* on October 6, 1917, he asked sarcastically,

> Does it matter?—losing your sight?
> There's such splendid work for the blind;
> And people will always be kind. (*War Poems* 91)

Although he chose to go back to the front upon being ruled fit for duty in order to be with his men (out of the loyalty for comrades-in-arms that Ferguson argues was the motivation for soldiers on both sides to continue fighting), Sassoon remained insistently critical of the war.

David Perkins's conclusion that "none of [Sassoon's] poems can compare with the best of Wilfred Owen" and "some of them are hardly more than journalism" (277) is perhaps judicious.[10] Some few have keen impact in their satiric bite or in the brutal vividness of their rendition of wounds, suffering, and the dead. But in my judgment Sassoon's best single poem is in a very different vein. In the sonnet "Dreamers," also written at Craiglockhart, he reined in his vitriol to let ordinary longings and simple dailiness convey, in a kind of urban Georgianism, their own unadorned pathos. Even in the midst of "flaming, fatal" action, his soldiers are "dreamers":

> . . . when the guns begin
>   They think of firelit homes, clean beds and wives.
>
> I see them in foul dug-outs, gnawed by rats,
>   And in the ruined trenches, lashed with rain,
> Dreaming of things they did with balls and bats,
>   And mocked by hopeless longing to regain
> Bank-holidays, and picture shows, and spats,
>   And going to the office in the train. (*War Poems* 88)

～

Wilfred Owen did not spring from the country gentry, like Sassoon, but from an economically straitened family struggling to retain a tenuous hold on gentility. He enlisted at the end of 1915 as a private. But his evolution in attitude and style resembles Sassoon's in its rejection of the old rhetoric of martial glory and his turn *toward*, but not *to*, pacifism.

As Stallworthy demonstrates, Owen's attitudes toward the war had begun to change even before his enlistment. In August 1915 he had written to his mother from France, where he was employed as a tutor, that "the guns will effect a little useful weeding"—a mouthing of the widespread notion that war would revitalize society by cleansing it of decadence (Stallworthy 109). Only a month later, having seen wounded French soldiers back from the front, he wrote to his brother about the horrible wounds and miserable filth he had seen, adding, "I deliberately tell you this to educate you to the actualities of the war" (Stallworthy 109–10). A year later, in the fall of 1916, he told his brother Harold that he would "conform" to military life "outwardly" and try to be a good soldier, but inwardly would remain apart. Largely this was a reaction to the coarseness of the men in his unit, over whom he now held the rank of second lieutenant (Stallworthy 146, 137). On December 30, 1916—at the end of the month in which Sassoon wrote "The Redeemer" and "The Prince of Wounds"—Owen's battalion crossed the English Channel on its way to front line duty in France. There his mental evolution would be dramatically accelerated.

On January 6, in freezing rain, Owen moved into the lines with the 2nd Manchesters regiment, which had seen punishing action during the late fall, and first heard what he called, in one of his frequent letters home to his mother, the "sublimity" of the guns (*Collected Letters* 423).[11] In another letter he reported a mean depth of two feet of water in the trenches and a "Gehenna" of artillery bombardment, and joked that he feared his writing style would become "bomb-shell-bastic" (*Collected Letters* 424–26). During the last week of January his platoon spent day after day in an advanced front line site exposed to cold and snow without so much as a trench to provide shelter (*Collected Letters* 13). He described this episode as being "marooned on a frozen desert" while having to watch one of his men freeze to death (*Collected Letters* 430). The experience produced "Exposure," probably his first poem in the new style of bitter disillusionment that would characterize his writing for the rest of his short life.[12] In eight stanzas whose adjectival slowness, overpunctuation, and hovering near-rhymes expertly convey the immobility of which the poem speaks, "Exposure" begins:

> Our brains ache, in the merciless iced east winds that knive us . . .
> Wearied we keep awake because the night is silent . . .
> Low, drooping flares confuse our memory of the salient, . . .
> Worried by silence, sentries whisper, curious, nervous,
> > But nothing happens. (*CP* 186)

After a recovery period at Abbeville, during which he went through a course to qualify him for transport duty, Owen returned to the front on March 1, 1917, but suffered a concussion on March 11, resulting in his evacuation four days later. In April he was back in the front lines twice more; then, in late April, after three and a half months on the Somme, he was injured by the close explosion of an artillery shell and invalided to the rear. Diagnosed as suffering a concussion and "neurasthenia," or shell shock, he was sent back to England.[13] He arrived at Craiglockhart Military Hospital in Edinburgh in late June and there, in August, met Sassoon.

The poem by which Owen is most often represented in anthologies, "Dulce et Decorum Est," was drafted two months later, in October 1917. It was famously dedicated in manuscript to Jessie Pope, the popular writer of jingoist verses urging young men—in greatly meliorated terms, of course—to go bravely into the horrors Owen records.[14] Titled from a line by the Roman patriot Horace meaning "it is sweet and fitting to die for one's country" (my translation; Owen wrote alternately "sweet and meet" or "sweet and decorous"), the poem is accurately described by Stallworthy as a release of "nightmare memories" (228).[15] The plight of a soldier caught in poison gas without his mask returns literally as a nightmare:

> But someone still was yelling out and stumbling,
> And flound'ring like a man in fire or lime . . .
> Dim, through the misty panes and thick green light,
> As under a green sea, I saw him drowning.

In all my dreams, before my helpless sight,
He plunges at me, guttering, choking, drowning.[16]

Even those not gassed are visually turned into nightmarish monsters with the donning of their masks. The poem's images of stooped and tattered, worn-out soldiers with "blood-shod" feet and the floundering of one who failed to get his "misty pane[d]" gas helmet on in time, and its elastically varying rhythms that accommodate spondees (double single-syllable accents) and running phrases according to the intensely emotional meaning, all invite reading aloud. Those who do (for instance, classroom teachers seeking to impress the poem's intensity on their students) will inevitably find their voices bending toward sarcasm at the end, where the Latin line is quoted in full—for the purpose, of course, of mocking it as a calculated lie:

If in some smothering dreams you too could pace
Behind the wagon that we flung him in
. . . .
My friend, you would not tell with such high zest
To children ardent for some desperate glory,
The old Lie: Dulce et decorum est
Pro patria mori. (*CP* 140)

The last word, "mori," to die, arrives with sardonic emphasis. It is, of course, Jessie Pope who is addressed facetiously as "my friend." Before the war, she had been a writer of children's books. Here, all those naive enough to believe her glorifying accounts of going to war are gathered up, rather sadly, under the rubric "children."

Owen's great outpouring of sometimes bitter, sometimes intensely sorrowing poems came in the fifteen months from his meeting of Sassoon until the end of his life in November 1918, only a week before the armistice, when he died in a doomed assault at the Sambre and Oise Canal. We can get a good conception of the nature of this outpouring from the nine poems later selected by composer Benjamin Britten as text for *War Requiem,* a memorial to the dead of both world wars.[17] These nine are "Anthem for Doomed Youth," an untitled fragment beginning "Bugles sang, saddening the evening air," "The Next War," "Son-

net (On Seeing a Piece of Our Artillery Brought into Action)," "Futility,"
"The Parable of the Old Man and the Young" (except for its startling
ending, a close rendition of Genesis 22: 1–19), "The End," "At a Calvary
near the Ancre," and "Strange Meeting." A reader who compares any
one of these, plus "Dulce et Decorum Est," to Owen's earlier poems will
see a dramatic growth in immediacy, authenticity, and rhythmic techniques along with an eruption of disgust at the war. If they differ from
Sassoon's characteristic poetry of the late war in their greater emphasis
on grieving and pity than on angry mockery, the difference lies mostly
in voice. The two were largely in agreement as to intention—so much in
agreement, in fact, that Owen could trust the older poet to discern his
thoughts without having to speak them. After he returned to the front
in September 1918, he wrote Sassoon, "What more is there to say that
you will not better understand unsaid" (*Collected Letters* 571).

"Anthem for Doomed Youth," written September to October 1917
at Craiglockhart, is probably the most traditional of the nine in language and form. Conveying the overwhelming grief Owen felt for the
young men "who die as cattle" in the war (*CP* 99), as well as for himself,
it contemplates the appropriate memorial observances of such deaths.
The trappings of traditional funerals—bells, prayers, choirs, candles, a
pall—are invoked only to be rejected. All these traditional trappings of
grief have been redefined by the war—bells turned into booming guns,
prayers "patter[ed] out" only by "stuttering rifles' rapid rattle," choirs
become the "wailing" of shells, and candles the light in the eyes of survivors who remember. Bugles, the traditional summons to battle, now
sound a futile summons home, "calling for them from sad shires." The
fragment ("Bugles sang, saddening the evening air"), the second text by
Owen used in Britten's *Requiem*, might almost have been an initial effort toward this better-known poem, with its sad bugles and despon-
dent, doomed "boys."

In "Anthem for Doomed Youth" the language of war poetry of the
past is explicitly inverted. Even so, by invoking such rejected trappings
within the traditional sonnet form the poem retains a nostalgic air that
belies its place in the excoriating new war poetry. But it belongs, finally,
with the new in its explicit rejection of the old language and in its refusal to lay claim to heroism or glory for these dead. The measured
last line—"And each slow dusk a drawing-down of blinds"—illustrates
Owen's increased poetic fluency and his ability to find (in T. S. Eliot's

later terminology) an objective correlative for prolonged mourning over the war's devastation of a generation. In his notes in the *Complete Poems*, Stallworthy points out that this last line may be an echo of Laurence Binyon's "At the going down of the sun and in the morning / We will remember them" (from "For the Fallen").[18] But its dusk and drawing-down of blinds are equally reminiscent of Sassoon's "Dreamers," written in the same year, 1917, with its picture of soldiers ruefully wishing for the dailiness of home. We might also note alongside Owen's rejection of traditional funerary observances as being inappropriate to these war deaths Wallace Stevens's similar, but characteristically more abstract, rejection in "Death of a Soldier" (1918):

> He does not become a three-days personage,
> Imposing his separation
> Calling for pomp.

> Death is absolute and without memorial . . . (97)

"The Next War," another sonnet chosen by Britten for the *War Requiem*, was written about the same time as "Dulce et Decorum Est." In a letter to his mother dated October 2, 1917, Owen mentioned that he was sending the poem for his younger brother, Colin—whose approach to draft age and interest in volunteering Owen found acutely distressing—to "read, mark, learn etc. it" (*Collected Letters* 550). The poem is a startling juxtaposition of surrealistic battlefield reportage with visionary hope:

> Out there, we walked quite friendly up to Death,—
>   Sat down and ate beside him, cool and bland,—
>   Pardoned his spilling mess-tins in our hand.
> We've sniffed the green thick odour of his breath,—
> Our eyes wept, but our courage didn't writhe.
>   He's spat at us with bullets, and he's coughed
>   Shrapnel. We chorused if he sang aloft,
> We whistled while he shaved us with his scythe.

> Oh, Death was never enemy of ours!
>   We laughed at him, we leagued with him, old chum.

No soldier's paid to kick against His powers.
    We laughed,—knowing that better men would come,
And greater wars: when every fighter brags
He fights on Death, for lives; not men, for flags. (*CP* 165)

The personification of death plays on the familiar representation of a cloaked figure carrying a scythe, but in Owen's line the grim reaper "shaves" rather than reaps the men; not yet cut down, they are merely subjected to close calls. Owen skillfully draws this conceit out for eleven lines before the striking turn in the twelfth, when the brittle laughter of the soldiers' effort to outface death suddenly becomes, instead, a visionary laughter of hope. It is a breathtaking poetic moment, positing a world free of war—the world Owen hoped for but no longer believed the present war would deliver. In that world, when better men will indeed fight, not for reasons of nationalistic chauvinism, against opposing armies, but for life, against death. To fight against other men "for flags," Owen's characterization of World War I, is actually to fight on the side of death; war, no matter how grandly organized, is a campaign of and for death. Thus the language of friendliness with the "old chum," a kind of defensive playacting, is at the same time a revelation that whatever the "flag" under which it fights, an army enlists on the side of death against life. With this abrupt expansion of meaning, Owen utilizes the traditional technique of the "turn" in the sonnet form, but combines it with matter-of-fact language ("old chum") and unpretty details (the spilled mess-tins, the smell of death) characteristic of modern verse. It is perhaps his finest achievement as a poet.

    The increasing flexibility in rhythms exhibited in Owen's work during this period of rapid maturation is also shown in "Futility," written in May 1918. A poem mostly of monosyllables and simple statements, its description of a paralyzed or dying soldier moves toward the less conversational polysyllabic "fatuous" in the next-to-last line, which suddenly, at that point of emphasis, shifts the import of the whole. In the first stanza the speaker urges some unnamed person or persons to "move him into the sun" in hopes its warmth will "rouse him" from his chill, or "snow" (*CP* 158). The word "snow" allies the condition of the (presumed) wounded soldier with the condition of the natural order—a subtle maneuver that prepares for the turn at the end. The second stanza invites us to consider the rousing effect of the sun's warmth, seen in the germination of seeds, in parallel with the warming of "the clays of a cold star" immensely long ago. The word "clay" links the soldier with the evolutionary processes of the universe by its reminder of the ordinary phrase "common clay." But still the trope remains inconspicuous, only hinted at. With the question "Are limbs, so dear achieved, are sides / Full-nerved, still warm, too hard to stir?" we relate the title, "Futility," to the futility of trying to reinvigorate the dying. Yet the evolutionary idea is again embedded in the question with the notion of animal limbs being "dear achieved." Then in the last three lines the meaning bursts outward to the cosmic level intended from the first:

> Was it for this [i.e., for needless death] the clay grew tall?
> —O what made fatuous sunbeams toil
> To break earth's sleep at all? (*CP* 158)

With these lines the war is positioned as an event of cosmic significance, and the whole of human and geologic process revealed as needless waste.

"The Parable of the Old Man and the Young," written, according to Stallworthy's dating, in July 1918, is a fulfillment of Owen's urge, documented in his letters, to challenge religious orthodoxy through parodies of familiar biblical language and stories. It is one of the great masterworks of twentieth-century poetry. In tone, it is much like his "Sonnet (On Seeing a Piece of Our Artillery Brought into Action)" with its first line "Be slowly lifted up, thou long black arm"—an apostrophe to one of the enormous artillery pieces developed during World War I—which ends in a curse on such weapons and on the human impulses that lead to their production. "Parable," too, is a poem of taut anger, yielding up Owen's characteristic sense of pity only indirectly, through its dramatization of situation.[19] We can only imagine the young poet's elation at finding himself able to render his anger and bitterness at the war in such terse and stunningly dramatized verse.

"Parable" reaches back to the ancient story of Abraham's willing obedience to God even to the point of sacrificing his son, Isaac. The presence of the war as secondary meaning in Owen's retelling of the story is suggested by the "belts and straps" with which the young Isaac is bound to the altar (recalling military uniform and paraphernalia) and the "parapets and trenches" Abraham builds in preparation for the sacrifice. Through twelve uninterrupted lines of flowing blank verse, Owen tells the familiar biblical story up to the point of the angel's call to spare the son and sacrifice, instead, the ram placed by God in a nearby thicket. Then comes the stunning couplet, tersely revealing the malice of the old against the young—the evil that Owen, Sassoon, and other poets saw behind the sacrifice of a generation:

> But the old man would not so, but slew his son,
> And half the seed of Europe, one by one.

It is a devastating, rending poem, its anger placing it in company with Sassoon's poetry of the late war. Here and in "Futility" and "The Next War" Owen had achieved his full power. We can only wonder whether he would have continued to move from masterwork to masterwork if he had outlived the war or would have tapered off as Sassoon knew himself to have done.

The last three poems of Owen's that would be set to music by Britten were "The End," "At a Calvary near the Ancre," and "Strange Meeting." "The End," composed over a period of more than a year, as Owen repeatedly returned to it, is another parable in quasi-biblical style, questioning the prophecy of Revelation that the dead will rise at the end and God will wipe away all tears from their eyes. And it appears the speaker of the poem is right to question, since in the sonnet's sestet the answer comes back that no, the scars caused by the war will not be "glorified" (*CP* 159). As a rejection of the biblical hope, the poem also rejects both religious and military rhetoric. Death is merely death. Ironically, Owen's mother chose part of this poem for his tombstone, but distorted the meaning. The passage as written by Owen was:

> Shall Life renew these bodies? Of a truth,
> All death will he annul, all tears assuage?—
> Or fill these void veins full again with youth,
> And wash, with an immortal water, Age?
>
> When I do ask white Age, he saith not so:
> "My head hangs weighed with snow."

And when I hearken to the Earth, she saith:
"My fiery heart shrinks, aching. It is death.
Mine ancient scars shall not be glorified,
Nor my titanic tears, the seas, be dried."

As compressed into the tombstone inscription, it reads:

SHALL LIFE RENEW

THESE BODIES?

OF A TRUTH

ALL DEATH WILL HE ANNUL (Stallworthy 288)

By being taken out of context and having the second question mark deleted, Owen's words were made into a message of hope rather than one of tough reconciliation.[20]

"At a Calvary near the Ancre" (a river near the fighting in which Owen played a role in January 1917) is another terse parable, again related to biblical texts though less directly so than "Parable" and "The End." It is the culmination—in verse, at any rate—of Owen's urge to depict the World War I soldier as a suffering Christ. More than a year later, in July 1918, he would write a last, more explicit statement of that trope in a letter to Osbert Sitwell:

> For 14 hours yesterday I was at work—teaching Christ to lift his cross by numbers, and how to adjust his crown; and not to imagine he thirst till after the last halt; I attended his Supper to see that there were no complaints; and inspected his feet to see that they should be worthy of the nails. I see to it that he is dumb and stands to attention before his accusers. With a piece of silver I buy him every day, and with maps I make him familiar with the topography of Golgotha. (*Collected Letters* 562)

In the poem, an adaptation (as Stallworthy notes) of the Gospel story, an unnamed "one" "ever hangs"—one imagines a corpse caught in the wire strung throughout no-man's-land—while the soldiers watch and the disciples hide. But in this story there are already priests near Golgotha, "stroll[ing]" with pride in their having been set apart from the soldier-Christs they observe.[21] Meanwhile, the "scribes," or writers, a group that populates many biblical stories, betray the public by "bawl[ing] allegiance to the state" (*CP* 134), while the soldier-Christs do not so much fight the war as meekly "lay down" their lives. Anger and pity are joined.

"Strange Meeting" is very different from these others. A long poem (forty-four lines) drafted partly out of earlier fragments in the early months of 1918, it was successfully submitted by Owen for publication. As Perkins points out (283), its diction is at times that of an outmoded romanticism, a language Owen had worked to eliminate from his poetry. He returns to that style apparently in order to convey a distancing from ugliness and misery that only death could provide. Here, the language works; it is no longer a sign of unthinking traditionalism. Indeed, by identifying echoes of precursors such as Dante by way of Shelley's *Revolt of Islam,* scholars have shown what *thinking* echoes of Romantic diction these are.[22] The title itself, "Strange Meeting," and the dead enemy's remembrance of how the speaker "jabbed and killed" him are direct allusions to Shelley's "one whose spear had pierced me, leaned beside . . . and all / Seemed like some brothers on a journey wide . . . whom now strange meeting did befall / In a strange land."

Once again Owen's mind is fixed on the sadness of the soldier's death. The war itself seems far away; only the sadness remains. Enemies, implicitly an English and a German soldier, meet after death, recognize each other, and agree to give up their enmity as they lapse into a permanent sleep. Even at this point of emotional detachment, however, they remain sad about their fate, because they have died before they could bring the world a message that might prevent future wars:

> . . . I mean the truth untold,
> The pity of war, the pity war distilled.
> Now men will go content with what we spoiled,
> Or, discontent, boil bloody, and be spilled.
> They will be swift with swiftness of the tigress.
> None will break ranks, though nations trek from progress. (*CP* 148)

As "The Parable of the Old Man and the Young" was a culmination of Owen's anger at the "old men" who made the war, so this poem, with its gentle redefinition of enemy as friend ("I am the enemy you killed, my friend"), is a culmination of Owen's objection to the nationalistic hatred underlying and compounded by the war. In its empathetic sense of the enemy's fears and its realization that the enemy's death is just as sad as the comrade's, it is reminiscent of Sassoon's poem "A Night Attack." Sassoon had written his poem in July 1916, more than a year before he was sent to Craiglockhart and met Owen. One wonders whether he showed it to the younger man who would do so much with the same theme.

Very late in his short life, probably in late May or early June of 1918 (Hibberd 317), Owen drafted a preface for an anticipated volume of war poems. Stallworthy regards this draft as "perhaps the most famous literary manifesto of the twentieth century" (266). It refers to his poems as "elegies," laments for the dead, but elegies that are "in no sense consolatory" but rather are intended as warnings (Stallworthy 266).[23] There can be no doubt that what they were intended to warn against was war itself. "My subject," he wrote, "is War, and the pity of War. The Poetry is in the pity." It was this emphasis on pity for passive suffering that led W. B. Yeats to regard Owen's verse as excessively emotional, not sufficiently hard-edged for inclusion among the documents of poetic modernism. Yet we now realize that modernism was not a single and uniform entity. Clearly, Owen as well as Sassoon, Read, Rosenburg, and other poets referred to here did develop, under the shock of their experience, a new kind of war poetry whose techniques, language, and willingness to confront unvarnished horrific facts constitute a turning against the romantic and genteel past. Later modernist verse could not have developed as it did without this break. It is clear, too, that by emphasizing pity and anger, Owen and Sassoon summoned the two rhetorical strategies that have often been thought the most likely to be effective in arguing against war—though they have so far failed in that purpose.

3

The Great Grief
Women Poets of World War I

"Fight on!" the Armament-kings besought:
Nobody asked what the women thought.
—S. Gertrude Ford, "'A Fight to the Finish'"

It is we especially who, in the domain of war, have our word to say, a
word no man can say for us.
—Olive Schreiner (1915)

Until recently, discussions of World War I poetry centered almost exclusively on male poets who actually served in the trenches—the soldier poets or trench poets considered in the previous chapter. Such an emphasis was understandable; their direct experience of combat privileged them as, seemingly, the war's authentic voices. But it was also a distorting and ultimately an invalid emphasis.[1] War is a far more encompassing social trauma than such an exclusive focus would indicate. To insist, as Hilda Spear does, that "second-hand experience cannot shatter illusions" (60), meaning secondhand experience of the battlefield, is not only to discount the validity of other kinds of direct experience— experience of the loss of loved ones, of wartime deprivations, of moral horror—but to disregard the value of writing based on contemplation. Most obviously, insistence on the primacy of the battlefield excludes women from having a voice about war.

In 1981 this critical disregard of women poets who wrote about the Great War was challenged by the Virago Press publication of Catherine Reilly's anthology *Scars upon My Heart: Women's Poetry and Verse of the First World War*—a fountainhead of rediscovery of this material. I urge readers to consult its pages for a sense of the plenitude of women's poetry from the war. Since the appearance of *Scars upon My Heart*, many fine studies have added to our awareness of women's war writing.

Nevertheless, a privileging of the male voice and the experience of combat still persists. Lorrie Goldensohn's pronouncement in her 2003 *Dismantling Glory* that the "antiwar inclinations" of soldiers are "compelling beyond" those of civilians implicitly devalues the antiwar writings of women (7), and indeed all opposition to war based on moral reasoning or the grieving of losses as opposed to combat experience. Even Margaret Higonnet, who has forcefully challenged the privileging of "actual battlefront experience," writes that women "were rarely situated where they could create war poetry" (Higonnet et al., *Behind the Lines* 14)—once again identifying war solely with the experience of battle. It appears, then, that the argument for inclusion of women's perspectives on war continues to have to be made. Moreover, attention to the war poetry written by women is essential if we are to achieve fullness and balance in our view of the landscape of war writing. No taxonomy (to shift the figure of speech from the geographic to the biological) can be valid that ignores entire phyla and their connections to the whole. My point is not that we should grant a modicum of attention to these poets out of a grudging sense of justice. On the contrary, disregarding the women poets of World War I deprives us of a great deal of thoughtful and compelling verse. The writings of these women—most of them necessarily excluded from the battlefield but keenly distressed by the encompassing social disaster of war—are fully as "essential" to our understanding of the cultural response to the war as those of the soldier poets.

If insistence on the primacy of the battlefield tends to exclude women, it does not in fact exclude *all* women. Despite the prevalence of assumptions that have "identified . . . the symbolic separation of the civilian zone from the militarized zone" with "the distinction between women's sphere and men's sphere" (Higonnet, *Nurses* xiii), the Great War battlefield was not an exclusively male zone if we include the presence of medical personnel in hospitals and especially in dressing stations near the front. In this "active zone" (Khan 106, quoting Lady Randolph Churchill, *Women's Work at War*) a number of women writers saw, if not combat itself, then its immediate results. Among these, as discussed by Nosheen Khan, were May Sinclair (1865–1946), who served with a Motor Field Ambulance Corps in Belgium in September 1914, at the age of forty-nine; Vera Brittain (1896–1970), who served as a V.A.D. nurse in France (Volunteer Aid Detachment, an organization that placed hastily trained, hard-worked, and poorly paid nurses, as well as cleaning women and other assistants, in hospitals at home and in the field); Mary Henderson (b. 1874), who served on the Eastern Front in Russia and Romania; Eva Dobell (1867–1963), who also served as a nurse; and May Wedderburn Cannan (1893–1973), who served with both the V.A.D. and the Intelligence Service. All these women were British. In addition, Mary Borden (1886–1968), an American married to a wealthy Englishman, drew on her own funds in organizing and personally directing a hospital unit attached to the French army and was awarded the Croix de Guerre and membership in the Legion of Honour (Khan 118). These and others wrote poems that might even be grouped with those of the soldier poets in that they emerged from direct experience near, if not actually on, the lines.

Women who provided battlefield support sometimes reported their observations with striking directness, in poems emphasizing the suffering they witnessed in hospitals and dressing stations. Several poems by Eva Dobell reprinted in Reilly's anthology ("Pluck," "Night Duty," "Gramophone Tunes") are good examples, giving the reader a strong sense of what it was like to work among the wounded trying to outface their pain (Reilly 132). One of the most notable of such poems is Mary Henderson's "The Young Serbian" (so titled in her 1918 volume *In War and Peace*, though shown as "An Incident" in Reilly's anthology). Henderson offers a particularly poignant version of the soldier as Christ with its image of

> . . . brave, shell-shattered hands—
> His boy hands, wounded more pitifully
> Than Thine, O Christ, on Calvary. (Henderson 15)

Mary Borden, who supervised her hospital in "the forbidden zone" for four years, wrote poems and sketches out of that experience that are not only strikingly original in form and style but also compellingly direct and factual in their vision. Borden thought many readers would find these "unbearably plain" (that is, plainspoken), but said she had actually "blurred the bare horror of facts and softened the reality" in spite of herself because she was "incapable of a nearer approach to the truth."

Ellen N. LaMotte, a nurse who worked in Borden's unit and appears in some of her sketches, published her own volume of sketches that was so hard-hitting it was subjected to censorship (Higonnet, *Nurses* 79, xiv).

May Sinclair also published keenly visual essays and verse reporting her experiences and observations during her month on ambulance duty in Flanders. A well-established writer long before the war, Sinclair was sufficiently accomplished as a poet to move beyond the jog-trot meters common among amateurs. Her "Field Ambulance in Retreat (Via Dolorosa, Via Sacra)" is one of the best of what we might call eyewitness poems. Beginning with a description of a stone road, then enlarging her view to the surrounding rural scene, then focusing on the agricultural laborers with their "great Flemish horses" who are the usual travelers of the road, she achieves a certain shock effect by suddenly shifting to the rush of war traffic and the priority given to a Red Cross ambulance:

> They and their quiet oxen stand aside and wait
> By the long road loud with the passing of the guns, the rush of
>   armoured cars, and the tramp of an army on the march forward
>   to battle;
> And, where the piled corn-wagons went, our dripping Ambulance
>   carries home
> Its red and white harvest from the fields. (Reilly 98)[2]

The word "dripping" conveys a fuller sense of the nature of the ambulance than one would imagine a single word could, and Sinclair demonstrates the depth of her educational and literary development in the way she turns the Latin of her subtitle ("Via Dolorosa, Via Sacra") into the English of her last line:

> . . . league after dying league, the beautiful, desolate Land
> Falls back from the intolerable speed of an Ambulance in retreat
> On the sacred, dolorous Way. (Reilly 99)

Sinclair's vivid evocation of the human cost of the war does not mean that she was an activist for peace; she supported the war effort. Terry Phillips usefully reminds us that although the "re-evaluation of attitudes to the Great War which began in the 1960s has contributed to a privileging of certain kinds of writing"—that is, of antiwar writing— not all women who wrote thoughtfully about the war fit that mold (55–57).

Poems that describe the reality of medical and relief work in the war, such as Sinclair's "Field Ambulance in Retreat," combine traditional feminine roles of caregiving with the newer roles entailing women's actual presence near the front. But women who served there did not always record their experience in terms of grief for the suffering they witnessed. As Gilbert and Gubar point out, their service at the front afforded women a degree of mobility and a sense of adventure they sometimes regarded as "glamorously dramatic," in contrast to their restricted activity at home and, indeed, males' enforced "immobilization" in the trenches or in hospitals. Such "unprecedented freedoms" sometimes brought "erotic release" (Gilbert and Gubar, *Sexchanges* 293–99). Sinclair, indeed, wrote of her experience at the front with a zest that seems to belie the heavy grief of "Field Ambulance in Retreat": "What a fool I would have been if I hadn't come. I wouldn't have missed this run for the world" (quoted in Gilbert, "Soldier's Heart" 215). Yet the predominant mode in poems by women who served on the front was the recording of what they saw and the expression of their grief, often joined to moral reflection. We see a terse combination of the two, keen visual presence plus expression of a solemn awareness, in Vera Brittain's "The Troop-Train," written, according to her note, in Boulogne in May 1917:

As we came down from Amiens,
    And they went up the line,
They waved their careless hands to us,
    And cheered the Red Cross sign.

And often I have wondered since,
    Repicturing that train,
How many of those laughing souls
    Came down the line again. (*Poems of the War* 31)

Brittain's focus and directness of statement belie the standard charge that women's poems of the war were excessively emotional and thus undisciplined. She was, of course, present as a V.A.D. at the scene she describes.

Yet to insist that women are entitled to add their voices to the war's poetry simply because they, too, played active roles near, if not in, the trenches is still to endorse too narrow a definition of war poetry. Such an argument of entitlement by actual presence was made, for example, by John Oxenham in a foreword to Mary Henderson's poems emphasizing her "experiences beyond most": "She has seen active service in Russia and Rumania, and had narrow escapes from capture by the enemy in the Dobrudja disaster. She made dangerous journeys carrying stores to her sisters at the distant eastern fronts . . . Those quiet fearless eyes of hers have seen many grim sights—have looked Death in the face, and have not shrunk before the horrors of modern warfare" (*In War and Peace* 5–6). Henderson herself celebrated the courage and staunchness of women who followed their "path of duty":

> I've seen you guiding over shell-marked ground
> The cars of succour for the shattered men,
> Dauntless, clear-eyed, strong-handed, even when
> The bullets flung the dust up from the road
> By which you bore your anguished, helpless load.[3] (*In War and Peace* 12)

Certainly one applauds the recognition of what such women did in the war; their roles have been unduly obscured. Yet celebrations such as these continue to equate war with the battlefield and to privilege experience over quality of thought and expression, implying that if a woman has not had such direct experiences near the lines (and of course relatively few did) her right to a voice will be open to question. Curiously, the same point never seems to be made about men who have written about wars without having fought in one. No one questions, for example, the authenticity and value of Stephen Crane's *The Red Badge of Courage*, though Crane was fully as removed from actual warfare as, say, Willa Cather, whose Great War novel *One of Ours* was ridiculed by male literati.

The idea of the exclusivity of those who were actually there is expressed with peculiar wit, and therefore with peculiar persuasiveness, by E. E. Cummings in ["lis / -ten / you know what I mean"] (*CP* 271) and ["my sweet old etcetera"] (275). In the latter, Aunt Lucy

could and what
is more did tell you just
what everybody was fighting
for

while the speaker's mother "hoped that / i would die etcetera / bravely"
and his father became "hoarse talking about how it was / a privilege
and if only he / could" while "my / self etcetera lay quietly / in the deep
mud." Cummings's main point, however, does not seem to be that others do not have a right to feel deeply about the war (and presumably to
express those feelings) but that most of them prefer to shut out the
awareness that might produce such involvement. They not only

don't and never
never
will know,
they don't want
to
no. (271)

Interestingly, Cummings's own basis for "knowing" was volunteer service in an ambulance corps—the kind of role that also allowed women
to know.

My larger point, then, is not that women did experience the battlefield and its immediate effects, but that it does not matter. War is a total
and totalizing social experience. Anyone who has lived through any of
its effects—loss of loved ones, a feeling for others' losses, economic disruption, political repression, horror and moral revulsion at the spectacle
of cruelty—has experienced some aspect of the total experience of war.
Authentic war poetry is written out of all these aspects of that total experience.[4]

To make this larger point, in the remainder of this chapter I emphasize poetry written by women who contemplated the war from a perspective at some remove from the front and who wrote about it in grief,
in moral reflection, and in exhortation. My intention is to reject equally
the privileging of direct experience and the common assumption that
women are inherently and necessarily poets of the more distant or re-

flective stance, not to say temperament. Often this latter assumption modulates into the idea that women are or must be protected from the horrors of the battlefield because they are by nature inadequate to it or, in an idealizing sense, too good for it. That idea, too, is a distorting and ultimately invalid one, premised as it is on the two-edged sword of assumptions about the nature of the sexes that limit, even as they purport to elevate, the female—while it also ignores the encroachment of the battlefield onto women's lives through bombing and earlier forms of the terrorizing of civilians. D. A. Boxwell, in an article entitled "The (M)Other Battle of World War One," has addressed this conundrum directly: "The essentialist notion that women are naturally peaceful sustains patriarchal conceptions of women as passive and protectively nurturing, granting them a kind of sentimentalized moral—but certainly not political—authority" (92). In short, gendered consideration of war poetry is a minefield onto which one steps with no little trepidation.

∿

Much, perhaps most, of the poetry written about the Great War by women is elegiac, a poetry of mourning. "Ours the sorrow, ours the loss," Diana Gurney insists in a poem called "The Fallen" (Reilly 45). As Judith Kazantzis points out in her preface to *Scars upon My Heart,* the grieving that women expressed in their poems might be either "personal" or "general." But in the case of a small volume by Margaret Postgate (1893–1980), later Margaret Postgate Cole, it is not always easy to distinguish between the two. Virtually her entire 1918 volume *Poems* is given up to verses of love and mourning, or love-and-mourning, together, with such a singleness of intent that, given its publication date, one is compelled to believe it is all war poetry whether the war is directly mentioned or not.

In some of Postgate's poems the presence of the war is explicit. "On a Pierrot Show," dated August 1914, envisions ordinary cheerful life as a "threadbare" tinsel star hung against the "black emptiness" of "war's dark ways" (29). "Spring Song, 1917" effectively takes up the by then commonplace contrast between spring's vitality and the death-dealing war—

> Ah, there was never a spring like this,
> For when was there a year like this,
> Or a people desolate as this,

> Whose captains in high places
>   Have stolen away the spring? (31)

Many observers in 1914, when an unusually lush spring and summer
gave way to the guns of August, had noted the ironic contrast Postgate
remarks on here. Ultimately it is a contrast between emblems of life and
of death. Several epitaphs and other poems gathered at the end of Postgate's volume comment on the war with pained irony. "Praematuri,"
with its effectively lengthened final line, tersely chronicles a generation
old before its time, mourning friends and lovers dead in their youth:

> When men are old, and their friends die,
> They are not so sad,
> Because their love is running slow,
> And cannot spring from the wound with so sharp a pain;
> And they are happy with many memories,
> And only a little while to be alone.
>
> But we were young, and our friends are dead
> Suddenly, and our quick love is torn in two;
> So our memories are only hopes that came to nothing.
> We are left alone like old men; we should be dead
> —But there are years and years in which we shall still be young. (33)

In 1916, about the same time that Postgate wrote "Praematuri," the
American poet Amy Lowell (1874–1925) wrote a poem called "Patterns"
that carries a similar sense of long, slow years of mourning stretching
ahead. Lowell achieves a dual exercise of the imagination in this poem—
imagining herself English and imagining herself heterosexual:

> I walk down the patterned garden-paths
> In my stiff, brocaded gown.
> . . . .
> Underneath the fallen blossom
> In my bosom,
> Is a letter I have hid.

It was brought to me this morning by a rider from the Duke.
"Madam, we regret to inform you that Lord Hartwell
Died in action Thursday se'nnight."
As I read it in the white, morning sunlight,
The letters squirmed like snakes.

. . . .

I shall go
Up and down,
In my gown.
Gorgeously arrayed,
Boned and stayed.
And the softness of my body will be guarded from embrace
By each button, hook, and lace.
For the man who should loose me is dead,
Fighting with the Duke in Flanders,
In a pattern called a war.
Christ! What are patterns for? (Lowell 75–76)

Much as Postgate's last line expands her poem to a vision of the persisting effects of war, Lowell's exclamatory and questioning last line abruptly shifts hers to one of protest.

Postgate punctures with sarcastic irony the commonplace claim that military training turns a youth into a man in "They Say—They Say":

They made a man of you this year, the sort
That England's rich and proud to own, they say
    —They say—they say—
And so they went and killed you. That's their way. (35)

The "they" here are the old men who sent the young to war, and like Sassoon or Owen she views that act as a kind of homicide: "they went and killed you."

Probably Postgate's two finest poems—and the only ones that are often reprinted, though *Scars upon My Heart* includes four—are the brief "Falling Leaves," captioned as November 1915, clearly a war poem though the war is not directly mentioned, and the wrenching "Veteran," captioned May 1916, which might have been written by Wilfred Owen except that his poetic vocabulary was rarely so colloquial. Here is "The Veteran" in its entirety:

> We came upon him sitting in the sun,
>   Blinded by war, and left. And past the fence
> There came young soldiers from the Hand and Flower,
>   Asking advice of his experience.
>
> And he said this, and that, and told them tales,
>   And all the nightmares of each empty head
> Blew into air; then, hearing us beside,
>   "Poor chaps, how'd they know what it's like?" he said.
>
> And we stood there, and watched him as he sat,
>   Turning his sockets where they went away,
> Until it came to one of us to ask
>   "And you're—how old?"
>   "Nineteen, the third of May." (32–33)

The only-too-common pathos of the ruined veteran and the unex- pected irony of this veteran's youth come together at the end of the swift narrative in a startling factual statement. Mourning for one be- comes a mourning for all. I find surprising Nosheen Khan's verdict that this poem, which to me displays a real gift for verse narrative, "fails to impress, being marred by its moralizing tones" (26). The moral point is in fact left unstated, though readily implicit in the simple drama. Margaret Postgate Cole did become an activist in the pacifist cause, even after having seen how her brother Raymond Postgate was persecuted for his pacifism, but her poetic capacity carries her beyond the dismissive label "moralizing."

As Lowell's "Patterns," Postgate's "The Veteran," and other poems quoted above demonstrate, the poetry of mourning, like the poetry of description, readily shaded into a poetry of moral reflection. Reilly of- fers numerous examples of both, from the strikingly perceptive and ca- pable to the banal if heartfelt effusions of amateurs who "use" poetry "to purge the soul of pain" (Tylee 226). Women did not, of course, have exclusive title either to banalities or to the mode of moral reflection in a poetry of mourning. Laurence Binyon's "For the Fallen" had launched such a mode in the opening days of the war. Interestingly, it was only nineteen days after the publication of Binyon's "For the Fallen" that Alice Meynell (1847–1922), relatively advanced in years, "already well known" for her religious verse, and well established in literary circles (Giddings 15), published "Summer in England, 1914" (*Times* October 10, 1914). In my judgment this is one of the most remarkable poems of the war.

In part it is Meynell's gifted variability and expressiveness of accent that makes "Summer in England, 1914" such a fine work, but in part, too, her ability to play on the reader's expectations by invoking a mode of beatitude and the familiar fondness of the English for the country-side, then using these as a context for harsh surprise and moral intensity. This "most happy year," 1914, when "the hay was prosperous, and the wheat" and "moon after moon was heavenly-sweet" and the flocks were "serried" (meaning, by dictionary definition, "compact, as soldiers in ranks"—an example of Meynell's skill in word choice) is the very year in which "armies died convulsed" (*Poems* 135). Meynell's revulsion appears to be both specific—for this war, in this year—and general, for humanity's perniciously repeated return to warfare:

> . . . And when
> This chaste young silver sun went up
>   Softly, a thousand shattered men,
> One wet corruption, heaped the plain,
> After a league-long throb of pain.
>
> Flower following tender flower; and birds,
>   And berries; and benignant skies
> Made thrive the serried flocks and herds.—
>   Yonder are men shot through the eyes.
>   Love, hide thy face
> From man's unpardonable race. (135)

Later in the war Meynell also wrote patriotic verse, praising the United States, for example, for listening as "nation unto nation calls" ("In Honour of America, 1917" 167). She applauded "conscripts" (as most of England's troops were, after the initial rush of volunteers had dwindled) for heeding the compulsory invitation and thus becoming eligible to be "crowned" with victory.[5]

> You, the compelled, be feasted! You, the caught,
>   Be freemen of the gates that word unlocks!
> Accept your victory from that unsought,
>   That heavenly paradox. (171)

Characteristically, the intensely religious Meynell casts the situation in biblical terms: the subtitle of "To Conscripts," first published in the *Dublin Review* in January 1919, reads "Compel them to come in—St. Luke's Gospel." Readers may variously think the device elevating, clever, or blasphemous.

Meynell also insisted on the strength and courage of women during the war. In "Nurse Edith Cavell," eulogizing a nurse at the front who was executed as a spy on October 12, 1915, she followed the ennobling vein of martial verse by announcing that "that day she met the Immortal Dead" (149). In "A Father of Women" she spoke with a kind of feminism born of cruel necessity, calling upon England's fathers to "approve, accept, know" their daughters, even if from beyond the grave, "Now that your sons are dust" (148).

Like Meynell, Vera Brittain, who is known for her memoir *Testament of Youth* (1933), took into her writing about the war a sensibility shaped by a Victorian idealism that she struggled to retain. But as Tylee writes, Brittain found the war "not only disillusioning" but "profoundly traumatic" (186). Working as a V.A.D. in severe conditions, helping to provide (as did Mary Borden) the first attention given to wounded men brought directly from the lines (Tylee 229), she was turned into what she herself described as an "automaton" of incessant work. When she returned to England to try to resume her previous life alongside people who had not suffered such an immersion in hell and who had "got on the better since we were away," she found herself "beginning to agree" that she and the others had been fools to go (*Poems* 64–65). It was almost two decades before Brittain could move beyond a preoccupation with the horror of the war into hope that future generations would have learned lessons from the vast spectacle of death, so it would not have been endured in vain. As Lynne Layton observes, Brittain's pacifism was not innate but hard won (72).

The final poem in Brittain's 1934 volume *Poems of the War and After,* "The War Generation: Vale," ends on a note reminiscent of Owen's "The Next War," with its visionary expectation of "better men" who in the future will fight "on Death, for lives; not men, for flags." Brittain's lines are even more explicit than Owen's:

> For nobler men may yet redeem our clay
> When we and war together, one wise day,
> Have passed away. (*Poems of the War* 94)

It was Brittain's poem "To My Brother," first published in her small 1918 volume *Verses of a V.A.D.,* that supplied the title for the anthology *Scars upon My Heart:*

> Your battle-wounds are scars upon my heart,
>   Received when in that grand and tragic "show"
> You played your part
>   Two years ago. (*Poems of the War* 42)

Ending the war—or ending war entirely—was a common thread in the poems of women who wrote reflective or hortatory verse. Not that all women who wrote poetry about the war were antiwar or pacifist in sentiment. The popular jingoist Jessie Pope wrote patriotic verse, and many poetic effusions sought to redeem the brutality of the war (so far as the writers knew it) through asserting a noble purpose. Their motivation to write such poems was often the need to reconcile themselves to the death of a loved one by regarding it as sacrificial. Accordingly, some expressed a belief that their dead had gone on to a transcendent glory, or that their ghosts were inspiring the living to be faithful to the cause, or that in any event they themselves would be reunited with them in the hereafter. Such effusions represent the widespread desire of wars' bereaved (as we still see) to find some acceptable meaning in their loss. But a poetry of moral reflection that either asserted or strongly implied the evil of war was also much in evidence. Elizabeth Daryush (1887–

1976) wrote of war as a "wasted era" and a "desert shore" haunted by "vultures" and "grim / Barbarian forms" ("For a Survivor of the Meso-potamian Campaign," Reilly 27)—in contrast to poems by her father, Robert Bridges, the poet laureate, that held to the official line and sup-ported the war as a solemn mission. Elizabeth Chandler Forman showed the futility and delusion of war in a short parable called "The Three Lads," in which a German, a Russian, and an English youth cheerfully ride off for war with virtually identical, and equally facile, slogans on their lips (Reilly 40).[6] Helen Hamilton (whom neither Reilly nor Khan is able to identify except as "schoolteacher"; dates are given for neither Hamilton nor Chandler Forman) wrote even more pointedly in a poem called "The Jingo-Woman," from a volume that appeared in 1918, the last year of the war:

> Jingo-woman
> (How I dislike you!)
> Dealer in white feathers,
> Insulter, self-appointed,
> Of all the men you met,
> Not dressed in uniform
>
> . . . .
> Do hold your tongue!
> You shame us women.
> Can't you see it isn't decent,
> To flout and goad men into doing,
>   What is not asked of you? (Reilly 47–49)

Perhaps it was easy to denounce the likes of Jessie Pope. But the senti-mental versifiers of war that Hamilton addressed in "The Romancing Poet" must have been nearer the nation's heart:

> I wish you would refrain
> From making glad romance
> Of this most hideous war.
> It has no glamour
>
> . . . .
> If you must wax descriptive,

Do get the background right,
    A little right!
The blood, the filth, the horrors,
Suffering on such a scale,
That you and I, try as we may,
    Can only faintly vision it.
Don't make a pretty song about it! (Reilly 49–50)

Teresa Hooley (1888–1973) wrote of her antiwar convictions in "A War Film" after seeing a newsreel of the week's war news and being overcome by dread that her own young child would also someday be "taken away / To War" (Reilly 56)—a dread many women have felt.

The consciousness of their own distance from the war and of being part of the "cause" for which the men were, however nonvolitionally, fighting, as seen in Hamilton's "Jingo-Woman" and "The Romancing Poet," is also a frequent note. Some used that distance to explain that they therefore saw the horror of the war in a detached, evaluative way, some deplored it, and some seem to have been caught up in a sense of guilt about it. One of the most famous poems of the war, Edith Sitwell's frequently anthologized "The Dancers (during a Great Battle, 1916)," is among the latter. Taking as her point of departure the contrast between men at the front and civilians at home, for whom there must inevitably be moments when they are enjoying life while soldiers are enduring slaughter, Sitwell raises that contrast to a level of surrealism in a kind of horrific vision collapsing the distance between the two:

The floors are slippery with blood:
The world gyrates too. God is good
That while His wind blows out the light
For those who hourly die for us—
We still can dance, each night.
. . . .
We are the dull blind carrion-fly
That dance and batten. (Reilly 100; also Giddings 89)

∼

The names of many of the poets I have mentioned here are unfamiliar to most readers. Some, such as Sitwell, Brittain, and Meynell, are more likely to be recognized. To end this chapter I single out three poets—no doubt, three from among many—whose names and work deserve to be familiar, even if they are not: May Wedderburn Cannan (1893–1973), Rose Macaulay (1881–1958), and Margaret Sackville (1881–1963).

May Wedderburn Cannan served during the war both as a V.A.D. and later in the Intelligence Service. She also lost her fiancé to the war; he died of influenza soon after armistice (Khan 130). Cannan is a good example of the kind of person who was caught between old beliefs or ideals and the new realities. Although she achieved a personal balance that remained affirming of the ideals of the war, from our vantage she is a figure of ambiguity.

Cannan's most frequently mentioned poem, "Rouen (26 April–25 May 1915)," conveys the sense of adventure she felt during her first period of overseas service, when she worked in a railway canteen. Written in November 1915, the poem has been seen as charming or nostalgic or even (by Philip Larkin, quoted by Khan) as "enchanting." Its rolling rhythms and skillful repetitions—"Can you recall . . . ," "Can you forget . . . ," "Can I forget . . . "—are indeed rather spellbinding. Together they create a strong sense of nostalgia:

> Early morning over Rouen, hopeful, high, courageous morning,
> And the laughter of adventure and the steepness of the stair,
> And the dawn across the river, and the wind across the bridges,
> And the empty littered station and the tired people there.
>
> Can you recall those mornings . . . (Reilly 17)

On the basis of this rather pleasant tribute, one might accuse Cannan of evasion or blindness to what it all meant. But if we look more closely we see that her emphasis throughout is on the pastness of that time. If her "heart goes out to Rouen, Rouen all the world away" and she "remember[s] our Adventure" there, it is because of what has come since, the realities that lie between the speaker and her "adventure." That adventure, after all, took place when the war was little more than six months old. The trains that she recalls with such affection ("Can you recall the parcels that we made them for the railroad . . . ") are indeed, as the last line says, trains "that go from Rouen at the ending of the day." They are gone. Which way did Cannan intend the poem? She seems to have been still flushed with the high aspirations of those early days. Yet Claire Tylee's assertion that "Rouen" expresses "imperialist patriotism" (81) strikes me as excessively absolute. Even if the youthful poet did feel zestful in her canteen work, and even if she continued to feel a certain zest in remembering it six months later, she nevertheless structured her poem with an emphasis on pastness and the departure of the trains. The poem speaks of a kind of patriotic imperialism that has left the station and not returned.

Another of Cannan's poems that Tylee reads as an expression of imperialistic ambition is "Lamplight," written in December 1916. Anthologized by Reilly as well as by Giddings, this poem, too, conveys a sense of separation from a zestful but, significantly, uninformed past. *Then,* in that past time, "you and I / Dreamed greatly of an Empire" (Reilly 16); the emphasis is again on the pastness of the past. When "you and I" dreamed that dream we were "young, and very wise"—a phrase gently mocking the self-assurance of the young. The direct contrast is drawn twice with a pointed "Now . . . " showing that none of what was expected has come to be. Instead, "You set your feet upon the Western ways" (that is, to the Western Front), and both the speaker and the one addressed are marked with crosses: the one a mark of death (and a "torn cross" at that), the other a mark of living grief. Contrary to Tylee, Khan reads this poem as a direct rejection of imperialistic patriotism, the contrast between then and now showing that a "private empire" (the young people's dream, perhaps not a political dream at all) has had to "make way to the stronger claims of the national empire" (168).

Cannan retained even to the time when she wrote her autobiography, published half a century after the war, a belief that "the Dead had kept faith" and had "saved England" and perhaps "the world" (quoted by Tylee, 79, 81–82). Yet it seems unduly harsh to use this expression as a basis for saying, as Tylee does, that her "imperialist faith remained unshaken." There is a considerable difference between, on the one hand, consoling oneself with the thought that the conflict of long ago had meant something and had prevented one's own country and others from being seized by an aggressor, and, on the other, cherishing an ambition to overrun other countries. Rather than being seen as a thoroughgoing imperialist despite the horrors of two world wars, Cannan might better be read as a woman regretful for a more pleasant world that existed before the first of those wars, distressed by the events that changed it, and willfully unclear about the value of it all. Her ambivalence demonstrates a thoroughly human muddle. Cannan's verbal skills as a poet were perhaps superior to her clarity of vision.

Margaret Sackville, mentioned dismissively by Perkins as one of those at whose feet Ezra Pound came to England to sit until he learned better (461), wrote for the most part a more traditional and sentimental style of poetry that is not likely, now, to hold much appeal. Yet among the eleven "War Poems" grouped together in her *Collected Poems* (1939) is one that would have to be counted among the most perfectly achieved of the many terse and highly visual poems that came out of the war. This poem, "A Memory," was written not from observation but from imagination:

> There was no sound at all, no crying in the village,
>   Nothing you would count as sound, that is, after the shells;
> Only behind a wall the low sobbing of women,
>   The creaking of a door, a lost dog—nothing else.
>
> Silence which might be felt, no pity in the silence,
>   Horrible, soft like blood, down all the blood-stained ways;
> In the middle of the street two corpses lie unburied,
>   And a bayoneted woman stares in the market-place.
>
> Humble and ruined folk—for these no pride of conquest,
>   Their only prayer: "O! Lord, give us our daily bread!"
> Not by the battle fires, the shrapnel are we haunted;
>   Who shall deliver us from the memory of these dead? (Sackville 264)

The last line should be read with a stress on "these." As in so many of the poems by women that either report or would seem to report observations of the war, this by Sackville is designed to evoke a sense of the wrong being done and the effect on noncombatants, as well as on sons and brothers in combat. It demonstrates that the poetry of descriptive statement could also be a poetry of persuasion as well as pathos. Sackville is represented in Robert Giddings's anthology by this one poem.

Noticed admiringly by Wilfred Owen in a letter to his mother (*Collected Letters* 497), Sackville was a pacifist who protested against the war from early on. The commonality in suffering of supposedly enemy peoples and the prevention of future wars were her passions, and they are the burden of her war poems.

Although "A Memory," with its stunning glimpse of silent streets of dead noncombatants, is perhaps Sackville's single best-achieved poem, the most remarkable insofar as its place in its social context is surely "The Pageant of War," written (according to its caption) in 1914, when the war was just beginning. At a time when the English were standing in line to enlist and cheering their opportunity to teach the Hun a lesson, Sackville already perceived the glory they sought as a delusion and a sham. She made her point compellingly and with heavy sarcasm in this long allegorical poem narrating an emblematic vision. Patterned, as Khan points out, on the pageant of the seven deadly sins traditionally found in medieval morality plays (33), "The Pageant of War" narrates a "slow, monotonous" parade along a mysteriously white road, which proves to be paved with "trampled bones"—

Trampled in since the world began,
Road of triumph—road of glory!
. . . .
Behold! since the world began,
This shining road—man's gift to man. (270–71)

The crowd shouts at the spectacle of the parade, and trumpets herald the main figure, War itself, coming "magnificently" down the white road (267). Seen up close, however, War is not magnificent at all but coarse-featured and so ugly that he wears a mask to disguise his "obscene countenance" (268). It is a statement of what many would discover in actual experience in the trenches. War's attendants include the "pitiful, bright army of the dead" who in past wars mistakenly followed, almost in pleasure, this leader "who had come to them disguised / In the garb sometimes of Peace, sometimes of Christ." (So much, then, for

the claim of a war to end all wars.) They did not see War's horrible
face because their eyes had been so dazzled by the "great splendour of
their fate"—a line so close to an elision of the first and eighth lines of
Laurence Binyon's "The Fourth of August" ("Now in thy splendour go
before us / . . . Into the grandeur of our fate") that one supposes it must
have been an intentional reference. Sackville might well have seen Binyon's poem in the *Times* on August 11, 1914.

The dead soldiers are followed, in Sackville's dream-vision, by the
"dim" shades of their mothers and by a repulsive company of war profiteers:

> High-priests of War, crafty and keen,
> With greedy hands and heavy-hanging chin,
> And down-cast eyes which veiled their laughter.
> These underneath
> Their arms clasped bursting money-bags,
> Hid from the prying eyes
> Of those who would disturb their privacies,
> In tawdry, many-coloured flags.
> For these the sword
> Was sign and symbol of a great reward. (269)

Sackville may not have been very innovative in the terms of her alle-
gory, but she does show an affinity for the plain words and direct statement characteristic of the new war poetry. In her focus on the tawdry
in war at a time when her country was wholeheartedly subscribing to
its painted pageant, she was purposeful and bravely satiric. Her satire
extends both to the social spectacle itself and to the elevated rhetoric
employed in selling it to a public as gullible as the cheering crowd in
her poem.

Rose Macaulay (1881–1958), the last of the three I am especially noting
here, was a prolific novelist who also wrote poetry. Like the heroine of
her novel *Non-Combatants and Others* (1916), she only reluctantly confronted the horrors of the war, actually volunteering at a local hospital
for men sent back from the fighting "in order to keep her thoughts off
the War" in spite of her tendency to vomit or faint at even the thought
of what they had faced, let alone the physical evidence (Tylee 116). Ma-

caulay seems to have resembled her fictional heroine, too, in "alternating" (as Tylee judges) "between cynicism and religiosity" (118). Tylee's criticism that Macaulay "found no new mental framework, no new literary language, to replace the old ones from which she was now alienated" (118) is perhaps severe. True, even in its late stages she would still be representing the war in the archaic image of a lance (in "Lady Day. 1917," from her 1919 volume *Three Days*). We might note, however, that Robert Frost also employed the archaic image of a lance even later, in a poem from his 1928 volume *West-Running Brook* called "A Soldier," which begins, "He is that fallen lance that lies as hurled" (332). And if we look more closely at "Lady Day. 1917" we see that its archaic images are combined with a very modern ambiguity and fragmentation, along with cryptically disorienting transitions. Beginning with the conceit "the world is a tent," Macaulay asserts mysteriously that the "Sons of God break through" when the tent is torn—

> Break singing through, as the winds of March
>   Lift a pennoned lance and run
> Tilting between the pale armies
>   Of beech-stems in the sun.
> So tilt, so run the Sons of God,
>   And set the world a-dance
> With a red banner of anarchy,
>   And a shivering piercing lance
> That breaks, that breaks . . . (*Three Days* 19)

The poem ends with a series of truncated questions raising the possibility of the death of God, the absence of any meaning in the "fierce battle" except the fact of "the shaft of a broken lance," and the irruption of "the Lord God of anarchy" (19–20). It is a challenging poem that pushes language to its limits in parallel with what she saw happening to humankind under stress of war.

An appealing (and more characteristic) aspect of Macaulay's poems, as well as her midwar novel, is their combination of realistic or ironic humor with momentary realizations of the misery of it all. This combination is evident in "The Shadow," a poem about a Zeppelin raid that begins with sinister visual description: "There was a Shadow on the

moon; I saw it poise and tilt, and go / Its lonely way" (*Three Days* 17).
Such raids leave "a hot rubbish-heap, / With people sunk in it so deep,
you could not even hear them swear" (18). From the sinister precision of
"poise and tilt" to the defensively deprecative "could not even hear them
swear" she moves quickly to the pathos of the battlefield in the concluding four lines:

> Death . . . Well,
> What then:
> Rim of the shadow of the Hell
> Of the world's young men. (*Three Days* 18)

In a move typical of Macaulay, who often lamented women's inability to
join their brothers at the front, this concluding echo of the reference to
the Zeppelin as a "shadow" transfers its meaning from the visual to the
thematic, as the pain and misery of the civilians victimized in the raids
is only a "pale shadow of the Pain that grinds / The world's young men,"
merely a "rim of the shadow" of their hell. Here, Macaulay *does* seem to
have found a new literary language for the war experience.

Besides "The Shadow," Macaulay is most often represented in anthologies (though only the specialized kind) by her fine poem "Picnic.
July 1917," where the dim booming of the guns across the Channel in-
sinuates the impingement of the fact of war on the minds of civilians.
The poem enacts in successive stages a movement from inherent matter-
of-factness or indifference, to a determination to shut out the knowledge that the sound of the shelling keeps bringing to mind, to a demonstration of the futility of trying to shut out that devastating awareness.
At first "We did not shake with pity and pain, / Or sicken and blanch
white" when hearing the guns, but merely commented that the sound
was carrying clearly (*Three Days* 11). As we came to know only "too well"
the hell going on in Flanders and Picardy, we clung to a desperate belief
that the danger on the Continent could not "break through" the walls
that kept us safe, and tried to shut out the sound "lest we run / Mad"
(12). But as the war went on, "we" noncombatants were less and less secure in our reliance on those walls and came to admit, in Khan's summary (95), "the ineffectiveness of efforts to shut out the war, the torture

of which the mind wishes to evade."[7] The fear of breaking beneath the anxiety and sadness of it all is powerfully conveyed in the last stanza:

> Oh, we'll lie quite still, nor listen nor look,
>> While the earth's bounds reel and shake,
> Lest, battered too long, our walls and we
>> Should break . . . should break . . . (11)

The succession of first walls, then minds becoming worn down by the battering guns and the anxiety and sorrow of a war that seemed interminable—also the theme of Macaulay's novel *Non-Combatants and Others*—appears again in her poem "New Year. 1918," with the repeated line "Whatever the year brings, he brings nothing new" (*Three Days* 21–23).

Perhaps the single poem that best displays Rose Macaulay's yoking of ironic humor with pathos is her autobiographical "Spreading Manure." Macaulay herself, after trying volunteer work in a military hospital, became a "land-girl," a wartime agricultural worker.[8] "Spreading Manure" records her experience of performing agricultural work in wintertime, suffering from the cold, in terms that range from the comical (satirizing the flatness of the supervisor's instructions, likening manure to marmalade) to the pathetic (with an ironic reference to the soldiers' comparative comfort) to Macaulay's characteristic sense of the unfairness of women's being restricted in the roles they were allowed in the war effort:

> When the heap is thrown, you must go all round
>> And flatten it out with the spade.
> It must lie quite close and trim, till the ground
>> Is like bread spread with marmalade.
>> . . . .
> I think no soldier is so cold as we,
>> Sitting in Flanders mud.
> I wish I was out there, for it might be
>> A shell would burst, to heat my blood.
>> . . . .

> I wish I was out there, and off the open land;
> > A deep trench I could just endure.
> But, things being other, I needs must stand
> > Frozen, and spread wet manure.

The language here may seem unadventurous, but it supports supple shadings of tone. Like some of the more pointed rejections of obfuscating, elevated rhetoric in poems by Sassoon and others, it rejects archaisms and ornamentation. Still, Macaulay is far from a modernist poet in any conspicuous way. And indeed, far from envisioning the revolution of poetic mind and language that would come in the wake of the war, she recorded in 1916, in the voice of a character whose views seemingly convey her own, an awareness only of the debilitation of literature by war's jingoism, and not of the possibilities for a new vision: "The flood of cheap-heroics and commonplace patriotic claptrap—it's swept slobbering all over us; there seems no stemming it. . . . Constructive force will be the one thing needed when the war is over . . . but where's it to come from? Those who aren't killed or cut to bits will be too adrift and demoralized and dazed to do anything intelligent" (*Non-Combatants* 47). We can scarcely condemn Macaulay for not foreseeing the work of, say, Pound and Eliot, though in retrospect it seems shortsighted to have been so certain there would not be a new art. She was deadly prescient, however, in foreseeing, in her poem "New Year. 1918," that even if the new year brought the end of the war (as it did), peace would be "war's orphan" and no more than the "ungrown mother of wars yet to be" (21).

4

Looking Back on the Great War

I do not hesitate to say that the war we have just been through, though
it was shot through with terror of every kind, is not to be compared
with the war we would have to face next time.

—Woodrow Wilson

Wars, one war after another,
Men start 'em who couldn't put up a good hen-roost.

—Ezra Pound, Canto XVIII (1928)

In Europe and America—perhaps around the world—people remained
haunted by the Great War. Its scale and technological horrors stunned a
generation.[1] A huge outpouring of cultural products by writers, composers, filmmakers, and visual artists expressed grief, revulsion, and despair coalescing in a consensus that the war marked a break point in history. As Willa Cather famously phrased it in her 1936 preface to *Not
Under Forty* (citing "1922 or thereabouts" as the moment of rupture),
"the world broke in two." Disillusion with the war was as widespread as
the grieving for those lost. It was widely doubted that any such noble
aims as had been declaimed in public rhetoric in the opening months of
the war or during the buildup to America's entry, in 1917, had in fact
been served. And the mood of disillusionment persisted. Siegfried Sassoon would write in *Siegfried's Journey* (1945), at the end of another
world war, "At the present time nobody needs disillusioning about war."
That job had been done. Retrospective views of the war frequently employed an ironic tone, ranging from the terse and brittle in Ernest Hemingway's *The Sun Also Rises* (1926) to the sarcastic in Ezra Pound and
E. E. Cummings. World War I and the disillusionment it produced remain a preoccupation of the artistic and literary imagination to this
day—witness Pat Barker's extraordinary trilogy of novels *Regeneration*,
The Ghost Road, and *The Eye in the Door*, published in the 1990s.

In the visual arts, the postwar years saw a flood of retrospection emphasizing ugliness and despair. A major resource for seeing this persistence of anxiety, grief, and anger is Richard Cork's *A Bitter Truth: Avant-Garde Art and the Great War*, featuring numerous color plates as well as analysis of works by artists of various nationalities, from the immediate postwar years to the late 1930s. The year 1919, in particular, saw a great outpouring of paintings in England, many of massive size, that reflected the nation's urge to find adequate modes of commemorating the stupefying event just past. These included, to name but three, American artist John Singer Sargent's *Gassed*, Paul Nash's *Menin Road*, and Christopher Nevinson's *Harvest of Battle*, which along with numerous others produced soon after the war emphasize its suffering, horror, and devastation. In the same year, 1919, a painting by the German artist Will Küpper, called *After the War*, shows a disheartened man, presumably a veteran, standing on crutches in a bleak room "utterly alone" (Cork 239). A "widespread German obsession with death" in the postwar years produced numbers of canvases in a grotesque and sometimes sadistic vein (Cork 242), such as Gert Wollheim's horrifying *Wounded Man* (also 1919), with its directly frontal, close-up view of a gaping stomach wound.

This outpouring of an art of horror and protest continued for years: in Max Ernst's *Celebes* (1921), with its mammoth machine-animal trampling the landscape; in Käthe Kollwitz's series of despairing woodcuts and her memorial sculptures such as *Memorial to the Fallen*, installed in 1932 at the soldiers cemetery in Roggevelde, near Diksmuide, Belgium (see figs. 6 and 7). The stone memorial consists of two mourners whose faces resemble those of Kollwitz herself and her husband, thus making the monument a representation of their own grieving—for their son, killed in the war and buried at Roggevelde. The outpouring continued, too, in the work of Otto Dix, who produced an extended series of horrific and grotesque paintings and etchings conveying the intensity of his horror at what he had seen in the war (see fig. 8). Dix was banned from exhibition in Germany after 1934, and his major painting *The Trench* (1920–23), directed at "those who were working so hard to rekindle thoughts of martial ardour and revenge among the German people" (Cork 273), was destroyed by the Nazis. It is impossible to calculate the impact on literature, let alone on culture generally, of visual images such as these, but we can at any rate measure it in this one in-

6. Käthe Kollwitz, *Memorial to the Fallen*, Soldiers Cemetery, Rogge-velde, near Diksmuide, Belgium, installed 1932. Photograph courtesy of Koen Blomme, Roeselare, Belgium.

stance. Dix's work was known and admired by Erich Maria Remarque, who stated that the images in his portfolio *War* anticipated much of *All Quiet on the Western Front* (Cork 279).

   In art music, the war produced Alban Berg's austere and shocking antimilitarist opera *Wozzeck,* which though set in the early nineteenth century obviously refers to Berg's experience in the Austrian army during

7. Käthe Kollwitz, detail of *Memorial to the Fallen,* Soldiers Cemetery, Roggevelde, near Diksmuide, Belgium, installed 1932. Photograph
courtesy of Koen Blomme, Roeselare, Belgium.

World War I. Berg began working on *Wozzeck* as early as 1917 and completed the orchestral score in the spring of 1922 (DeVoto 11). It was first
performed in 1925 in Berlin, where one reviewer called it a "musical . . .
capital offence" (quoted in DeVoto 12), and was quickly repeated in
Prague (where it provoked riots), Leningrad, Vienna, and other cities.
Wozzeck came to New York and Philadelphia in 1931. The work's gloom,

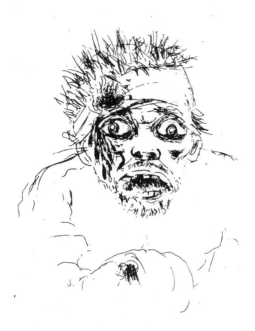

8. Otto Dix, *Wounded Man Fleeing (Battle of the Somme, 1916)*, 1924. Courtesy of British Museum, London.

brokenness, and harsh depiction of the degradation of military life propelled it into notoriety and wide musical influence.

The war also produced a little-known retrospective art song by Charles Ives, the angry and bitterly disillusioned "Nov. 2, 1920," alternatively titled "An Election" (*114 Songs* 50–55; *Nineteen Songs* 26–31). The headnote to the song in Ives's published volumes explains that it is the "soliloquy of an old man whose son lies in 'Flanders Fields'"—a reference that links it inescapably to his startling setting of John McCrae's "In Flanders Fields" (1917, revised in 1919), in which the note of protest is more ambiguous. In "Nov. 2, 1920," characterized as "sardonic" by the Cowells (79), Ives's disillusionment in the wake of the war is clear. Primarily he denounces the American national election of November 1920 when Woodrow Wilson's agenda, including support of the League of Nations, was rejected by voters. In the words of the song, the reason was that the "hog-heart" of greed "came out of his hole." After this overtly disillusioned response, with its denunciation of cynical self-interest, Ives wrote no more retrospectives on the Great War until 1942, when, with U.S. entry into World War II, he added new touches to his World War I song "He Is There!" rendering it, unlike the earlier version, clearly anti-war in intent.

It is in popular music, though, that we can most readily see the variety of musical memorializing of the war and the persistence of war-concern in the general public. Popular music of wartime is a subject of its own that can only be touched on here, but it is as important an expression of a culture's responses, anxieties, and needs as art music and other "high" arts. Frank Huggett observes that some of the songs popular in England during World War I had a tone of "moralistic command" rarely heard in those of the Second; he cites as an example "We Don't Want to Lose You (But We Think You Ought to Go)" (9). Such obviously occasional songs as this quickly dropped out of the public memory, though a number of the more morale-boosting type were later revived to satiric antiwar effect in the Vietnam-era multimedia play *Oh What a Lovely War.*[2] Sentimental love songs from the war, since they more readily express a variety of human situations, remained standard in the popular repertoire for singing and humming. It was not the propaganda songs urging men to fight and women to support them that stayed in people's minds, but songs lamenting the war or expressing loneliness and the yearning to be reunited.

Among postwar songs reflecting on the war, one of the oddest and most frivolous but ultimately (though unintentionally) most ironic is Cole Porter's "When I Had a Uniform On," from the 1919 musical production *Hitchy-Koo.* With a bizarre humor that can now only seem poignant, the singer comically laments that whereas he got lots of attention from girls when he was wearing his uniform, now that he's "in civilians" the girls pass him by. His solution to the problem: to "start another war." Porter could not have foreseen that what sounded like a preposterous joke in 1919 would become a reality only twenty years later.[3] A 1922 hit by Walter Donaldson and Gus Kahn, "My Buddy," remembered the war in a very different way, the general vein of grieving for the lost. "My Buddy" has remained a sorrowful standard, since its reference to the war was not explicit. And in 1926—a year that produced what Modris Eksteins calls a "small wave" anticipating the "flood of war books and other material dealing with the war" at the end of the decade (277)—

another song explicitly referring to the war, this one as bizarre in its own way as Porter's "When I Had a Uniform On" and equally forgotten by later generations, became a big hit: "My Dream of the Big Parade," music by Jimmy McHugh, lyrics by Al Dubin, recorded by the Peerless Quartet.

Possibly stimulated by the hit movie *The Big Parade,* the song begins with what seems to be a dream of a victory parade, but the dream quickly turns into a nightmare-vision of the maimed and bereaved. After an opening verse setting the idea of the dream, the chorus enters:

> I saw buddies true,
> Marching two by two,
> In my dream of the Big Parade.
> I saw angels fair
> With the Red Cross there,
> In my dream of the Big Parade.
> I saw Gold Star Mothers, sisters and brothers,
> What a sacrifice they made;
> I saw one-legged pals coming home to their gals,
> In my dream of the Big Parade.

As if the reference to the "one-legged pals" has triggered his memory, a member of the quartet then speaks the next verse in a heavily emotional rubato style:

> Millions of soldiers, millions of men
> All going over—I see them again.
> Oceans of water, submarines, too:
> Millions of sailors helping them through.
> Millions of doughboys landing in Brest,
> Marching, marching, never a rest.
> Millions of bullets thundering past.
> Millions of bodies, wounded and gassed.
> Valleys of ruins, mountains of mud,
> Beautiful rivers and rivers of blood.
> Airplanes flying, bombs coming down.
> Millions of cooties crawling around.
> Pieces of shrapnel, pieces of shell,

Many a cross where somebody fell.
Fighting and fighting a horrible war,
And God only knows what you're fighting it for.
Then came November, that Armistice Day . . .

But unfortunately, "all that went over didn't come home."

We may question the precision of the lyrics at some points, such as "thundering" bullets, but the cumulative effect is of a harrowing ordeal. The line "God only knows what you're fighting it for" reflects a common sentiment of the time; it is rendered on the recording in a tone of wrenching lament. The reference to those that "didn't come home" slows to a mournful solemnity. The quartet then repeats the last four lines of the chorus with its vision of Gold Star Mothers (an insignia indicating that a son had died), sisters, brothers, and sweethearts.[4] The grieving continues, and the memories of the war called up in the song are colored by the disillusionment and regret that were by that time widespread.

❧

Retrospectives on the war in poetry were written both by those who had been in combat and those whose involvement was less direct. Edmund Blunden, one of the more prolific of the soldier poets, served in the British army from 1915 to 1919 and was awarded the Military Cross. A friend of Sassoon, he went on to a long and successful academic career. His memoir *Undertones of War* was published in 1928. In some of his wartime poems, notably "Third Ypres," Blunden conveyed the horrors and misery of his experience with a bluntness verging on brutality. In general, though, his poetic voice was quieter and more conventional than either Sassoon's or Owen's and was characterized by a pastoral note conveying his yearning to return to the English countryside. Despite both these strains in Blunden's war poetry, his direct presentation of the horror of battle and his repeated expressions of nostalgia for rural England, his retrospective poem "1916 Seen from 1921" expresses a surprising nostalgia for the war itself.

What Blunden misses about it is not, certainly, any pleasure in killing or in contributing to the winning of the war, but its opportunities for heightened feelings of affection among comrades. "Tired with dull grief, grown old before my day," he writes, he thinks of "lost intensities of hope and fear" and feels as dead as "the men I loved" (32). Estranged by his battlefield experiences from ordinary life at home, he recalls with yearning those times when he and his "friend of friends" would slip away from the horror for quiet, implicitly homoerotic moments, even if only a few minutes of exhausted sleep: brief pockets of time within the brutalizing crush of events, found in pockets of surviving pastoral land-scapes. "1916 Seen from 1921" is perhaps Blunden's most fully ironic poem, not in its overt tone but in an underlying recognition of how his life's greatest misery was intermingled with its deepest joy.

Seventeen years after Blunden's "1916 Seen from 1921," in a 1938 poem titled "Recalling War," Robert Graves likened his persistent memories of the war to the aching of an old wound. The recurring pain reminds him of how he viewed the war in its early days, before experience had taught him its harsher lessons. He recalls the beginning of the conflict through a series of metaphors: first as an epidemic, "an infection of the common sky"; then as a mindless return to an "antiqueness" of romanticizing—"tasty honey oozing from the heart" while the mind was "waived"; and, most startlingly, as a collective hard-on, as "oppressed" by the infected sky he and his contemporaries "thrust out / Boastful tongue, clenched fist and valiant yard"—that is, yardarm. With a complex irony he sees this erasure of mind in the service of a deluded and militant physicality as having been, at the same time, an erasure of ideals that may have been false but were at any rate sustaining:

> War was foundering of sublimities,
> Extinction of each happy art and faith
> By which the world had still kept head in air . . . (Giddings 174)

Without these props, the discovery of the miseries of the flesh and of the fact that acquaintance with "life's . . . transitoriness" isn't thrilling, after all, becomes, for Graves, a "duty to run mad." Enlightenment is at once a gain and a loss.

The last stanza of "Recalling War" is a madly sarcastic representation of artillery and machine-gun fire as a wanton sort of child's play:

> And we recall the merry ways of guns—
> Nibbling the walls of factory and church
> Like a child, piecrust; felling groves of trees
> Like a child, dandelions with a switch!

Machine-guns rattle toy-like from a hill,
Down in a row the brave tin-soldiers fall:
A sight to be recalled in elder days
When learnedly the future we devote
To yet more boastful visions of despair. (Giddings 174)

Like Rose Macaulay in "New Year. 1918" and Wilfred Owen in "The Next War," Graves foresees future wars—"yet more boastful visions of despair" —and seeks to warn against them: remember the soldiers falling! His voice, though, unlike theirs, is one of wit underlain by seriousness. By speaking of the guns and soldiers as toys, he elicits from the reader a response of protest that no, this wasn't a game; real soldiers suffered when they fell down. Writing two decades after the end of the war, he piles irony on irony in a series of contrasts between an elated sickness and a dull wellness, between adventurous intensity and intensity of suffering, between horror and play, between involuntary flashbacks and boastful recall that reduces the memory to unreality. One of the great retrospective works on the war, the poem's metaphoric naming of memory as the aching of a wound is all the more effective in light of Graves's recognition that his own poetry written during and immediately after the conflict had at times adopted elaborate strategies for blocking the war out of consciousness (277).[5]

An echo of Graves's "Recalling War" resounds in Philip Larkin's frequently cited and reprinted "MCMXIV," written in the 1960s, not just years after the war it refers to but years after the Second World War. Graves's "Never was such antiqueness," compressing the idea that pastness had never before been felt by his generation, is echoed in Larkin's "Never such innocence":

Never such innocence,
Never before or since,
As changed itself to past
Without a word . . .
Never such innocence again. (28)

Through a technique of tight focus on a few selected details, Larkin resuscitates the imagined quality of life in England on the brink of the war, as discovered in photographs and written retrospectives. More importantly, he resuscitates the *significance* of those details: the grins on the faces of men waiting in line to enlist because they had been sold a bill of goods and had no idea what awaited them, the holiday atmosphere because people believed they were embarking on a collective opportunity for glory, the tradition of naming children after England's monarchs in expression of a general faith in authority that would sink under a spreading resentment of elder leaders, pubs open all day because wartime restrictions had not yet been imposed in order to keep defense workers at their jobs and alert. All these innocent (remembering that "innocent" means literally not-knowing) aspects of life would be wiped out.[6]

Larkin has been taken to task for his supposed blindness to the defects of English society in the prewar years and the falseness of many Britons' early notions of what the war would mean, as if he truly regretted that the world can never again be as it was then or (perhaps) can never enjoy the beginning of a new war. Claire Tylee writes that he employs a romanticizing and mythologizing mode, ignoring the "great social unrest and . . . miserable poverty in industrial or agricultural slums" of prewar England in order to lament "the loss of innocence" and "Britain's lost imperial splendour" (245). But surely this is a tone-deaf reading not adequately attuned to the complex balance of his regretful ironies. To be sure, prewar British life is rendered in "MCMXIV" with a tinge of (imagined) nostalgia. Larkin views Georgian England across the great divide of not one but two world wars, the first of which was fought before his birth. His account is always already located in the sorrow of subsequent events, in comparison to which it is easy to write with longing for supposedly prelapsarian times when those events had not yet happened. He knows, and he writes in the knowledge that we his readers will know, that the "archaic" faces in photographs taken in early August 1914 are the faces of those doomed to horror. Such regret scarcely deserves the accusation of being militaristic, considering the contrast between their careless cheer—however outmoded and false the jingoistic ideal upon which it was based—and the rude awakening that awaited them. One wants to pull these carelessly cheerful children back from the fire, not because they and their lives and ideals were so admirable but because one hates to see any child burned. That,

I believe, is the tone of Larkin's poem. It is only in contrast with what was to come and its aftermath that prewar English lives glimpsed in "MCMXIV" look so idyllic. So far as Larkin's supposed endorsement of a system of hierarchical social class—a system that was, if not entirely done away with, at any rate greatly attenuated by the effects of the war—the poem's reference to "differently-dressed servants / With tiny rooms in huge houses" provides, in its terse and quietly ironic language, a clue that we are not to suppose he truly wishes to return to what was.

These three poems by Blunden, Graves, and Larkin illustrate the tone of wistfulness heard in much of the poetry of the backward glance—certainly not a wistfulness for the ordeal itself (other than for the male bonding it sometimes entailed)[7] but for what the war eradicated. A great sadness haunts this poetry, a wish that the war generation had been spared the knowledge and disillusion brought by the catastrophe that destroyed so many. Seldom do we see any note of praise for such traits as courage in battle.

∼

We do hear praise of courage in a remarkable, painful poem by E. E. Cummings from 1931, ["i sing of Olaf glad and big"], but the courage he celebrates is not that of a soldier but of a war resister. It has been said that the participant-poets writing about the Great War tended, in retrospect, to exaggerate their opposition to the war (Caesar 68). Probably that is natural. But Cummings is not claiming that the heroic opposition he depicts here was his own, but rather that of an imagined "conscientious object-or." Combined with his praise of Olaf is an intense anger at society's demands for unquestioning support of its militaristic goals. Cummings's ["i sing of Olaf"] is both unusual among retrospective Great War poems and one of the great triumphs of the genre, all the more so in that its appalling sketch of Olaf's torture while he stubbornly resists—"I will not kiss your fucking flag" and "there is some shit I will not eat"—also exposes and critiques American racism.[8] The poem exhibits with great clarity Cummings's distinctive gifts for achieving a voice combining black-comic satire with lyricism, particularly at the point five lines before the end where the satiric tone suddenly breaks into the lyrical:

our president,being of which
assertions [i.e., Olaf's defiances] duly notified
threw the yellowsonofabitch
into a dungeon, where he died

Christ(of His mercy infinite)
i pray to see; and Olaf, too

preponderatingly because
unless statistics lie he was
more brave than me:more blond than you.[9] (340)

The war's evils and sufferings are seen here as having spread far beyond
the trenches.

In the same year that Cummings wrote about the war in *The Enormous Room* (1922), a semifictionalized account of his arrest and deten-
tion in France, where he was serving as a volunteer in the Norton-Harjes
Ambulance Corps, he published the volume *Tulips and Chimneys,* where
the war is explicitly recalled in only a single group of five short poems.
Of course, we may well regard the preoccupation with death and with
prostitutes throughout *Tulips and Chimneys* as a reflection of his wartime experience. The group designated "La Guerre" includes the pointedly fierce ["Humanity i love you"], which ends with the raw exclama-
tion "i hate you," and the more understated ["the bigness of cannon"]:

the bigness of cannon
is skillful,

but i have seen
death's clever enormous voice
which hides in a fragility
of poppies. . . . [10] (55)

Death hid, that is, in Flanders, whose poppies had been famously memorialized in McCrae's "In Flanders Fields," but not with Cummings's
light touch.

In 1926, eight years after armistice, with the publication of Cummings's volume *is 5,* this bare trickle of war poems became a flood of vituperation targeting colonels and generals, war profiteers (in ["the season 'tis,my lovely lambs"]), and politicians who "chatte[r] about Peacepeacepeace" (in ["opening of the chambers close"]) (265–66). In at least two of these poems Cummings aggressively parodies the empty wartime rhetoric of chauvinistic speakers who don't themselves go to fight. In ["my sweet old etcetera"], which charmingly conveys the sexual fantasies of the soldier lying "quietly / in the deep mud" and dreaming of "Your smile / eyes knees and of your Etcetera)," the speaker's family members at home mouth patriotic platitudes so inane as to be mere verbal prefabs. His mother hoped he would "die etcetera / bravely of course," while his father got hoarse from "talking about how it was / a privilege and if only he / could" (275). The speciousness of the father's wish that he could serve is, of course, a statement of the enmity of the young men in the trenches toward the old men who sent them—that is, very much a sentiment in the spirit of Wilfred Owen, despite the difference of style. Even more directly targeted toward debased rhetoric in wartime is Cummings's portrait of the platform speaker in one of his characteristic free-spirited sonnets:

> "next to of course god america i
> love you land of the pilgrims' and so forth oh
> say can you see by the dawn's early my
> country 'tis of centuries come and go
> and are no more what of it we should worry
> in every language even deafanddumb
> thy sons acclaim your glorious name by gorry
> by jingo by gee by gosh by gum
> why talk of beauty what could be more beaut-
> iful than these heroic happy dead
> who rushed like lions to the roaring slaughter
> they did not stop to think they died instead
> then shall the voice of liberty be mute?"
>
> He spoke. And drank rapidly a glass of water. (267)

Having seen ambulance duty, Cummings knew that the "heroic happy dead" were not beautiful. His sly inclusion in the speaker's jumbled rhetorical flood of the fact that those who died "did not stop to think" could scarcely be a more pointed warning (by Cummings, though not, of course, by the speaker) for the next time. A similar sarcasm appears in his portrait of the youth who heeds the call of duty "for God for country and for Yale" in ["come,gaze with me upon this dome"] (272). The youth is, notably, blond—that significant coloration of true Americanness in ["i sing of Olaf"].

In four of the *is 5* war poems (268–71), Cummings's tone approaches Owen's goal of presenting the pity of the soldier's experience, but with his characteristic facetiousness. These are, first, ["it's jolly"]—that is,

jolly
odd what pops into
your jolly tete when the
jolly shells begin dropping jolly fast

—and second, ["(look at this)"], which points to but does not describe what a .75 shell did to what was "my particular / pal." Third,

first Jock he
was kilt a handsome
man and James and
next let me
see yes Will

—so many killed that it becomes a puzzle just to keep them straight. And fourth:

lis
-ten

you know what i mean when
the first guy drops you know
everybody feels sick or

> when they throw in a few gas
> and the oh baby shrapnel

Cummings's agitation over his own and others' war experience and what he saw the war as having done to American society continued into his 1935 manuscript *No Thanks* and beyond, as war became one of his recurrent themes, along with sex and spring and snow and loving. By 1940, in his volume *50 Poems*, he was writing with disgust about the wrongs of new dictators and the coming of a new war.

~

The point that Cummings made in ["i sing of Olaf"] and elsewhere—that war's evils and sufferings extended beyond the battlefield—is one that had been made during the war itself primarily by women poets. American leftist and prolabor writer Genevieve Taggard (1894–1948) continued in that line, linking women's sorrows over the war with the struggle for economic justice. In a poem of 1936, almost two decades after the war, she seems simply to take antiwar sentiments as an assumption in writing of the goals of women participating in a march:

> Last, walking with stiff legs as if they carried bundles
> Came mothers, housewives, old women who knew why they abhorred war,
> Their clothes bunched about them, they hobbled with anxious steps
> To keep with the stride of the marchers, erect, bearing wide banners. (5)

The phrase "knew why" leaves no doubt that their reasons were sound, though we are left to imagine what they were. For Taggard, peace was as much a social justice issue as equality. It was not an issue that went away when the Depression came on:

> Women are conservative. That is
> They want life to go on . . . Groceries
> Are important, and milk delivered each morning.
> I must feed my children. Keep the peace. (54)

Keeping the peace is as much a matter of welfare for children as keeping them fed. The impetus toward peace that Taggard attributed to working-class women sprang naturally from their experience of loss and grieving.

Another poet calling for social justice in the postwar years was Sterling A. Brown, who receives far less attention than his enormous gifts and thoughtful appraisal of American society deserve. Folklorist, poet, editor, and longtime professor at Howard University, the son of a father born in slavery, Brown pointed to one of the bitterest ironies of postwar America in his poem "Sam Smiley." Most African Americans who served in the war—in segregated units, of course—were kept unarmed and were put to heavy labor such as unloading ships in French ports. Some, like the "boys" in Brown's poem "Raise a Song," "slog[ged] through the mudholes" and were "flung smack in the teeth of death" (S. Brown 212).[11] But when black soldiers came home they were received, not with celebration and praise, but with a resurgence of repression and lynching, perhaps because white people feared that their experience outside the country, wearing military uniforms, conscious of having assisted measurably in the victory that was often seen as America's alone, would make them "uppity." Well aware of this injustice, Brown wrote the ballad "Sam Smiley" about such a returning soldier who has learned dangerous lessons:

> The whites had taught him how to rip
>   A Nordic belly with a thrust
> Of bayonet, had taught him how
>   To transmute Nordic flesh to dust.
>
> And a surprising fact had made
>   Belated impress on his mind:
> That shrapnel bursts and poison gas
>   Were inexplicably color blind.
>
> He picked up, from the difficult
>   But striking lessons of the war,
> Some truths that he could not forget,
>   Though inconceivable before. (45)

The rest of the poem follows the happily "buckdancing" Sam Smiley home, where—in Brown's typically stark, slightly melodramatic, but realistic storytelling—he finds his sweetheart in jail, soon to be executed

for killing a baby bred on her by a white man. Smiley's reaction reflects
the lessons of war:

> And he remembered France, and how
>   A human life was dunghill cheap,
> And so he sent a rich white man
>   His woman's company to keep.

What immediately follows is the inevitable result (in that time and
place) of such an action, with a final chilling fillip characteristic of
Brown's mastery at poetic narrative:

> The mob was in fine fettle, yet
>   The dogs were stupid-nosed, and day
> Was far spent when the men drew round
>   The scrawny woods where Smiley lay.

> The oaken leaves drowsed prettily,
>   The moon shone down benignly there;
> And big Sam Smiley, King Buckdancer,
>   Buckdanced on the midnight air. (46)

Lynching is a recurrent theme of Brown's—a fact of American experience that in blues music and other black-authored texts is often treated
with cautious indirectness but in Brown's verse is confronted directly
and disturbingly.[12] But in spite of his fixation on these injustices, Brown
could still envision (in the poem "Honey Mah Love") a time when
"there will be a truce from quarreling" and we will attain "something
nearer peace" (246).

∽

Ezra Pound also insisted, in his retrospectives on the war, that its evils
and sufferings extended beyond the battlefield. As we turn to Pound and
T. S. Eliot, and to the traces of the war in this body of poetry that has
been taken to constitute the highest of high modernism, we see again
how false is the conception that World War I poetry consists solely or
even primarily in the writings of the trench poets.

Pound's recurring preoccupation with the evils and aftereffects of the war are not so much with the poison that spread into individual lives through the medium of militarism (as Cummings's is) as with what might be called the macro effects on civilization.[13] That is, at any rate, his burden in the fourth and fifth sections of "Hugh Selwyn Mauberley." Written between 1915 and 1920, at the same time as he was writing the first seven of the cantos (Perkins 473),[14] "Hugh Selwyn Mauberley" employs, for the most part, a mode of tautly ironic juxtapositions that allow the poet's own attitude to emerge, if at all, from the reader's judgment of the significance of their contrasts. In sections four and five, however, as if his pent-up distresses were finally bursting through the wall of ironic detachment and ambiguity, Pound "cries straightforward invective against war" (Perkins 481) in one of the most powerful and most pained of all denunciations of the debacle. I quote the two familiar sections in their entirety to let us experience once again Pound's angry voice:

iv

These fought in any case,
and some believing,
        pro domo, in any case . . .

Some quick to arm,
some for adventure,
some from fear of weakness,
some from fear of censure,
some for love of slaughter, in imagination,
learning later . . .
some in fear, learning love of slaughter;

Died some, pro patria,
        non "dulce" non "et decor" . . .
walked eye-deep in hell
believing in old men's lies, then unbelieving
came home, home to a lie,
home to many deceits,

home to old lies and new infamy;
usury age-old and age-thick
and liars in public places.

Daring as never before, wastage as never before.
Young blood and high blood,
fair cheeks, and fine bodies;

fortitude as never before

frankness as never before,
disillusions as never told in the old days,
hysterias, trench confessions,
laughter out of dead bellies.

    v
There died a myriad,
And of the best, among them,

For an old bitch gone in the teeth,
For a botched civilization,

Charm, smiling at the good mouth,
Quick eyes gone under earth's lid,

For two gross of broken statues,
For a few thousand battered books. (*Personae* 190–91)

The Latin, of course, echoes for bitterly satiric purposes the celebrated phrases of the Roman poet Horace. Translated, they are: *pro domo*—for home; *pro patria*—for homeland or nation; *non "dulce" non "et decor"*— not "sweet," not "and fitting." The term "wastage," in line 20 of iv, was used for deaths in the trenches from routine enemy fire when no assault was in progress.

    Here we cannot suppose the poet guilty of nostalgia for prewar days. The civilization that sent "a myriad" to die was "botched," a civilization marred by money hunger and the glorification of nation-states as well as, implicitly, by falsehood in such public manifestations of its values as books and statues. (The last two lines are, however, elusive, since in his usual way Pound may also be mocking the denseness of those who would not think art worth dying for.) We can hear in these lines not so much an echo of Sassoon's and Owen's cries of enmity between the corrupt old and the victimized young, and of Owen's mocking allusion to Horace's "old lie," as a near-simultaneous voicing of the same idea. "Hugh Selwyn Mauberley" was published in 1920, the same year as the first collection of Owen's poems.

At virtually the same time as Pound was writing "Hugh Selwyn Mauberley," Eliot was writing the poetry in his early style that has been taken to define high modernism. "Portrait of a Lady," written around 1910, and "The Love Song of J. Alfred Prufrock," written in 1911 and published during the war, in 1917, present a curious contrast with Larkin's "MCMXIV" in that they show a society with none of the innocent optimism and liveliness that Larkin imagined, but rather a society of the living-dead.[15] One might suppose that if Eliot saw England in the way he presented it in "Prufrock," as a cycle of meaningless patter or as a kind of "patient etherized upon a table" (saw it, that is, in the imagination; he was still a student at Harvard at the time), he might well have viewed the war as a perverse rescue from such a condition.

That he did not is quite certain, not from his having written any explicitly antiwar poems but from the abundant images of brokenness that accumulate in his postwar poetry and the implications we can see in many of its abstract statements. Until recently, scholarship on Eliot has customarily emphasized psychoanalytic and philosophical influences and their traces in his poetry, rather than his place within the public context of his times. With a redirection of emphasis toward historicism, we can see that lines such as the following from "Gerontion" (in *The Sacred Wood* [1920])—

After such knowledge, what forgiveness? Think now
History has many cunning passages, contrived corridors
And issues, deceives with whispering ambitions,
Guides us by vanities. (22)

—may refer at least in part to the public rhetoric of the war, the knowledge that the war yielded, and the "cunning passages," "contrived corridors," and "whispering ambitions" of the Treaty of Versailles. The cry of the backward-looking speaker in "A Cooking Egg," also from *The Sacred Wood*—"Where are the eagles and the trumpets? / Buried beneath some snow-deep Alps" (27)—may well refer to the war's burial of the old notions of martial glory, perhaps as a parallel to the burial of Hannibal's militaristic ambitions in the snows of the Alps. Certainly it is not hard to see in the image of "stony rubbish" in *The Waste Land* (1922) the all-too-real imagery of the war's destruction. Sandra M. Gilbert, who reads the "ravaged terrain" of *The Waste Land* as "a figure for No Man's Land itself . . . littered with the shards of the English elegy," sees Eliot and his persona Tiresias as "an impassioned witness to the woes of a world shattered by (and for) the war's shattered armies of the night."[16] Gilbert points out that the work was written out of personal grief for a beloved friend lost in the war, a young French medical student named Jean Verdenal, killed at Gallipoli on May 2, 1915.[17] That Pound's influence on *The Waste Land* was profound is well known, and Pound was passionately engaged with the effects of the war, but Eliot had his own reasons for writing a war elegy.

Although none of the first seven cantos that Pound was writing at about the same time as "Hugh Selwyn Mauberley" displays the kind of direct concern with the war that "Mauberley" does, references to the war would enter the cantos for years. In Canto XVI (published in 1925), which begins "And before hell mouth," there are long passages of tortured memory and anger, including an outburst against "that son of a bitch, / Franz Josef of Austria" (*Cantos* 71). Memorializing literary figures who served in the war, Pound recalls that

> They put Aldington on Hill 70, in a trench
> dug through corpses
> With a lot of kids of sixteen,
> Howling and crying for their mamas,
> And he sent a chit back to his major:
> I can hold out for ten minutes
> With my sergeant and a machine-gun.
> And they rebuked him for levity.

And Henri Gaudier went to it,
    and they killed him,
And killed a good deal of sculpture,
And ole T.E.H. he went to it,
With a lot of books from the library,
London Library, and a shell buried 'em in a dug-out,
And the Library expressed its annoyance.
    And a bullet hit him on the elbow
 . . . gone through the fellow in front of him,
And he read Kant in the Hospital, in Wimbledon,
in the original,
And the hospital staff didn't like it.(*Cantos* 71)

The anecdote about T.E.H. refers to T. E. Hulme, the philosopher of imagism, killed in September 1917, and to wartime prejudice against the German language and anything else that smacked of Germany (such as the dish sauerkraut, sometimes called "victory cabbage" during the war). "And Wyndham Lewis went to it," Pound continues,

With a heavy bit of artillery,
    and the airmen came by with a mitrailleuse [machine gun],
And cleaned out most of his company,
    and a shell lit on his tin hut,
While he was out in the privvy,
    and he was all there was left of that outfit. (*Cantos* 71–72)

Much of Pound's declamation deflates, as this passage does, any notion of nobility in the proceedings. Like Owen's and Sassoon's poetry, it also tends to elevate the common soldier to the detriment of senior officers. The anger of enlisted men toward officers is, of course, a classic theme of derisive songs sung by soldiers. We might compare Pound's attention to the common soldier with the harsh pathos of Cummings's ["the season 'tis,my lovely lambs"], ending:

. . . Colonel Needless
To Name and General You Know Who
a string of pretty medals drew

(while messrs jack james john and jim
in token of their country's love
received my dears the order of
The Artificial Arm and Limb) (265)

Pound's Canto XVIII, published in 1928, includes satiric lines about a
war profiteer, leading up to the disheartened pronouncement, "War, one
war after another, / Men start 'em who couldn't put up a good hen-
roost" (*Cantos* 83). A hen-roost, if a humble structure, is at least useful.
Canto XIX continues the idea, adding sarcastic reminiscence about the
good old days of British imperialism in India. As late as Canto XLII
(1937) Pound was still returning to 1918, "the fifth / et cetera year of the
war," to launch another diatribe against usury—"A mount, a bank, a
fund a bottom an / institution of credit" (*Cantos* 209)—which he saw as
the root cause of such social miseries as the war, started by men who
"couldn't put up a good hen-roost."

5

Uneasy Interlude
Visions of the Approach and Renewal of War

... Listen, listen. The step
Of iron feet again. And again wild.
> —Gwendolyn Brooks, "Gay Chaps at the Bar"

Who is not afraid? Who wants war?
> —Glenway Wescott, *Fear and Trembling* (1932)

It is difficult to determine exactly when world events clearly began to presage the coming of the Second World War. In retrospect we can see the planting of the seeds at the Versailles Conference, when world powers reverted to their hereditary practice of carving up territories. Perhaps unusually prescient observers might have seen the signs in 1927 when Chiang Kai-shek launched the struggle for a unified China that would evolve into civil war between Nationalist and Communist forces. Or perhaps in 1931, when, coming into the unstable situation in China, Japan took over Manchuria and created the puppet state of Manchukuo. Essentially, Asia was in a state of war from that time on, with massive Japanese bombing of China (for example, of Shanghai in 1932) causing many deaths.[1] It was also in 1931 that events occurred which would lead to the Spanish Civil War. In April of that year the people of Spain voted into office a majority of Republican legislators, and the Spanish royal family defected. After a prolonged period of unsettlement, during which there was street fighting between Loyalists (monarchists) and Republicans, the full-scale Spanish Civil War erupted in July 1936 when Gen. Francisco Franco set up a fascist government and attacked the Republican army with superior forces, with assistance from Italy and Germany. Some 1 million people would lose their lives in this struggle.[2] But the definitive start of the war in Europe came on September 1, 1939, when Hitler's Germany invaded Poland. Britain and France declared war two days later. W. H. Auden would use the date September 1, 1939, as the title of one of the great poems of the decade or perhaps of the century, a meditation on the "low dishonest decade" that had eventuated in the invasion that launched all-out war in Europe.

Certainly there had been apprehension about the threat of another world war before the invasion of Poland. In 1937, a Pulitzer Prize–winning political cartoon by C. D. Batchelor showed a hideously diseased prostitute labeled "War" inviting a young man in uniform labeled "Any European Youth" to come upstairs with her. The caption reads, "Come on in, I'll treat you right. I used to know your Daddy." As Michael Sherry observes in his book on the militarization of the United States since the 1930s, *In the Shadow of War,* the cartoon is evidence that "most Americans understood war as an external force bearing down on them" (84). How clearly they understood that it was bearing down on them *at that moment* is hard to say, but astute cultural leaders were voicing their concern.

American novelist Glenway Wescott, quoted in the second epigraph to this chapter, was writing about the fear of renewed war by 1932. His friend Katherine Anne Porter, who arrived in Berlin on a Guggenheim Fellowship in late 1931 and remained in Europe until the fall of 1936, repeatedly expressed, throughout that period, a sense of foreboding. Porter's little-known poem "After a Long Journey" recounts her feelings during the bitterly cold winter of 1931–32 as she contended with language barriers and cultural unfamiliarity and struggled to feed herself on her Guggenheim stipend, to write, and to resist amorous vexation. All around her she saw the miseries of the German people, suffering impoverishment in the wake of the First World War and the ensuing economic collapse. The poem draws a parallel between Porter's physical coldness (from the chilly climate and inadequate indoor heating) and her emotional coldness ("kisses freeze in our mouths . . . ") and parallels both to the frozenness of a society "petrified" by its "catalogues of defeat, advantages, stratagems, warfares" and its devotion to "medals, ribbons, citations" (Porter 493). It is arguably an effective, even important poem that merits wider reading. Porter's letters from Europe during the 1930s confirm that she saw the disruption of the German economy and social order as a root cause of the war she felt was imminent.

E. E. Cummings began to warn in 1935, in a manuscript volume called *No Thanks* (included in his *Complete Poems*), of what the renewal of war would do to the resistant spirit he consistently celebrated. Beware, he cried, of "politisions" and

> beware of folks with missians
> to turn us into rissions
> and blokes with ammunicions (405)

What precisely "rissions" are I cannot say, though the word is surely a play on "Russians," but we all know only too well what "blokes with ammunicions" are. Instead, he implies, what we need is more people like the determinedly resistant Olaf of ["i sing of Olaf glad and big"]. Such heroes are rare—"there are possibly 2½ or impossibly 3 / individuals every several fat / thousand years" (514, from the 1940 volume *50 Poems*). Despairing of the general run of folk who

> simply
> can't)
> won't(most
> parent people mustn't
> shouldn't)most daren't (412)

he slyly likens such nonresisting conformists (rissions, perhaps?) to the controlled masses of Soviet Russia:

> kumrads die because they're told)
> kumrads die before they're old
> (kumrads aren't afraid to die
> kumrads don't
> and kumrads won't
> believe in life)and death knows whie
>
> (all good kumrads you can tell
> by their altruistic smell
> moscow pipes good kumrads dance) (413)

The Communist reference of the word "comrade" was well established by that time, of course, but the word was also commonly used for one's fellows in war. Here, as so often, Cummings is whimsical and elusive.

But in the same 1935 collection he denounced the times directly and
with heightened emotion:

> loudly for Truth have liars pled,
> their heels for Freedom slaves will click;
> where Boobs are holy,poets mad,
>
> . . . .
>
> if Hate's a game and Love's a fuck
> who dares to call himself a man?
>
> King Christ,this world is all aleak;
> and lifepreservers there are none:
> and waves which only He may walk
> Who dares to call Himself a man. (438)

Long a war-resister, Cummings found the mid-thirties a deplorable and
alarming time.

W. H. Auden also found the times "aleak" well before World War II
actually erupted in September 1939. Along with others of his set of socially engaged poets in England, he was deeply engaged in the troubles
of the thirties. In Edward Callan's words, he turned his "clinical, clipped
phrases, sharp ironical eye, and deft control of line and rhythm" on the
"infected spots on the body politic" during this decade-long "quagmire
of war and depression" (14). Auden visited the war zone in Spain in 1937,
and in 1938 went to observe the war in China, where, though he did not
witness combat, he did meet and photograph Chou En-lai (Callan 22).
Following these visits, he wrote of the turmoils of the return-of-war decade in both nations and their parallel courses of civil war and interfer-
ence by foreign powers, in *Spain* (1937) and *Journey to a War* (1939).

The result is a poetry at once engaged and detached. In "Sonnets from
China" Auden writes with a poignant weariness of "our global story"
when "Austria died, when China was forsaken, / Shanghai in flames and
Teruel [in Spain] re-taken" (*Collected Poems* 155).[3] The most frequently
noted of the sonnet sequence from China is the twelfth, which begins
"Here war is harmless like a monument; / A telephone is talking to a
man." How far from harmless he saw it as being, however, is evident in
the "living men in terror of their lives, / Who thirst at nine who were to

thirst at noon . . . And, unlike an idea, can die too soon." Auden's lines
bear the imprint of a great weariness of war. Reminiscent of Hemingway's famous manifesto that abstractions had lost all meaning and only
the names of places on the map held significance, the sonnet ends

> And maps can really point to places
> Where life is evil now,
> Nanking, Dachau. (153)

If it seems puzzling that Dachau should appear in this poem written
(according to the dated groupings in Auden's 1976 *Collected Poems*) in
the mid- or late 1930s, we must remember that although the full extent
of operations at the Nazi death camps was not generally known until the
end of the war, the existence of concentration camps in Germany was
known by the mid-thirties. Heinrich Himmler announced the establishment of Dachau on March 21, 1933. At first it was political opponents of
the regime, notably Communists, who were imprisoned there, then such
official undesirables as gypsies, homosexuals, and Jehovah's Witnesses.
Jews were sent to Dachau after Crystal Night in November 1938.[4]

∽

At virtually the same time as Auden was writing about Spain and
China, and Cummings was denouncing the conformity with which the
world's masses were being led back into war, Louis MacNeice was also
writing about the localized war in Spain and the prospect of another
world war. "Autumn Journal," a little-known masterwork written between August and December 31, 1938, conveys the deep foreboding that
weighed on MacNeice and others in England during these ominous
weeks. During the time chronicled in this poetic journal, the Spanish
Civil War reached a point of climax at Barcelona, and the Munich accord (the culmination of an unsuccessful British and French policy of
appeasement) was signed, giving the Czech Sudetenland to Germany.
Both events serve as points of reference in the poem. In the last canto,
on New Year's Eve, the last night of 1938, he looks forward toward the
new year fearful of what it will bring. As we know, his fears were amply
justified.

In parallel with his anxiety and depression over the public events,
MacNeice also recounts in "Autumn Journal" his anxiety and depression

over events in his personal life, specifically, his divorce. As in Katherine Anne Porter's poem "After a Long Journey," the public and the personal are aligned or even intertwined. What distinguishes MacNeice's use of this rhetorical strategy from Porter's is the fullness with which he establishes voice, the incisiveness with which he aligns vocabulary with occasion and with form, and his maintenance of these techniques at a high level of fulfillment over an extended span. A work of more than 2,200 lines in twenty-four cantos varying from 56 to 128 lines each, "Autumn Journal" is an intensely personal record of the poet's state of mind as he contemplates his own troubles and, at the same time, world events and the all-too-evident approach of the coming war.

To give anything like a full reading of this lengthy work that MacNeice himself called a lyric inclining toward the didactic would almost require a book in itself. What I provide here is a brief summary or road map emphasizing how the approach of war weaves its way into the whole, in the hope of conveying a sense of MacNeice's voice in this highly individualized pronouncement on the state of London society and the larger world on the brink of war.

Technically, in its prosody, "Autumn Journal" is unusual to the point of peculiarity. It is written in lines of varying length, made up mostly of trochaic feet (accented-unaccented, as opposed to the iambic, or unaccented-accented, that is more usual in English-language verse) that give the whole a falling rhythm. Line endings generally alternate between masculine (ending on an accented syllable) and feminine (ending on an unaccented), with the masculine endings usually rhyming. But the principle of purposely tedious alternation goes even further. The cantos themselves alternate between beginning with a masculine-ending line and beginning with a feminine-ending line—but again, not consistently: the eighteenth canto begins the "wrong" way. We may well wonder what possible end is served by this elaborate scheme. Why did MacNeice bother setting up so big a work in so contrived a form? In part, it may have been simply for the sake of structure itself. The poem was truly a journal of daily events and feelings, a kind of writing that could easily sprawl into formlessness. But beyond that, the regularity of the alternations sets up a sense of expectancy, almost of suspense. The pattern is so nearly unvarying that when it does break, when the succession of masculine-feminine endings suddenly turns around, the quiet change comes with something like a thud, like the muffled sound in a dark house that one has been tensely listening for. Together, these peculiarities of form and versification sustain a thoroughly individualized voice that nevertheless convincingly establishes itself as the voice of its time. It is a voice characterized by irony, weariness, and uneasiness, conveying a complex but generally valedictory mood—an "autumnal air" in every respect (O'Neill and Reeves 181).

MacNeice had used the pattern of alternating feminine and masculine line endings earlier in a short lyric, "The Sunlight on the Garden," published that same year, 1938. With its images of church bells, sunlight and garden, and a sky "good for flying" (MacNeice 104), this poem is far more celebratory of daily experience, far less cuttingly ironic than "Autumn Journal." Even so, it too is permeated with lurking anxiety. The pleasures of ordinary life are either mentioned in the past tense (the sky *was* "great for flying") or caught at the moment of passing ("the sunlight on the garden / *hardens* and *grows* cold"). Given its historic context, we have to read "The Sunlight on the Garden," like most of MacNeice's writing of the mid- to late 1930s, as a poem of the approach of war.

Canto I of "Autumn Journal" begins by casting British society as a "spinster sitting in a deck-chair picking up stitches / Not raising her eyes to the noise of the 'planes that pass" (121). This quickly set note of averting one's eyes or seeking distractions from the signs of impending war will be continued in various sequences of pleasure-seeking scattered throughout the poem. Also quickly established is the suggestion that the death of the poet's marriage mirrors a more general social decay. As he rides on a train, the rhythm of the wheels "becomes the ad nauseam repetition / Of every tired aubade," or dawn song of love, a genre he quickly parodies (in lines that constitute one of the rare variations of the masculine/feminine alternation of line endings):

> I loved my love with a platform ticket,
> > A jazz song,
> A handbag, a pair of stockings of Paris Sand—
> > I loved her long.
> I loved her between the lines and against the clock,
> > Not until death
> But till life did us part . . . (122)

Oppressed by anxiety and a depression approaching suicidal levels, he feels afraid "in the web of night / When the window is fingered by the shadows of branches." He mouths hopeful phrases turned upside down— "Glory to God in the Lowest, peace beneath the earth"—and wonders "whether anything is worth / The eyelid opening and the mind recalling," but reminds himself perfunctorily that he must "go out to-morrow as the others do / And build the falling castle" (123).

In Canto III, as he sees Londoners returning from holiday at the end of August, he ponders the contrast between haves and have-nots, between the suntanned pleasure-seekers able to afford holiday trips and those "ninety-nine in the hundred who never attend the banquet" but must "wash the grease of ages off the knives" (125). A concern with social injustice and a sense that such inequality is a root cause of wars will recur throughout the poem. Too honest with himself not to realize that he, too, has "the slave-owner's mind" and would prefer to "sleep on a mattress of easy profits" and inhabit a "niche at the top," he nevertheless rebukes himself for thinking that "victory for one implies another's defeat" (125). In Canto IV he pays tribute to his lost love, who particularly enjoyed the autumn of the year. But in V, as a beautiful autumn day dawns, the morning news is troubling:

> . . . posters flapping on the railings tell the fluttered
>> World that Hitler speaks, that Hitler speaks
> And we cannot take it in and we go to our daily
>> Jobs to the dull refrain of the caption "War"
> Buzzing around us as from hidden insects
>> And we think "This must be wrong, it has happened before,
> Just like this before, we must be dreaming;
>> It was long ago these flies
> Buzzed like this . . . " (128)

It was, of course, the sense of repetition (underscored here in verbal repetitions) that bred such intense despair in the public generally.

MacNeice had expressed the idea of the repetitiveness of war in another poem of the 1936–38 period, "Chess":

> The victor is a cypher once the war is won.
> Choose your gambit, vary the tactics of your game,
> You move in a closed ambit that always ends the same. (111)

He was haunted during those years by a sense that the same horror was erupting again.[5]

Still in Canto V, the poet stops by a bar in the evening where the talk is of sports—another of those efforts at self-distraction—but with a "heavy panic" running under it. When he and his friends leave and go out into the streets, the special editions of the newspapers strike fear and a sense of futility. Anxiety so infects every perception with metaphors of war that even the carpet sweepers pushed by restaurant workers seem to "advance between the tables after crumbs / Inexorably, like a tank battalion" (129). In bed at last, trying to go to sleep in his flat on Primrose Hill, "whose summit once was used for a gun emplacement / And very likely will / Be used that way again," MacNeice feels history closing in:

> And at this hour of the day it is no good saying
> > "Take away this cup";
> Having helped to fill it ourselves it is only logic
> > That now we should drink it up. (129)

His sense of personal participation in obscure moral causes of war strikingly resembles Marianne Moore's in "In Distrust of Merits"—"There never was a war that was / not inward." Moore's poem has been roundly condemned by some of her contemporaries and many later critics as sentimental and scolding. Yet MacNeice states much the same idea and so far as I know has not been faulted for softheaded or sentimental thinking.

In Canto VI he recalls his 1936 visit to Spain and realizes how imperceptive he was at the time, not to see the signs of a more encompassing war on the horizon. But in VII these signs have become inescapable:

> Conferences, adjournments, ultimatums,
> > Flights in the air, castles in the air,
> The autopsy of treaties, dynamite under the bridges,
> > The end of *laissez faire*. (132–33)

Seeing public opinion turning in favor of war, he thinks gloomily of the enormous number of casualties likely:

> Think of a number, double it, treble it, square it,
> > And sponge it out
> And repeat *ad lib.* and mark the slate with crosses . . . (133)

Events hurry along. "Hitler yells on the wireless," and the government is indeed "cutting down the trees on Primrose Hill" because the crest is wanted for antiaircraft guns—"the guns will take the view" (133). Ordinary things begin to seem pointless:

> And I come back here to my flat and wonder whether
> > From now on I need take
> The trouble to go out choosing stuff for curtains
> > As I don't know anyone to make
> Curtains quickly. Rather one should quickly
> > Stop the cracks for gas or dig a trench
> And take one's paltry measures against the coming
> > Of the unknown Uebermensch. (134)

The lessons in disillusionment taught by the First War seem to have been forgotten, since

> . . . we who have been brought up to think of "Gallant Belgium"
> > As so much blague
> Are now preparing again to essay good through evil
> > For the sake of Prague . . . (134)

As the ax chopping down the trees outside his apartment "keeps falling," the hill "grows bald and bleak." But "maybe," he observes with a touch of the sardonic, "we shall have fireworks here by this day week." The swing of emotions as MacNeice records his responses to the daily news during this period of gathering storm clouds is recognizably human. The diary is grittily personal. He wants to save himself; he wants to live long enough to enjoy new curtains; he reminds himself of how stupid the slogans of early World War I appeared in the post-Somme world; he warms to the thought of defending the oppressed on the Continent; he tries to dismiss his own belligerent feelings by labeling the prospect mere "fireworks."

In Canto VIII, as London braces itself, MacNeice recalls how he rambled around the city in 1931 (he would have been twenty-four at the time). People took no notice then of how the train (of history) "ran down the line / Into the sun against the signal" (135) or how the poorer

classes were suffering during this period of postwar economic hardships. As a member of the classics-educated upper middle class, he was
cushioned from such deprivations, even if he sometimes ran short of
funds, and he took "no look back to the burning city" (136). Now once
again he sporadically seeks to fill his hours with distractions such as
comic stage shows, but the "zero hour approaches" and the "eagles
gather." Things briefly look better (we have a keen sense of Londoners watching each new issue of the newspaper and grasping at hope)
while "we feel negotiation is not vain— / Save my skin and damn my
conscience"—a revulsion against appeasement that notably contrasts
with his earlier mockery of the rhetorical rallying around Prague:

> And negotiation wins,
>   If you can call it winning,
> And here we are—just as before—safe in our skins;
>   Glory to God for Munich
> . . . only the Czechs
>   Go down and without fighting. (137)

The reference to the Munich Conference here is so direct that one could
almost call this occasional poetry if its weightiness did not so exceed the
usual meaning of that term.

In Cantos IX through XIV the poet ponders his own life, his school
days, his return now to his university teaching, his hopes that his wife
will come back to him in the spring. But throughout he keeps thinking
of himself as one of "those who are about to die." The private life does
not exist apart from the public life; the two interpenetrate. Seeking out
more and more frenetic amusements to distract himself from the impending disaster and from his personal problems, he is nevertheless
haunted by ghosts of the First World War:

> O look who comes here. I cannot see their faces
>   Walking in file, slowly in file;
> . . . .
> But something about their faces is familiar;
>   Where have we seen them before?
> Was it the murderer on the nursery ceiling

> Or Judas Iscariot in the Field of Blood
> Or someone at Gallipoli or in Flanders
>   Caught in the end-all mud? (151)

He calls for music and jokes, to no avail:

>   Tell them as often as you like and perhaps those horrible stiff
> People with blank faces that are yet familiar
>   Won't be there when you look again, but don't
> Look just yet, just give them time to vanish. I said to vanish;
>   What do you mean—they won't?
> . . . .
>   Now I think you may look, I think the coast is clear.
> Well, why don't you answer?
>   I can't answer because they are still there. (152)

The ghosts won't go away. He is haunted by history.

As Christmas approaches, he recalls his childhood in Ireland and his happiness with his wife, now departed. He crosses the Channel to the "brittle dance of lights in the Place de la Concorde" (170) but presses farther south, to Spain. There, in Barcelona, the one city trying to hold out against the Fascists in the prolonged Civil War, he sees true deprivation where people still

> . . . manage to laugh
>   Though they have no eggs, no milk, no fish, no fruit, no tobacco,
>   no butter
> Though they live upon lentils and sleep in the Metro,
> . . . .
> Life being more, it seems, than merely the bare
>   Permission to keep alive and receive orders. (170)

As the year ends, MacNeice breathes an invocation, almost literally a prayer, for gentleness and generosity in the year to come, but the effect is one of great wistfulness, because the poem itself has already established the inevitability of quite the opposite. Yet in XXIV, the final canto, he insists on disavowing the past and dreaming a dream of a better future that can only seem far off:

> What is it we want really?
>   For what end and how?
> If it is something feasible, obtainable,
>   Let us dream it now,
> And pray for a possible land
>   Not of sleep-walkers, not of angry puppets,
> But where both heart and brain can understand
>   The movements of our fellows;
> Where life is a choice of instruments and none
>   Is debarred his natural music,
> Where the waters of life are free of the ice-blockade of hunger
>   And thought is free as the sun,
> Where the altars of sheer power and mere profit
>   Have fallen to disuse,
> Where nobody sees the use
>   Of buying money and blood at the cost of blood and money. (174)

The year 1939 begins, and "the die is cast." He can only face the grim fact that "there will be time to audit / The accounts later" while hoping that "there will be sunlight later / And the equation will come out at last" (175). The reference to sunlight reminds us poignantly of his 1938 poem clinging to the preciousness of the everyday in the face of war's alarms, "The Sunlight on the Garden."

It has been observed that MacNeice was "unique" in his poetic set (a set composed primarily of Auden, Stephen Spender, and C. Day Lewis) in "conveying a sense of total doom" (T. Brown 51). That may not seem like a gift designed to evoke celebration, but it is an important one. We can at least say that his words caught the sense of the time as it struck an observer of singular intelligence, honesty, and verbal gift.

～

Like "Autumn Journal," W. H. Auden's "September 1, 1939" is both a reflection of and a reflection on the "instability and uncertainty" of the "historical moment" (Bryant 100). First published in October 1939 in the *New Republic,* it quickly became one of the "more celebrated" of Auden's works (Callan 141). Auden, however, became convinced that the poem was guilty of "theatrical gestures" and sentimentality (Callan 156), and omitted it from his massive *Collected Poems,* published in 1976. He also dropped the equally noted "Spain," in which he had called on readers to "build the just city" (*Collected Poetry* 183). Readers who knew "September 1, 1939" protested, but he insisted that his decision, a rejection of romanticism and of activism, was the right one. We are free to doubt his judgment on this point.

Despite the memorable quality of many of its passages, "September 1, 1939" is not an easy or obvious poem. One must view the response of readers to the clipped language and the restrained despair of the work as a measure of their realization of its significance. The date referred to in the title is, of course, the day Hitler's Germany invaded Poland. Auden, a displaced Englishman, sits in a bar in New York much as Mac-Neice had sat gloomily in a bar in London a year earlier. Fussell comments that the opening reference to "one of the dives / On Fifty-second Street" (*Collected Poetry* 57) as the setting of his meditation on the outbreak of the war "seems evocative of the alcoholic atmosphere" of the war years (*Wartime* 97). Perhaps. More appositely, the lowness of "dives" —both the word itself, in relation to standards of usage, and the kind of establishment it signifies—effectively sets up the reference, four lines later, to the "low dishonest decade" now ending. A sense of shabbiness spreads over everything. Also, the poet's dispirited recourse to a bar is a fitting evocation of his depression at seeing war come around again. As Fussell concedes, "There's clearly something about fighting another war against the same enemy fewer than twenty-five years later so depressing and cynical making as to propel anyone toward the saloon" (*Wartime* 97). Thus, the poet sits

> Uncertain and afraid
> As the clever hopes expire
> Of a low dishonest decade:
> Waves of anger and fear
> Circulate over the bright
> And darkened lands of the earth,

> Obsessing our private lives;
> The unmentionable odour of death
> Offends the September night. (*Collected Poetry* 57)

The odor of death that he senses arises, of course, from his premonition of the mass deaths of the coming conflict. As we know, only two days later England and France would declare war.

At this point, however, Auden does not condemn Germany alone for dragging the world into this plight. Rather, looking back at the previous war, he sees the cause in a more general moral failure. "Imperialism's face / And the international wrong" stare back at one from the mirror, much as MacNeice's implication in social injustice had stared back at him and as Moore's sense of her inner spirit of war stared her in the face. All three poets take the role of conscience for their time. If the wrongs Auden perceives are in part the harsh peace imposed on Germany at Versailles, they would also seem to include the wrongs committed by Germany against others. It is a circle of hurts, like a playground squabble:

> I and the public know
> What all schoolchildren learn,
> Those to whom evil is done
> Do evil in return.

All have participated in the circling exchange of wrong.

Using the first-person plural, Auden describes the pervasive moral state and the resulting anxiety in terms of the bar, this temporarily homelike "fort" where he sits watching and thinking:

> All the conventions conspire
> To make this fort assume
> The furniture of home;
> Lest we should see where we are,
> Lost in a haunted wood,
> Children afraid of the night
> Who have never been happy or good. (*Collected Poetry* 58)

As in MacNeice's "Autumn Journal," the tone is one of weariness as a generation faced the renewal of what was still entirely too fresh in their memories. "We must suffer them all again," the poet laments, including in his "all" the debased speech that accompanies war—a debasement Cummings had lamented with respect to World War I rhetoric in ["next to of course god america"]. Against the rhetorical falsifications and "militant trash" in the air, the duplicity of those in authority and the falsehoods of the ordinary individual, Auden can counterpose only "a voice." At the end he grimly hopes to be one of those who "show an affirming flame" by helping to send out honest, or just, messages (*Collected Poetry* 59). It is a tautly restrained ending, but perhaps for that very reason an example of the honest communication for which he calls, since anything more, on the evening of September 1, 1939, would seem unwarranted. The poem ends not so much with an affirmation in the face of impending war as with a bare "wish to affirm" (O'Neill and Reeves 162). Here as in his elegy written only seven months earlier, "In Memory of W. B. Yeats," Auden's hope is centered in the courageous voice of the honest poet.

One such voice was that of Theodore Roethke. Perhaps the least topical or political of all twentieth-century American poets, Roethke, too, wrote a poem about the coming of war—the only Roethke poem I know of that comments on current events. Like Auden, he explicitly located his poem in time, calling it "Lull (November, 1939)." Roethke's term for the historical moment, "lull," captures its uneasiness and insecurity from the perspective of an as yet nonbelligerent American. He saw it as a time of cold "winds of hatred," "intricate phobias," and "malignant wish[es] / To spoil collective life" (29). Like MacNeice, he acknowledged that "we," in such a time of insecurity, "think of our separate skins," and like Auden he was angered by the ineffectualness of public leaders:

> The arbitrators wait;
> The newsmen suck their thumbs.
> The mind is quick to turn
> Away from simple faith
> To the cant and fury of
> Fools who will never learn.

Roethke, too, saw that a time of war meant degeneration of language—
the poet's lifeblood.

∽

Composer Charles Ives was also beset by moral concerns over the
"low dishonest decade" and a fear that World War I had not taught
people the lessons they needed in order to avoid such calamities in the
future.[6] During the 1930s he produced a variety of writings arguing for
the establishment of a world democracy in which any consideration of
war would be put to a universal referendum. What he hoped was that
ordinary people would proclaim "No more war in the world." At some
point in the late '30s Ives drafted, but apparently did not send, a letter to
Pres. Franklin D. Roosevelt denouncing wars fought to aggrandize national holdings. In the draft of that letter he once again employed language he had used in his post–World War I song "Nov. 2, 1920": any
country that fought a war of aggrandizement, he said, was like a hog trying to "get 'his' in the pigsty" (Houtchens and Stout, " 'Scarce Heard' " 93).

In the first days after America's entry into the new war, in a striking
parallel to his composition of "In Flanders Fields" in the very week of
entry into the first, Ives composed a redaction of his World War I song
"He Is There!" calling the new work "They Are There!" A song in two
verses and two distinct choruses, it reuses, with only slight changes, the
words of the third (final) verse and chorus of the original, then adds a
verse and chorus made up of newly written lyrics. In its very structure,
then, "They Are There!" exemplifies the continuity of the two wars. In
"Nov. 2, 1920" Ives's imagined speaker had exclaimed sarcastically "To
hell with ideals!" when he saw the "hog-heart" of greed come "out of his
hole." These words seem to indicate that Ives would not again bring
himself to support a military undertaking if he believed the "hog-heart"
was in evidence. "They Are There!" shows precisely such a belief. In this,
his only known direct comment on World War II in music, Ives's stub-
born insistence on opposing his voice to what he seems to have regarded
as an obvious wrong reaches a culmination.

The changes that Ives made in redacting his earlier war song give the
new work a visionary quality. He prophesies a world not only where
all may have a say, as in the earlier version, but "where all *will* have a
say" (emphasis added). In the chorus, where the "yankee boy" of "He Is
There!" had joined the Allies in "beat[ing] up all the warlords," the Al-

lies are now expected—in terminology echoing Ives's previous rhetoric against war fought for greed and profiteering—to "beat up all the warhogs." These "warhogs" may include political leaders like Kaiser Wilhelm or Hitler, Mussolini, and the Japanese prime minister Tojo, making war for reasons of national aggrandizement, but as the second verse indicates, may also include munitions makers, perhaps American businessmen.

Ives's musical and lyrical texts are at times, of course, ambiguous; it is uncertain whether he is composing martial patriotic songs or satiric ones. But in "They Are There!" he voices directly and forcefully a hatred of the present war and a hope for a future free of war. In the words of the new verse—again, written by Ives himself—he denounces it as a "cursed war . . . started by a sneaking gouger / Making slaves of men" and calls on all people together to "rise, / and stand together in brave, kind Humanity." Generalizing to wars in general, he asserts that they are usually "made by small stupid selfish bossing groups / while the people have no say" but prophesies that "there'll come a day / Hip hip Hooray" when people will "smash all dictators to the wall." Here the second verse ends and the new chorus enters:

> Then it's build a people's world nation, Hooray,
> Ev'ry honest country's free to live its own native life.
> They will stand for the right,
> But if it comes to might
> They are there, they are there, they are there.
> Then the people, not just politicians,
>   will rule their own lands and lives.
> Then you'll hear the whole universe
>   shouting the battle cry of Freedom.
> Tenting on a new camp ground.
> Tenting tonight,
> Tenting on a new camp ground.
> For it's rally 'round the Flag
>   of the people's new free world,
> Shouting the battle cry of Freedom. (*Nine Songs* 22–24)

While the verse is set to stridently bellicose music, the chorus makes it clear that Ives's purpose is considerably larger than merely winning the renewed world war. To the extent that he supports the war effort, he does so, it seems, for the sake of creating a new world in which war will be obsolete.

As if the words and musical ideas on the page were not clear enough, a recording of Ives himself performing "They Are There!" shows him further revising the text to add emphasis.[7] In this improvisational rendition featuring a spirited combination of ebullient untrained singing and peculiarly aggressive piano playing, his musical and textual interpolations make even clearer the visionary implications of the song and provide additional support for reading it as an antiwar text. Ives intensifies and accentuates the dissonances and rhythmic distortions of the composition through his slapdash playing to the point of utterly undercutting the conventions of the war song as a musical genre. At the words "smash all dictators to the wall," for instance, his dense tone clusters exceed what is indicated on paper, which is already very far from the straightforward harmonies of traditional martial music. When he sings the second verse, after the words "cursed war / All started by sneaking gougers" (not "a sneaking gouger" as in the published text), he tosses in a barely audible aside: "goddamn them!" In both choruses he adds an epithet prefaced by a sharply articulated tone cluster on the piano: "They are there, they are there, they are there (goddamn thief!)." In the second chorus, rather than "Most wars are made by small stupid selfish bossing groups," as in the published version, he sings "selfish bossing goops," using a now-obsolete slang expression meaning stupid oafs or simpletons. Together, the plural "goddamn them" and "selfish warring goops" (or even the tamer "groups," as printed) imply not so much a blaming of one or another national leader as a blanket derision of the members of military, political, and corporate business establishments who take nations to war. At minimum, "They Are There!" reveals a large measure of uncertainty, of conflicted feelings. Like others of his generation, Ives was caught in a weary agony, instinctively taking up a degree of patriotic sentiment while at the same time feeling the disheartenment of a renewal of the ordeal they themselves, or at any rate the slightly older generation, had already gone through.

6

Poetry and Music Enlist

Patriarchal poetry is the same as Patriotic poetry is
the same as patriarchal poetry is the same.

—Gertrude Stein

Accentuate the positive.

—Harold Arlen and Johnny Mercer

Although Americans are given to recalling World War II as "the good war," a conflict entered into for the righteous cause of resisting Nazism and Hitler's abuse of Jews and others persecuted under the Third Reich, the American public did not in fact widely support entry into the war for such reasons, but rather for reasons of self-defense and revenge after the Japanese bombing of Pearl Harbor. By and large, the people of the United States preferred to let Europeans fight their own war, and the nation's political leadership had a difficult time marshaling support for any direct involvement in another conflict in Europe. In 1939, even after Hitler's Germany had invaded Poland and after England and France had declared war, Franklin Roosevelt was still assuring the American public, in his radio broadcasts, that he would not lead the country into war. Even the supplying of war matériel to the Allies did not have wide support in public opinion until after the fall of France in the spring of 1940 (Blum 7). But there had been a long history of prejudice and discrimination against Asians in this country, and after Pearl Harbor public opinion shifted overnight.[1] War against Germany still had little popular support except insofar as it was recognized that declaring war on Japan necessarily entailed declaring war on its allies. A massive propaganda effort was necessary to "increase American antagonism to Nazism" (Schweik 17).[2]

Although most of the serious poetry and music considered in the following chapters was antiwar or at least antimilitary in impulse, there were exceptions. And the popular media "enlisted for the duration" (Beidler 8).

The domestic propaganda effort, coordinated by the Office of War Information, devolved largely on the motion picture industry, since movies were so popular and persuasive a form of entertainment. But the industry itself, wishing to forestall direct intervention, acted aggressively on its own hook to "tell the American people about the war," "build morale," and "*keep 'em smiling*."[3] Thus the purposes of domestic propaganda were carried out without the direct control that, as Blum shows, the president wished to avoid. The Bureau of Motion Pictures of the OWI did, however, as Fussell demonstrates, make "suggestions"— which were reinforced by the armed services' possession of the equipment film studios needed in order to make movies showing combat (*Wartime* 162).[4] In the late-thirties' climate of public reluctance to support the preparedness effort being promoted by the government, Hollywood "presented the interventionist view" (M. Sherry 54).

The campaign to mobilize public sentiment also extended to music and literature. Maxene Andrews, of the celebrated Andrews Sisters, recalls in an offhand way (in a coauthored memoir called *Over Here, Over There*) that the Office of War Information "exercised the strongest kind of wartime government control over America's radio stations," concerning itself, for example, with the frequency with which the popular hit "Praise the Lord and Pass the Ammunition" was played on the air, because it didn't want people to tire of it (82).[5] Actually, the domestic function of the OWI was virtually eliminated by Congress in 1943, only a year after the song came out and the same year it was recorded by Kay Kayser (Blum 41). Even so, whether at the government's direction or with its encouragement, the entertainment media and the arts did widely enlist in the war effort. Such committed support was less pervasive in literature, but increased after the fall of Paris in 1940. In July 1942 Katherine Anne Porter, a writer who throughout her career staunchly resisted any efforts to bend art to the service of a political agenda, published a patriotic piece called "American Statement" (later retitled "Act of Faith") in *Mademoiselle* magazine. She was doing her war work. This does not mean that Porter was insincere in what she wrote. Her loudly bruited pacifism had shifted to a reluctant and then a strongly emotional support of the war effort after the fall of France.

The situation was entirely different in England, which was fighting for its life. There, the arts were especially important for maintaining public morale.[6] There are many recorded instances of concerts or poetry readings that continued while bombs were falling, thereby becoming gestures of defiance and national determination. Patriotic and sentimental doggerel, or newspaper verse, was not lacking on either side of the Atlantic, of course. Such material had indeed "enlisted."

A more notable example of poetry that rallied the determination of civilians in England was *The White Cliffs*, published in 1940. In Schweik's words a "call for England's defense" (59), it was written by a woman originally from the United States, Alice Duer Miller, who had married a British subject. Duer Miller's sequence of poems tells of the loss of her husband in the First World War and her son's enlistment early in the Second. Her purpose, stated in the opening poem, is to tell her love story and the story of her acculturation to British society and her love for England "in the hour of trial and danger" (3). She had chosen to remain in England after her husband's death despite many difficulties and irritations. As another war approached she felt overcome with dread, but again chose to remain because her son declared he "would tread the very same / Path his father trod" (65). England was worth dying for, he said—despite his mother's recognition that the nation's leaders during the '30s "bade the English believe / Lies as the price of peace" (67). At the time Duer Miller writes, her son has gone to the fighting, and she has become reconciled to sending him to war when she contemplates the glories of English history:

> . . . I am American bred,
> I have seen much to hate here—much to forgive,
> But in a world where England is finished and dead,
> I do not wish to live. (70)

It is a classic call to patriotism and courage in arms, and readily lent itself to being made into an MGM movie in 1944 similarly aimed at rallying American morale.

Only a year after the publication of *The White Cliffs* the song "[There'll Be Blue Birds over] The White Cliffs of Dover," words by Nat Burton, music by Walter Kent, became a great hit. I am not aware of any direct link between Duer Miller's poems and the song, but there didn't need to be; the cliffs of Dover had long been a symbol of England's defensive power. From the vantage of today, and perhaps also from the vantage of some who heard it in 1941 and during the rest of the war, the song's references to "peace ever after . . . Tomorrow when the world is free" are only too reminiscent of similar hopes expressed during the Great War, which went unrealized.

∽

Popular music is an important index of social attitudes and provides listeners "a way of managing the relationship between our public and private emotional lives."[7] We can see this mediating function between the personal and the public in the songs that were popular during World War II. For a widely dispersed audience who nevertheless shared the experience of anxiety created by the war, popular songs provided a means to the commonality that Ray Pratt calls a "social space" (23). In Fussell's words, a shared familiarity with song titles and lyrics created "notable social cohesiveness" (*Wartime* 188).

Most of the popular music of the war years fell into one or the other of two categories: rousing, sometimes comical morale boosters or else sentimental ballads about separation and the hope of being reunited. Both categories tended to serve what Pratt refers to as "conservative/hegemonic uses" rather than "emancipatory" ones (9, 14). That is, they reinforced a sense of sharing in the goals and activities being determined by governmental authority, not of resisting them. So far as I am aware, there was no genuinely popular (widely circulated, widely enjoyed) music that expressed opposition to this war and its aims as there would be during the Vietnam era. The media "spoke with one voice" (Fussell, *Wartime* 180).

Charles Hamm insists that in the United States, at any rate, music directly addressing the war in any way made up only "a tiny percentage of the songs written during the war years" (*Yesterdays* 377).[8] Even so, some of those that did were quite popular. For the most part, they encouraged perseverance and reassured their listeners that victory would be achieved if we all did our part, and they did so in a cheery way—for example, Irving Berlin's "Any Bonds Today?" recorded by the Andrews Sisters in 1941 and by others throughout the war. Frank Loesser's "The Road to Victory" (1943) similarly exhorted civilians to "buy another bond today" (*Frank Loesser Song Book* 56). It was a recurrent theme. "We Did It Before and We Can Do It Again," by Cliff Friend and Charlie

Tobias (1941), invoked the precedent of the First World War when (so Americans liked to believe) U.S. doughboys had prevailed in a struggle the European Allies were powerless to win. Other flag-waving morale boosters were "Remember Pearl Harbor," by Don Reid and Danny Kaye, written and recorded less than two weeks after the attack in December 1941, and "Comin' in on a Wing and a Prayer," by Jimmy McHugh and Harold Adamson, recorded by the Song Spinners in 1943. Fussell lists one that made bald-faced use of the kind of racist language widely accepted at the time: "The Japs Don't Have a Chinaman's Chance" (*Wartime* 185). "Over There," George M. Cohan's World War I "inspirational song," as Andrews and Gilbert term it (6), was revived.

World War II had its own inspirational song, however—or rather, what would seem to be its own: Irving Berlin's "God Bless America." Actually, "God Bless America" was also in a sense a revival, having first been drafted by Berlin for his World War I stage show *Yip! Yip! Yaphank*, from which it was dropped as being too solemn for the purpose.[9] First performed by Kate Smith during a radio special for Armistice Day in 1938 but not recorded until August 1940 (Andrews and Gilbert 18), it became one of the two most important patriotic songs of the war years. So intense and so widespread was its impact that Kate Smith, whose recording was not only the first but the signature version, was received at the White House and introduced to the king of England.[10]

Irving Berlin became, in fact, what his biographer calls a "minstrel of war" with his patriotic songs in support of the war effort. He had responded in much the same way and reaped much the same harvest of publicity and popularity toward the end of World War I, with his fabulously successful revue that raised some eighty-three thousand dollars for the Army Emergency Relief Fund (Bergreen 163). With the return of war, Berlin volunteered to write and stage another "morale-boosting revue" for the benefit of the Army Relief Fund. The result was *This Is the Army*, which opened on July 4, 1942, with an all-male (sometimes in drag), all-army cast and production crew. Remarkably, for the time, it included both white and black performers, who by working and living together constituted the first integrated unit in the U.S. military (Bergreen 396–97). After a prolonged run on Broadway, the show toured nationally and abroad, with performances in such far-flung theaters of war as New Guinea, Guam, Iwo Jima, and Rome. In addition, Warner Brothers made *This Is the Army* into what Bergreen calls a "bombastic ... propaganda film" with a tacked-on romantic story line starring Ronald Reagan (425). In the film and in many of the tour performances, Berlin again performed (as he had in *Yip! Yip! Yaphank*) his hit number "Oh, How I Hate to Get Up in the Morning." Other songs in the "rousing" score were the rhythmically upbeat "This Is the Army, Mr. Jones," "That's What the Well-Dressed Man in Harlem Will Wear," and "I Left My Heart at the Stage Door Canteen," plus topical numbers such as "The Fifth Army's Where My Heart Is" and "Heaven Watch the Philippines" added at various times for specific tour venues (Bergreen 438). But Berlin's biggest hit of the war years, surpassing even "God Bless America," was not written with the war in mind at all; that was "White Christmas" from the movie *Holiday Inn*, filmed in 1941 but not released until '42. With its tone of wistful nostalgia, it became a huge hit both stateside and among American servicemen overseas, for whom it expressed a deep longing for home.[11]

Second in popularity only to Bing Crosby's recording of "White Christmas" was the patriotic song "Praise the Lord and Pass the Ammunition," words and music by Frank Loesser. "Praise the Lord" became a hit in 1942 in its first recording (by the Merry Macs) and achieved hit status again in a 1943 recording by the Kay Kayser orchestra (Andrews and Gilbert 81).[12] Although some might see blatant irony in the song's linkage of religious expression with artillery bombardment of the enemy, such a linkage was absolutely standard in the country's sense of its war mission. Invocation of religious purpose of the God-is-on-our-side variety has been standard war rhetoric immemorially.

Morale was, in Fussell's words, one of the Allies' "unique obsessions" throughout the war, and popular music was seen as "invaluable" for maintaining it (*Wartime* 143, 184). Motivational numbers might deliver a direct exhortation to listeners to persevere to the victorious end that was sure to come, but upbeat songs utterly without reference to the events of the day also served as morale boosters by providing distraction from the worries of the war. Bing Crosby's advice to "accentuate the positive and eliminate the negative," in his spring 1945 hit recording of the Arlen and Mercer song, is a perfect example. But probably the most widely recognized and popularly sung of such numbers in the United States, next to "Praise the Lord and Pass the Ammunition," was "The

Beer Barrel Polka," with its happy proclamation, "We've got the blues on the run." Fussell refers to it as "the Allied song of the war" (*Wartime* 187). Frank Huggett, who drew on the memories of numerous ordinary citizens in writing his book *Goodnight Sweetheart* about music in England during the war years, reports that by the summer of 1939 "The Beer Barrel Polka" was so popular as to be often sung in parodies (182, 145). One of Huggett's informants mentioned group singing of "Roll Out the Barrel" as well as "Pack Up Your Troubles in Your Old Kit Bag" by prisoners of war in Germany (164). In England as well as the U.S. "bright and breezy" radio fare was preferred by the public, who badly needed a lift in spirits (52–53).

Another of the most conspicuous of what Maxene Andrews calls the "happy songs and novelty tunes" that distracted both civilians and soldiers from the cares of the war was the irresistibly upbeat Andrews Sisters hit "Boogie Woogie Bugle Boy of Company B" (written by Don Raye and Hughie Prince). Recorded by the famous trio in 1941 and sung in their movie *Buck Privates* (and again in the movie *Swingtime Johnny*), it became a standard feature of the Andrews Sisters' act as they toured the country performing at bases, hospitals, and canteens for the USO (United Services Organization). "Boogie Woogie Bugle Boy" captured in one lively package both the topic of the day, military service, and the newest rage in style, a combination of boogie-woogie beat and big band sound. Along with the Andrews Sisters' energetic delivery, the song's lively beat and infectious alliteration made it a natural hit.

Similar morale-boosting hits, to mention only a few, were "Juke Box Saturday Night," the lively "Chattanooga Choo-Choo," now a classic, and "Pack Up Your Troubles in Your Old Kit Bag" (and smile, smile, smile), a reprise of a World War I song. One of the most unusual was a comic number recorded by the irrepressible Spike Jones and his City Slickers, "Der Fuehrer's Face" (1942), featuring rude sound effects in "we go [Bronx cheer] right in the fuehrer's face." Huggett admits that "Der Fuehrer's Face" had "some vulgar success" in England as well (49). Comic songs in mock-rueful style directed at the woes of army life were not so numerous as one might expect. Irving Berlin's "This Is the Army, Mr. Jones" (1942) and "Oh, How I Hate to Get Up in the Morning," with its comic promise "Some day I'm going to murder the bugler," are notable examples. Frank Loesser's "What Do You Do in the Infantry?"

(1943) answered its own question, "You march, you march, you march." But for pure silliness as distraction from wartime cares, what could surpass "Mairzy Dotes and Dozy Dotes"? And who that lived through those years could forget it?

Sentimental love songs emphasizing themes of separation, loneliness, and hopeful anticipation of being reunited were also widely sung. Among the Andrews Sisters' recordings, the 1920 song "[I'll Be with You] In Apple Blossom Time," by Neville Fleeson, became an early and major hit in November 1940. At that point, the only connection to the war was awareness of what was going on in Europe, but with the rampant separations that occurred after the United States declared war the song took on added significance. The trio followed up with the more bumptious "Don't Sit under the Apple Tree"—that is, "with anyone else but me" (by Lew Brown, Sam H. Stept, and Charlie Tobias), a straightforward statement of the widespread anxiety about infidelity often expressed in more sentimental numbers. Other ballads that reflected wartime separation or took on new resonance when the war came were the forlorn "For All We Know (We May Never Meet Again)," lyrics by Sam M. Lewis and music by J. Fred Coots (1934), "I'll Be Seeing You (in All the Old Familiar Places)", by Irving Kahal and Sammy Fain (1938), "I'll See You Again," by Noel Coward (1944), and "I'll Be Home for Christmas," with its drawn out "if only in my dreams," words by James "Kim" Gannon and music by Walter Kent (1943).[13] A Bing Crosby recording of "I'll Be Home for Christmas" in the late fall of 1943 was almost as big a hit as "White Christmas" the year before. Duke Ellington's "Don't Get Around Much Any More" (1942) must have struck a responsive chord with many of both sexes; its recording by the Ink Spots was number two on the chart for two weeks in the spring of 1943 and as recorded by Ellington's band occupied the top spot again only two months later for three weeks. "Till Then," by Guy Wood, Eddie Seiter, and Sol Marcus, a song of anticipated reunion, occupied the number one spot on the Billboard chart in August 1944 in a recording by the Mills Brothers. Another favorite was Cole Porter's "Ev'ry Time We Say Goodbye" (1945).

Laments of the social-sexual deprivations of the war usually focused on the serviceman's loneliness, though love songs lamenting the absence of a beloved were often appropriate for the perspective of either a male or a female singer. The more rarely voiced feelings specific to the lonely and frustrated woman at home were heard in "No Love, No Nothin'" ("until my baby comes home") by Leo Robin and Harry Warren, and the comic but all too realistic "They're Either Too Young or Too Old," by Frank Loesser and Arthur Schwartz.[14]

In none of these sentimental songs of loneliness, sorrow, and anticipation of reunion do we hear a note of resistance against the war itself. Singers might lament the woes of wartime, but they did not demur from the war effort as, for instance, a Vera Brittain or a Margaret Postgate Cole, writing poems of grief during World War I, had done. It is one thing to sing "My darling, please wait for me" or "Pray that our loss is nothing but time" ("Till Then") and quite another to go on record as opposing the cause of the separation.

USO tours taking music to the servicemen, along with comedy, magic, and other variety acts, began in May 1941 when Bob Hope put on a show at March Field in California.[15] Impresario Billy Rose began sending troupes of entertainers to military bases that same month. The content of USO Camp Shows was heavily controlled for morality and good cheer (though Hope was known for slipping in an element of raunchiness). Any commentary on the war itself was carefully scrutinized, even when performances were put on in close proximity to actual combat. The roll call of well-known singers, musicians, and actors who performed with the USO is extensive and varied, with such names as the Andrews Sisters, Al Jolson, George Burns and Gracie Allen, Ed Wynn, operatic sopranos Lily Pons and Kathryn Grayson, violinist Isaac Stern, Mickey Rooney, Milton Berle—it is impossible to give a genuinely representative sampling. Novelist Willa Cather was proud to report in a 1943 letter that her young friend Yehudi Menuhin had flown to England on a bomber to entertain the troops (Stout no. 1639). Many of the big bands performed USO shows, and the army exploited the popularity of the sound by organizing its own big band and sending it on tours. Big bands provided, in Andrews's and Gilbert's words (38), "an important morale boost to Americans . . . in every corner of what people were calling our 'war-torn world.'" Clearly, music was serving a deeply felt cultural need.

In the concert hall, Aaron Copland's *Fanfare for the Common Man* and *A Lincoln Portrait*, both composed in 1942 as Copland's "response to the surge of patriotic fervour" (Butterworth 91), served similar needs in a directly patriotic way. The *Lincoln Portrait* was intended, in Neil Butterworth's summation, to exemplify "characteristics of the national spirit—courage, dignity, strength, simplicity and humour" (87). Given the spirit of the time, cultivating such a self-conception on the part of Americans would naturally bolster their determination to support the war effort. Copland's *Fanfare* was even more explicitly a work designed for wartime; commissioned by the Cincinnati Symphony Orchestra, it was one in a series of ten "patriotic fanfares" performed during the orchestra's 1942–43 season (Butterworth 96). The open brass patterns of the piece, in combination with its title, are indeed rousing.[16]

∽

Poets did not enlist in the war effort to the extent movies and popular music did. Probably the two most notable examples of those in America who did are the prominent public figure and playwright-poet Archibald MacLeish and the immensely popular while also critically respected Edna St. Vincent Millay.

MacLeish headed the governmental Office of Facts and Figures for its one year of existence prior to being folded into the Office of War Information in 1942, at which point he returned to his prewar post as librarian of Congress. He had been a voice for preparedness since long before Pearl Harbor, labeling as "irresponsible" intellectuals who did not support military buildup in the late '30s (M. Sherry 36).[17] His 1937 verse radio play *The Fall of the City*, broadcast by CBS at a time of strong isolationist sentiment in the country, urged a stance of preparedness. In 1938 a second verse play by MacLeish, *Air Raid*, used the bombing of Guernica, in Spain, as a cautionary tale for Americans. Later in the war, his poem "The Young Dead Soldiers" voiced sentiments much like those of the dead infantrymen of "In Flanders Fields," from the First World War, calling on those left behind to continue the fight until the goal of victory was accomplished.

Fussell sarcastically derides MacLeish both for his own wartime writing and for his praise of Carl Sandburg, who wrote a newspaper column that Fussell describes as being full of "folksy optimistic anecdotes and exhortations." Sandburg also bent his book on Abraham Lincoln toward representing Lincoln as religious in order to provide encouragement to Americans then greatly in need of the solace of secure beliefs (*Wartime* 174). To praise such a time-server, Fussell argues, was the mark of an inferior literary mind. A very different view of MacLeish, however, is given by John Morton Blum, who, while conceding that the poet met "strong opposition from those of his fellow writers who considered political advocacy a corruption of art," still regards him as having brought to his work as director of the Office of Facts and Figures a set of "humane sensibilities" and a "strategy of truth" (22–23).

Edna St. Vincent Millay's enlistment in the wartime work of producing what she herself regarded as propaganda is at least equally notorious and surely more distressing. The strain of knowing she had compromised her poetic standards, even for what she considered a very good cause, may have contributed to Millay's mental breakdown in 1948. Her radio verse play *The Murder of Lidice* (1942), apparently influenced by MacLeish's works in that genre, was written at the behest of the Writer's War Board.[18] A dramatization of the fate of a Czech village that was razed by the German army because of its suspected sheltering of the assassin of a German officer, *The Murder of Lidice* heightens the horrors of the event in order to stir up American listeners to hatred of the Nazis. According to Schweik, in the course of the town's destruction, atrocities actually were committed, including the killing of 173 males, the deportation of 203 women to a concentration camp (143 of whom lived to return), and the dispersal of 104 children allegedly to German families, though 81 of the 104 were in fact killed in gas chambers. It was, to be sure, a horrifying incident and was widely publicized. One can scarcely fault Millay for expressing the horror she felt. But a text that includes such standard propaganda elements as the bayoneting of an infant, as this one does, can scarcely be regarded, in retrospect, with admiration.

The Murder of Lidice was not alone among Millay's works in its expression of a hortatory brand of patriotism. Her 1940 volume *Make Bright the Arrows* had sought to forge a spirited determination to defend goodness and justice against the attacks of (to use Ronald Reagan's term anachronistically) an evil empire. The volume was disparaged by critics who viewed her as having sold out her poetic gift to a time-serving purpose. Millay herself regarded the poems in *Make Bright the Arrows* as ephemera that did not belong among her serious literary work and was distressed when they were issued in the same format as her other poetry (Schweik 63). Only two of the *Make Bright the Arrows* poems are in-

cluded among her collected works: "To the Maid of Orleans," a call to
Joan of Arc to return from the dead and lead France in its present danger, and "Memory of England (October 1940)," a tribute to the dear and
good in rural England. The latter expresses satisfaction that her mother
had died without knowing that the countryside of her ancestral origins
had been bombed by Germany. Neither poem is memorable. More satisfying, perhaps, because it bears the trace of Millay's characteristic
wit and flamboyant lifestyle, is a poem from the early war period, "To
S.V.B.—June 15, 1940," expressing grief over the disruption of her beloved Paris by warfare. The title dedication is to the influential owner of
Shakespeare and Company Books in Paris, Sylvia Beach.

Millay had long been an occasional poet as well as a writer of serious,
or aesthetic, verse. She had written, for example, a baccalaureate hymn
for Vassar College in 1917, the year of her graduation from that institution. In her role as occasional poet she now wrote an "Invocation to the
Muses," which was read at the Public Ceremonial of the National Institute of Arts and Letters at Carnegie Hall, New York, on January 18, 1941,
beseeching the immortal nine somehow to be present to soldiers on the
battlefield and prisoners in concentration camps (*CP* 407). Her public
stature was still high, despite negative critical reaction to *Make Bright
the Arrows*. And it remained high in 1944, when on D-day, June 6, the
celebrated actor Ronald Colman read a poem by Millay, "Poem and
Prayer for an Invading Army," over the NBC radio network.

"Poem and Prayer" is a curious document, more of an effusion than
a poem. After calling on (presumably) God to be with the troops then
assaulting the beaches in Normandy, Millay invokes the divine presence
to be with those "here" who work to supply war matériel. Whitman-
like, she then addresses these workers themselves in series. "You men
and women working in the workshops, working on the farms . . . you
workers in the shipyards, building ships . . . you who have stood behind
them to this hour": all of these are called on to stay the course. "This is
the hour, this the appointed time," she urges, "for we know well they
will not all come home, to lie in summer on the beaches"—an oddly
trivializing detail. Those who will mourn them are directed to remember that they died putting an end to a "guilty" period of history. She
then, after a break, invokes the help of the "Lord of Hosts" in "exorcis-

ing from the mind of Man" the "beast" called War (*CP* 421). That is, the idea of a war to end wars persists in this ceremonial statement. In traditional terms she prays, as the voice of the many,

> Oh Lord, all through the night, all through the day,
> keep watch over our brave and dear, so far away.
> Make us more worthy of
> their valour; and Thy love. (*CP* 422–23)

None of this is surprising or remarkable on such an occasion. What *is* surprising, as well as politically astute, given the McCarthy years soon to come, is the section of the prayer that then follows. Millay uses the occasion to warn against domestic fascism. After the heart cries out "Let them come home!" the "thoughtful mind" prays:

> ["]Now look you to this matter well: that they
>   upon returning shall not find
> seated at their own tables,—at the head,
> perhaps, of the long festive board prinked out in prodigal array,
> the very monster which they sallied forth to conquer and to quell;
>   and left behind for dead." (*CP* 423–24)

After the closed quotation mark, ending the collective prayer of the presumably collective "mind," she underscores the point by continuing without quotation marks, thus presumably in her own voice:

> Let us forget such words, and all they mean,
> as Hatred, Bitterness and Rancor, Greed,
> Intolerance, Bigotry . . .

It was a commendable and surprising use of her public lectern, which Millay reconciled to the public purpose by ending with an urge to "all great and noble" of the earth to win the victory over the Axis: "Hold high this Torch, who will. / Lift up this Sword, who can!" (424)

The genuineness of both Millay's and MacLeish's concern about the necessity to fight fascism and therefore the need to marshal public support for that fight cannot be questioned. MacLeish himself said that he was "frightened for the Republic" (quoted by Blum 23), and there is no reason to doubt his words. The plight of the writer who wishes to advance a prevailing political view, especially such a totalizing view as war sentiment, which traditionally evokes a rhetoric of exaggeration, is real, and the task of writing such expressions of general belief while maintaining literary or artistic distinction is a difficult one indeed. Still, the spectacle of accomplished poets bending their sharply honed creative intelligence and craft to the purpose of cant expression is a troubling one.

Although *The Murder of Lidice* was written at the behest of the Writer's War Board, that is by no means true of all of Millay's "enlisted" poetry, nor of such poetry in general. *Lidice* exists at a kind of far extreme. Such a work as Muriel Rukeyser's "Letter to the Front" (a long poem in her 1944 volume *Beast in View*) is a very different matter, neither opposed to the war—it is indeed, in Schweik's words, "strongly antifascist"—nor unthinkingly committed to it. "Letter to the Front" centers on the Spanish Civil War, in which Rukeyser's lover, Otto Boch, was killed fighting on the Loyalist side and in which she herself had wished to fight (Schweik 141, 143).[19] Rukeyser's long poem, as well as other war poetry she wrote during the 1940s and afterward, occupies a difficult and ambiguous middle ground, expressing the wish both to prosecute a war such as that in Spain for clear ideological reasons (she wrote also of resisting the Nazi persecution of Jews before most Americans were even acknowledging it) and, at the same time, to invalidate war itself. Her poetry explicitly regards "women and poets" as the visionaries who see truth, including the truths of disasters while they are yet approaching, and who may be able to discern better ways than repression and armed conflict for achieving social ends. Rukeyser was one of many important figures whose war poetry deserves more extensive attention that it can be given here.

Rukeyser's "Letter to the Front" consciously responds to and revises a convention of the war years, the poem as soldier's letter home, *from* the front.[20] As a genre, the poem as letter home continues the traditional privileging of direct experience of combat, and thus necessarily of the masculine voice, that characterizes war poetry more generally.[21] Rukeyser, for one, was explicitly challenging that privileging. As Schweik points out, the genre is both exemplified and elaborated upon, or complicated, by Karl Shapiro's poem "V-Letter." In the hands of a skilled writer like Shapiro it takes on poetic sophistication, but it could also be used—and was used—by the unsophisticated and thus came to be a popular recurrent form. The poem as letter home "allowed published poetry the 'latitude' of patriotism" because its rhetorical stance of personal, not public, expression gave it the air of authenticity rather than of cant (Schweik 89). It was a form that could enlist without taking on the onus of blind chauvinism.

On what basis can we distinguish, with respect to literary value, between such patriotic verse and the more generally oppositional poetry treated in the next chapter? On this basis, for one: that an art which "enlists" runs the risk of becoming an art that simplifies, that reduces a complex situation such as war, or a complex issue such as the political and social imperatives summed up in war aims, to a simple statement, the imperative to fight on. It is an art that, whether wittingly or not, engages in what A. P. Foulkes terms "integration propaganda," the kind of communication that is "self-reproducing," or widely distributed among members of a group and is designed to promote stability or "conformity" with generally assumed public myths and causes (Foulkes 44, 11).[22] I reject the oversimplification of the complex on artistic as well as ethical grounds. But I recognize that even if this is a standard that frequently validates both the ironic and the resistant, it is by no means infallible or a standard that necessarily aligns "enlisted" art on one side and resistant or uncommitted art on the other. The poets discussed in the following chapter were in many cases both—both enlisted in the war and at the same time committed to honesty, often a harsh honesty, about their experience.

7

Weariness and Irony
A Poetry of Fact

I have seen our failure in
Tibia, tarsal, skull, and shin.
—John Ciardi, "Elegy for a Cave Full of Bones"

. . . to be able to hold in the mind these ghastly facts and poetry at the
same time is a great achievement.
—Robert Bly, "The Work of Louis Simpson"

It has been said that although the First World War produced an abundance of high-quality poetry, the Second did not. Margot Norris broadens this slighting generalization to a belief that the First was "a quintessentially *literary* war" but the Second "was *not*" (99). But in fact World War II produced a rich array of excellent poetry: by Elizabeth Bishop, Gwendolyn Brooks, John Ciardi, James Dickey, Hilda Doolittle (H.D.), Richard Eberhart, T. S. Eliot, Randall Jarrell, Robert Lowell, Marianne Moore, Karl Shapiro, Louis Simpson, Edith Sitwell, Dylan Thomas, Richard Wilbur . . . and the list could be greatly expanded. Moreover, the poetry of World War II was by no means so unidimensional as it has sometimes been characterized, but instead displays a great variety of response to the social ordeal out of which it grew. In addition to a tight-lipped poetry of fact, there was an extensive poetry of grieving and of social comment and moral meditation.

To be sure, the poetry that came out of the Second World War usually differed from that of the First, even from the poetry of disillusionment that appeared after the debacles of 1916 and essentially came to define modern war poetry. In Michael Sherry's judgment this "shift in tone and substance" came about because of an anxiety of influence—that is, because writers of the Second World War and the years leading up to it "sought to extend rather than simply replicate" what had gone before, and the way in which they did so grew out of an "emphasis in American culture during the interwar years on machine-age dehumanization and cosmic purposelessness" (96). In any event, World War II poetry did not often linger so much on overt pity or anger as the poetry of the Great War did. In the war poetry of the 1940s that Susan Schweik calls "anti-war soldier poetry" or "soldier poems of the modern ironic type" (99, 51), the tone flattened, became more factual, more gritty, less bent on rhetorical mission, seemingly more resigned to reportage. At its extreme it took on, as W. R. Martin has observed, "a detachment so great that it almost seems as if esthetic distance has become callous indifference" (38–39). The harshness of the truths the poet had to utter was taken for granted. The trope of the soldier as Christ, suffering because of the sins of the world, yielded to a trope of the soldier as workman doggedly and resignedly doing his job.

It is verse of this nature, a poetry of fact, a kind of utterance springing out of the ironic, often bitter poetry of late World War I but with far less apparent emotional investment, that is usually regarded as the defining mode of World War II poetry—and rightly so, if we remember that this was not the only, or even the only important, mode. There was an equally significant body of work of a more meditative sort, which I take up in the following chapter. The two are not such distinct and separate categories as this division into chapters might imply. Much of what I designate the poetry of fact is also characterized by a strong moral sensibility and readily shades into a poetry of meditation, especially as soldier-observers confront problems of guilt and innocence. Randall Jarrell's fine poem "Eighth Air Force," for example, one of the rare recurrences of the trope of the soldier as Christ, invokes biblical imagery not to emphasize the soldier's suffering but to question his all too ambiguous guilt or guiltlessness.

What is most striking in this terse and factual mode of World War II verse is what W. R. Martin calls its "remarkable . . . sharpness" of "observation" (38), a visual acuity so pronounced that envisionment—specific acknowledgment of the existence of what is observed—becomes at times the entire poetic statement, in a kind of poetry of objectification. Martin traces this sharpness of focus on the visual to Eliot and Auden, and beyond them to Sassoon and Owen, but an even more important linkage might be made to Hemingway's fiction about World War I and its aftermath. At times, all meaning becomes reduced to the fact, the thing. When there is a significant content of lament, grieving, or denunciation, such emotional and rhetorical effects are generally achieved through, not separately from, the fact, the object. Hortatory purpose is minimized or disguised. A certain flatness of tone implies weary but not unfeeling acceptance of the fact of painfulness and debasement, or even surrender to the inevitable, a kind of giving up.

Probably the clearest and most familiar example of this factual mode is Randall Jarrell's frequently anthologized "Death of the Ball Turret Gunner," with its shocking and unforgettable last line, "When I died they washed me out of the turret with a hose" (144). Almost equally familiar is the terse ending of Richard Eberhart's "The Fury of Aerial Bombardment," where the poet distances his grief and fury over the deaths of the trainees he has taught by a self-defensive focus on things in their thingness: "But they are gone to early death, who late in school / Distinguished the belt feed lever from the belt holding pawl" (90). The larger machine of war enjoined a mechanical discipline focused on machinery. Such a restriction to fact is overtly parodied in the formulaic singsong of the instructor's voice in British poet Henry Reed's "Naming of Parts."[1] While the more aesthetically or humanistically inclined inductee finds his attention wandering to the springtime outside the window, the instructor drones on mechanically:

To-day we have naming of parts. Yesterday,
We had daily cleaning. And to-morrow morning,
We shall have what to do after firing. But to-day,
To-day we have naming of parts . . . (49)

It was a war of thingness, even soldiers themselves being reduced to the status of things or substances to be washed out of the ball turret, for instance, with a hose. But the mode of matter-of-factness could sometimes break apart and allow intense emotions to show through, as it does for Eberhart, for instance, in the poem "World War." Eberhart's anger at the entire undertaking is expressed in his summation of what war demands:

Strike down, batter! shatter! splinter!
Destroy! fracture! cripple! butcher!
Knock! beat! whack! cuff!
Ruin! gash! smash! blast! (96–97)

Another of the many poems that could be offered as defining examples of the poetry of fact, the predominant mode of Second World
War poetry, is "When a Beau Goes In" by the British academic poet
Gavin Ewart. Like Eberhart, Reed, and Jarrell, Ewart also served in the
military, though not necessarily in combat, during the war. His poem
tells about the crash of a Beaufighter (a two-man observation/fighter
plane) without comment, or with what might better be called a deliberate and ironic absence of comment.

When a Beau goes in,
Into the drink,
It makes you think,
Because, you see, they always sink
But nobody says "Poor lad"
Or goes about looking sad
Because, you see, it's war . . .

Even though "it's perfectly certain / The pilot's gone for a Burton,"

You shouldn't cry
Or say a prayer or sigh.
In the cold sea, in the dark,
It isn't a lark
But it isn't Original Sin—
It's just a Beau going in. (*Selected Poems* 11)

Like others of this tight-lipped genre, "When a Beau Goes In" makes a
great show of suppressing emotion, partly by its pose as a mere statement of fact and partly by its use of slang ("into the drink," "gone for a
Burton"). It is instructive to compare a poem like this with one of, say,
Wilfred Owen's, in which there are palpable designs on the reader for the

purpose of eliciting agreement that for the soldiers in the trenches the experience of the war was nightmarish and that the poetry of war really is in the pity of it. In Ewart's poem whatever effort there is to arouse pity is submerged in the ironic clipping off of expressive or directive language. The pity arises from the contrast between what is said and what we can imagine we would feel in the pilot's, or even the observer's, place. Not told, it emerges from the presence of absence.

No other defining example of the terse poetry of fact, however, is as visually focused as Jarrell's "The Death of the Ball Turret Gunner," which stands as a kind of outpost at the further extension of the type. It would probably be fair to say that most of the artistically and humanistically successful poetry of the war written in this mode of reportage achieved its success through adopting the factual vision and then, in whatever way, moving beyond it. Jarrell himself moves beyond the minimalism and visualization of "Ball Turret Gunner" in poems where he ponders the guilt or innocence of bomber pilots. In poems of both sorts he draws on his own war experience in the air corps as a control tower operator working with the crews of B-29 bombers. Though not a bomber pilot himself and, as Goldensohn points out, never stationed outside the United States, he was well acquainted with those who were and the issues they dealt with.[2] His three years at an air force training camp gave him abundant insight into the culture and routines of the military.

∽

A great body of battle poetry of World War II was written about the war in the air. It is a subgenre inviting a study of its own. Airplanes had been used in battle in the First World War and briefly, before that, in the U.S. invasion of Mexico, but the use of bombing, fighter planes, and air transport greatly expanded in the localized wars of the so-called interwar years and then in the Second World War, radically redefining the nature of warfare while extending it irreversibly to civilians. Sven Lindquist writes in his *History of Bombing* that in protesting the Japanese bombing of Natao, China, in 1937, which wounded the British ambassador, the British Foreign Office declared that such an act was "inseparable from the practice, illegal as it is inhumane, of failing to draw that clear distinction between combatants and noncombatants in the conduct of hostilities, which international law, no less than the conscience

9. Paul Nash, *Totes Meer*, 1940–41. Courtesy the Tate Gallery, London.

of mankind, has always enjoined" (47; see also 50–52, 71). But as Lindquist points out, the British had bombed civilians in Egypt in 1916, in
India in 1917, and in Baghdad in 1923; the Spanish had bombed civilians
in Morocco in 1925; France had bombed civilians in Syria in 1925; South
Africa had bombed civilians in southwest Africa in 1925 and succeeding years—and so forth. The point is not merely that Britain's protest in
1937 was hypocritical but that conflicts and bombing, with consequent
erosion of the "clear distinction" the Foreign Office invoked, had been
widespread between World Wars I and II.

In a 1940–41 painting by the insistently antiwar Paul Nash, *Totes Meer*,
airplanes are viewed as the emblem of the war's mechanistic lack of mo-
tivating ideal (see fig. 9). Nash uses a sea of wrecked planes as a symbol
of the dead-endedness of war itself. More commonly, though, the image of the airplane, pilot, and crew retained the romance that had surrounded their far fewer numbers in World War I. In part this was because air combat had the image of a clean war—though certainly not for
those on whom the bombs fell. Howard Nemerov uses the phrase "clean
war" in his retrospective World War II poem "The War in the Air," ex-
plaining that its "saving grace" was

we didn't see our dead,
Who rarely bothered coming home to die
But simply stayed away out there. (Stokesbury 92)

Nemerov's adoption of the stance of a somewhat uninformed spectator, despite having been a pilot himself in two nations' air forces (Canada and the United States), can be regarded as an ironically transparent strategy of self-protection. He writes as if he could distance himself from more disturbing awarenesses.

Randall Jarrell adopts the collective but nevertheless personalized group voice of the B-29 pilots with whom he worked in his poem "Losses" to express what would become a recurrent note in World War II poetry—a sense of guilt for actions performed in the course of duty. The speaker (for it becomes clear that there is one speaker despite the use of the plural "we" to indicate the group) remains anonymous though clearly identified as a bomber pilot.[3] "It was not dying," the poem begins, "Everybody died. / It was not dying: we had died before / In the routine crashes" (145). The repetition of "it was not dying" raises, of course, the question of *what* was not dying, or it was not dying that *what*. An apparent answer, though it will prove not to be the final answer, comes quickly in the first stanza's reference to the impersonal way in which their deaths occur or perhaps the fact that they occur because of blunders:

We died on the wrong page of the almanac,
Scattered on mountains fifty miles away;
Diving on haystacks, fighting with a friend,
We blazed up on the lines we never saw.

The tone here is flat, accepting of the facts of the matter, but still ironic in its reporting of how things were.

. . . our bodies lay among
The people we had killed and never seen.
When we lasted long enough they gave us medals;
When we died they said, "Our casualties were low."
They said, "Here are the maps"; we burned the cities. (145)

Those who gave out the maps were officers; following what had by then become the usual mode of war writing, Jarrell speaks for those who carry out the orders.

When the original assertion of "Losses" reenters at the end of the poem, with its undefined "it," the answer to the implied question is finally given. The problem, the "it," is the posthumous speaker's sense of guilt over the devastation he and others like him have caused those on the ground. The guilt of those who said "here are the maps" and sent him out is implied but not voiced.

> It was not dying—no, not ever dying;
> But the night I died I dreamed that I was dead,
> And the cities said to me: "Why are you dying?
> We are satisfied, if you are; but why did I die?" (146)

The final word is that of the flyer's collective victims, "the cities." It is they who ask the last question in quotation marks, "why did I die?" If we as readers are brought to question why the pilot and his fellows died (he speaks for the dead), we have no answer other than the fact that he was sent. But the question of why the civilian victims, the "cities," had to die is even less answerable and goes far toward raising the deeper question of why wars exist.

"Losses" is very much a poem of the Second World War, with its vast civilian casualties. In the cities' question lurks a wholesale condemnation of the entire enterprise. True to the minimalist, modernist governing principles of the World War II war poetry of fact, that condemnation is not voiced. Buried in a more limited complaint that is buried, in turn, in a question, it emerges from the tacit communication of writer and reader. Judgment is left unstated, suspended in ambiguity. Indeed, as Goldensohn writes, Jarrell never reconciled such events as the fire-bombing of Dresden and Tokyo and the doubts they raised about "the morality of our behavior" with "his own sense of the larger justice of the Allied position" (*Dismantling Glory* 224). A far cry, this, from Archibald MacLeish's overtly rallying treatment of a similar topic in "The Young Dead Soldiers," where, in the voice of the dead, he enjoins the living, "We leave you our deaths. Give them their meaning. . . . We have died.

Remember us." One imagines that the Writer's War Board would have been pleased with MacLeish's poem, but perhaps not with Jarrell's.

Jarrell begins with a seemingly flat statement of fact and moves beyond it. Similarly, James Dickey, who wrote a great deal of fine poetry on the war, often begins with factual detail and moves beyond it.[4] In "Drinking from a Helmet," for example, this move beyond reaches a sense of communion with the dead and he weeps for them (185–90). In "The Performance," Dickey offers a little parable of limited human meaning-making in which the act itself (in this case, a captured pilot's small repertoire of gymnastic feats culminating in a handstand) is all one can offer in this life (58–59). John Ciardi, who wrote a masterpiece of terse factuality in his poem "Elegy for a Cave Full of Bones," also pushes beyond fact itself to the concluding moral pronouncement "I have seen our failure in / Tibia, tarsal, skull, and shin."

Karl Shapiro, whose 1945 volume *V-Letter and Other Poems* won a Pulitzer Prize, is another soldier poet (he served in the Pacific) who wrote rhetorically resonant poetry grounded in flat fact, as in "Troop Train" and "Elegy for a Dead Soldier."[5] A major work that knowingly and articulately builds on traditional conventions, "Elegy for a Dead Soldier" memorializes a casualty of the action on a Pacific island and voices resistance to the war's impersonality:

> However others calculate the cost,
> To us the final aggregate is one,
> One with a name, one transferred to the blest;
> And though another stoops and takes the gun,
> We cannot add the second to the first. (*CP* 90)

Even so, the poem retains its grounding in the factual mode. Beginning with a "white sheet on the tail-gate of a truck" that "becomes an altar," it ends with notice of the heaviness of the coffin, before proposing a brief epitaph to mark the grave:

> Underneath this wooden cross there lies
> A Christian killed in battle. You who read,
> Remember that this stranger died in pain;

And passing here, if you can lift your eyes
Upon a peace kept by a human creed,
Know that one soldier has not died in vain. (*CP* 92)

Clearly, this soldier's creed has not availed for such a purpose. Shapiro's short poem "Human Nature," a retrospective on his wartime experience from the perspective of the college professor of English that he became after the war, also begins with the vividly remembered fact of the "battle-gray Diesel-stinking ships" he rode during the war, paralleling that memory to the "Diesel-stinking bus" he drives behind on his way to work.[6]

We can find many examples, then, of poets who start with the factual mode of reportage tinged with irony and use it as a foundation for wider-ranging rhetorical purposes. Yet the visual and factual thingness of such poems and the minimalism of their expression of irony remain the defining quality of this body of writing of battle. (One hesitates to say writing of the battlefield, considering the far-flung nature of World War II combat zones, which as the war went on were extended more and more to combat on civilians.) The factual mode remained dominant long after the war years, so that when Edward Hirsch, who was not born until 1950, looked back on the war in "Leningrad (1941–1943)" in the voice of a survivor of that city's miseries, he employed a rhetoric of naming appalling facts almost without comment, to rouse the reader's indignation and aversion. In the heyday of the new criticism, which exerted a powerful influence on academic poets in the 1940s and '50s, this was called showing rather than telling.

∽

A number of poets have been mentioned here who wrote about World War II and are identified, some more and some less, with the tradition of terse, ironic factuality. Before turning to the tradition of meditative verse about the war, I will give somewhat more extended attention to the work of two of these figures, John Ciardi and Louis Simpson.

Ciardi was one of the most accomplished and probably most underrecognized poetic voices of the century. He, too, served in the army air corps during the war, as a gunner on a B-29 stationed in the South Pacific on Saipan (an island in the Marianas, east of the Philippines, that saw heavy fighting), and wrote poems that directly reflect his war experience. His "Elegy for a Cave Full of Bones" deserves to be regarded as one of the great poems of the war.[7] With its clipped language, it is a sustained example of the hard-edged mode. In its subtitle, "Saipan / Dec. 16, '44," even the terms identifying place and time are abbreviated, minimal. Here is the first stanza:

Tibia, tarsal, skull, and shin:
Bones come out where the guns go in.
Hermit crabs like fleas in armor
Crawl the coral-pock, a tremor
Moves the sea, and surf falls cold
On caves where glutton rats grow bold.
In the brine of sea and weather
Shredded flesh transforms to leather,
And the wind and sea invade
The rock-smudge that the flame throwers made.

After pondering this residue left in the cave by men who were "certain" of their cause but who "stood to die / Passionately to prove a lie"—a piece of heavy irony that, together with the emphasis on brute facts, places the poem squarely at the center of the dominant tradition of World War II poetry—the poet realizes that he is inescapably embroiled in a guilty act, if not as perpetrator then as victim:

I shall murder if I can,
Spill the jellies of a man.
Or be luckless and be spilled
In the wreck of those killed. (575)

The spondaic measure of "those killed" perfectly conveys the bluntness, the factuality, of what has happened and will happen again, while the poet's realization of his own implication in the evil he witnesses recalls similar realizations by Louis MacNeice, W. H. Auden, and others. These lines also prepare for the subdued meditation of the last two lines: "I have seen our failure in / Tibia, tarsal, skull, and shin" (576). Not our victory, despite the evidence of victory in a narrow military sense, but our moral failure.

In "Return,"[8] a poem about bomber pilots and thus, again, directly reflective of his own war experience, Ciardi implies a comment similar to that in Jarrell's "Losses":

> Under the celebration of the sky
> Still calling home the living to their pause
> The hatches spill the lucky and returned
> Onto the solid stone of not-to-die
> And see their eyes are lenses and they house
> Reel after reel of how a city burned. (Stokesbury 73)

This focus on the returning bomber crew is elaborated to visionary levels in the poem "V-J Day," as bombers out on a run beyond Iwo Jima celebrate the end of the war by jettisoning their bombs—an emblem, perhaps, of the hope of jettisoning all future warfare. And the dead of the war, as if they too are pilots and crews returning from a run, come back: "On the tallest day in time we saw them coming, / Wheels jammed and flaming on a metal sea" (Ciardi 57). In its hope for magical return, it is a moment comparable to that in Kurt Vonnegut's *Slaughterhouse Five,* when the firebombed city of Dresden reassembles itself and the un-exploded bombs fly upward and are folded back into the belly of the bomber—an idea wrenching in its poignance and its yearning to reverse time and eradicate what has happened. Such a visionary note is sel-dom heard in World War II poetry. It can be sustained, in a generation schooled in particularity and irony, only by a poet enormously skilled in walking verbal tightropes—as Ciardi was.

It is difficult to understand Fussell's reference to Ciardi as one of the men of letters of that time who "became silent" (*Wartime* 134), since he was in fact a prolific author of both poetry and criticism for many years. Fussell bases that statement on a comment by Karl Shapiro, who in-cludes himself in the assertion: "We all came out of the same army and joined the same generation of silence" (quoted by Fussell, *Wartime* 134). Among other things, this interesting statement enforces a distinction between "we" who were in the armed forces and outsiders who were not—perhaps between "we" men and you, or they, women. That is, it maintains the privileging of direct experience of battle that has been a central thread in the history of war poetry. It then uses that insider-outsider distinction as the basis for a paradoxical authorization to speak

—a kind of catch-22, because those who do speak are shown by that very fact not to be among the authorized, whereas those who are authorized may speak because they have first chosen silence. But in fact Shapiro himself was not silent either. He wrote a great deal of very fine poetry about the war, most famously, perhaps, his sonnet "Christmas Eve: Australia" (*CP* 61).

Ciardi also wrote poems of reflexive self-examination, poetic self-portraits in which he maintains an ironic detachment that communicates itself to the reader as a fragile shield against anxiety. "Elegy Just in Case" pretends not to be bothered by what would be the facts ("fractured meat and open bone") in case he crashed. In so doing, it reminds us of "Elegy for a Cave Full of Bones," with its attention to remains:

> Here lie Ciardi's pearly bones
> In their ripe organic mess.
> Jungle blown, his chromosomes
> Breed to a new address.
>
> Was it bullets or a wind
> Or a rip cord fouled on chance?
> Artifacts the natives find
> Decorate them when they dance.
>
> Here lies the sgt.'s mortal wreck
> Lily spiked and termite kissed,
> Spiders pendant from his neck
> And a beetle on his wrist. (45)

Learned, as Dickey and Shapiro were, in the conventions of the elegy, Ciardi summons nature to share his (self-)mourning, though in fact the somewhat unprepossessing representatives who appear do not mourn: "Bring the tick and southern flies / Where the land crabs run unmourning." Whimsically extending the convention, he also summons elements of his recent military career, expressing the soldier's conventional resentment of the brass with a humorous ambiguity:

> And bring the chalked eraser here
> Fresh from rubbing out his name.

Burn the crew-board for a bier.
(Also Colonel what's-his-name.) (45)

It is not clear whether the colonel is "also" being summoned or "also" being disposed of. Besides recalling the traditional elegy, Ciardi's "Elegy Just in Case" also invokes the more recently established genre of the V-letter, through a brief address to an unnamed woman, possibly representing many women:

Darling, darling, just in case
Rivets fail or engines burn,
I forget the time and place
But your flesh was sweet to learn (46)

—a passage that effectively evokes yet another of the continuities of the soldier's experience.

A second self-portrait, "On a Photo of Sgt. Ciardi a Year Later," conveys more directly the idea already detected in "Elegy Just in Case," that the bomber pilot–poet maintained a determined but brittle pose of tough indifference. Standing "newsreel-jawed" in leather jacket, he "doesn't give a damn" but merely "waits to see the fun"—fun being, presumably, a euphemism for another bombing run. In the last two stanzas the idea is made explicit:

The camera always lies. By a law of perception
The obvious surface is always an optical ruse.
The leather was living tissue in its own dimension,
The holsters held benzedrine tablets, the guns were no use.

The careful slouch and dangling cigarette
Were always superstitious as Amen.
The shadow under the shadow is never caught:
The camera photographs the cameraman. (61)

Our images of war, Ciardi says, are fictions in which purveyors, actors, and consumers are all complicitous in a plot to misrepresent the unseemly facts.

〜

Born in 1923 in Jamaica, Louis Simpson was a student at Columbia College when his degree work was interrupted by the outbreak of the war. He served in the U.S. Army, both in a tank corps and in the infantry of the 101st Airborne Division. After being "among the first to go ashore at Normandy" (Stitt 349), he was discharged with "a Bronze Star, a Purple Heart, and United States citizenship, not to mention frozen feet and delayed shock" (Gray 174). Subsequently, he pursued a successful academic career as poet-scholar and was awarded the Pulitzer Prize in 1964. The following year, he joined a number of other writers and artists in supporting Robert Lowell's public refusal of Pres. Lyndon Johnson's invitation to a White House Festival of the Arts, on grounds of opposition to the war in Vietnam.[9] Simpson's war poems have been called "some of the best" (Cox 193) or even "*the* best" poems to come out of World War II experience (Moran 22; emphasis added).

Simpson is singled out for discussion here not only because of the interest and seriousness of his work but also because he is so clearly transitional between the two broad categories of World War II poetry we have been tracing. Some of his poems about the war could be used as defining illustrations of the first of these types. Seemingly impersonal, they are poems of reportage; their rhetorical or expressive functions are concealed behind a seeming limitation to facts. Simpson himself stated in an essay called "Dogface Poetics" that he "wanted people to find in my poems the truth of what it had been like to be an American infantry soldier" (quoted by Hummer). His poems often succeed in this aim. On the other hand, his work sometimes seems, as another critic has termed it, "more subjective than objective," offering a "repersonalization," a directness of communication, "between reader and writer" (Gray 174–75). Not at all confined to facts and visual presences, it then "touches upon a reality beyond the compass of any trust in rationalism and 'hard facts'" (Cox 195). Yet the hard facts are there, too. Reading lines like the following, from a poem called "On the Ledge,"—

I can see the coast coming near . . .
one of our planes, a Thunderbolt, plunging down
and up again. Seconds later
we heard the rattle of machine guns.

> That night we lay among hedgerows.
> The night was black. There was thrashing
> in a hedgerow, a burst of firing . . .
> in the morning, a dead cow (Simpson 272)

—it is hard to understand the judgment by one of his critics that Simpson's war poems do not "blister with immediate, felt experience" (Stitt 349).

Simpson's first book, *The Arrivistes: Poems, 1940–1949* (1949), has been faulted for excessively rigid formal structures.[10] Jarrell, while expressing confidence in Simpson's promise, said there wasn't "a good poem" in it (quoted by Moran 40). One of the poems in the volume, however, is "Carentan O Carentan," which another of Simpson's critics has designated as perhaps his best war poem (Cox 194). Robert Bly goes further, calling it "the best poem written yet [as of 1958] about World War II" (Bly 24).

In summary, "Carentan O Carentan" begins with soldiers walking two by two along a "shining green canal," much as, in the past, lovers had walked two by two along that same canal (Simpson 23). As the soldiers enjoy the brightness of the early summer day, the seemingly idyllic scene, and their temporary respite from combat, they are lulled into letting down their guard. To be sure, a little smoke hangs in the blue sky where "ships together spoke" (a verb of striking and ironic understatement) to "towns we could not see" (23). But that is off at a distance and easy to ignore. As they walk or even "stroll" along and admire trees such as they "never knew," the soldiers look as innocent and unwary as "farmers out to turn the grass, / Each with his own hay-fork." But the hay-forks are rifles, and the company is deployed at "combat-interval"— details indicating that their relaxation is ill judged. They are in fact walking into an ambush. Camouflaged, or leopard-suited, "watchers" cannily wait for best advantage, then aim "between the belt and boot / And let the barrel climb."[11] The speaker, hit in the knee, remains in a mode of denial as he first assesses his situation, then imagines a letter he wishes he could write to his mother:

> I must lie down at once, there is
> A hammer at my knee.
> And call it death or cowardice,
> Don't count again on me.

Everything's all right, Mother,
Everyone gets the same
At one time or another.
It's all in the game. (23)

Although these two stanzas have been cited as illustrations of just how clumsy Simpson's lines could be (Hummer 338), they seem to me quite artful; I take them to be designedly awkward to reflect the naive young speaker's resort to empty formulas in attempting to fathom his situation.

Clearly one of the "dogfaces" whose experience Simpson wanted to convey, the soldier-speaker of "Carentan O Carentan" then turns to a succession of authority figures—master sergeant, captain, and finally lieutenant—for orders. But each has become "a sleeping beauty, / Charmed by that strange tune," the "whistling in the leaves" that is "not the wind" (24)—that is, they are all dead. A transparently euphemistic language, almost the language of fairy tale, continues to the final stanza, when in simple declarative statement the speaker utters his mature realization:

Carentan O Carentan
Before we met with you
We never yet had lost a man
Or known what death could do. (24)

The speaker's voice, which had begun in the plural but switched to the singular when he was hit, has again become plural, a "we" rather than an "I," joined with the voices of those with whom his fate and his consciousness are identified. Because of his sudden unwelcome awakening, it is also now a more mature voice. By employing a naive language bordering on humor, Simpson sets up, by contrast, the reader's realization of the shocking brutality of the war. Throughout "Carentan O Carentan" a contrast is constructed between language and underlying realization.

In his later volume *Good News of Death and Other Poems* (1955), Simpson uses more supple rhythms and achieves stronger effects than in most of the poems of *The Arrivistes*. Best, perhaps, is "The Battle" (53), which compresses into four quatrains an account of a multiday engagement in combat by focusing on visual details, on facts as experienced by a "they" so depersonalized that in the first two lines they are merely marching objects—"Helmet and rifle, pack and overcoat / Marched through a forest." Animalized by war, they sink into the "clammy earth" like "moles" at the sound of artillery fire. The only trace of personal presence is a single occurrence of the pronoun "I" in the last stanza, where the speaker acknowledges his presence in the scene and his impression of the condition of his comrades. Otherwise our understanding of their ordeal comes strictly from reprortage of facts.

> . . . Their feet began to freeze.

> At dawn the first shell landed with a crack.
> Then shells and bullets swept the icy woods.
> This lasted many days. The snow was black.
> The corpses stiffened in their scarlet hoods.

> Most clearly of that battle I remember
> The tiredness in eyes, how hands looked thin
> Around a cigarette, and the bright ember
> Would pulse with all the life there was within. (53)

Of course, they are very artfully selected facts and details, especially the way the color red moves from the red glow of the night sky "like the circle of a throat" to the "scarlet hoods" of the casualties (interrupted by the black of dried blood that once was red) to the red end of the cigarette that burns with the sum total of a soldier's vitality.

Also memorable, from the same 1955 volume, is "The Heroes." The title itself mocks the cant language of the war, since in fact the so-called heroes spoken of in the poem are never individualized either by name or by deed, as we would expect. Using a darkly comic irony, the poem shows that in their handling by the government these "heroes" have the status only of damaged goods:

> They shipped these rapscallions, these sea-sick battalions
> To a patriotic and picturesque spot;
> They gave them new bibles and marksmen's medallions,
> Compasses, maps, and committed the lot. (54)

With the idea of their being "committed," Simpson recognizes the psychological damage done to many soldiers.[12] The jaundiced view of the cant of heroism seen here is also evident in "The Ash and the Oak,"

where, with an equally pointed but more solemn irony, Simpson asserts
that at Verdun (in the First World War) a hero was in fact "a fool" and
death "nothing if not dull" (55).

Many writers, seeing World War II approaching, pondered the dreadful continuity between their historic moment and that two decades earlier. This awareness is powerfully present in Simpson's 1959 volume *A
Dream of Governors,* in "I Dreamed That in a City Dark as Paris," a
poem in the traditional dream-vision mode that links the two world
wars. An awareness that the same thing was happening yet again might
well, and often did, generate in writers a tone of cynicism, as if they said
to themselves, what's the use. In "I Dreamed That in a City Dark as
Paris" it instead generates a sense of fellowship across the years. Imagining himself lost from his army, alone in a dark city, with an artillery
battle going on in the distance, the speaker senses a magical interpene-
tration between himself and a French soldier of the earlier war:

> The helmet with its vestige of a crest,
> The rifle in my hands, long out of date,
> The belt I wore, the trailing overcoat
> And hobnail boots, were those of a *poilu.*
> I was the man, as awkward as a bear. (83)

Assuming that the identification and awareness he feels are also felt by
the long-dead poilu, he addresses the "confrere / In whose thick boots
I stood," asking whether he too is "amazed" by their crossing of the
boundaries of time and death. He offers an explanation of this supernatural moment by reference to the times in which he lives, whose dev-
astations destroy even the natural order:

> The violence of waking life disrupts
> The order of our death. Strange dreams occur,
> For dreams are licensed as they never were. (83)

But the moment depicted in supernatural terms also makes a rational
point. Despite differences in the trappings of warfare, the two soldiers'
experiences have an essential sameness. The point of "I Dreamed That
in a City Dark as Paris" is that the world is still in thrall to world war;
things are as they were.

Another important theme Simpson treats is the continuing presence of the war for the veteran. In a sense, virtually Simpson's entire mature corpus of work was pervaded by a postwar consciousness; he became a thoughtful, often sad, commentator on history and on the manifold failures of America to live up to its own dreams of itself. "How sad it is, the end of America!" he wrote, in "Lines Written near San Francisco," from the 1963 volume *At the End of the Open Road* (*CP* 166). We can well believe that such a weary wisdom was rooted in the disheartenment brought about by his war experience. In the poems "On the Ledge" and "A Bower of Roses" he writes explicitly of the ongoing effects of the war—or perhaps, the ongoing damage to himself.

"On the Ledge," from the 1980 volume *Caviare at the Funeral*, shows the position of a group of soldiers, first on an invasion coast and then on an inland embankment where they are pinned down "like infantry in World War One / waiting for the whistle to blow" for an assault (*CP* 272). Their plight is compared to that of a character in Dostoevsky who is given a choice between death and having to continue standing on a narrow ledge forever. Presented with such a predicament, one would presumably gain a sharpened perception of life beyond the ledge, perhaps a perception honed even to the point of observing an individual butterfly "as it drifts from stem to stem." The story of the soldiers is anticlimactic, though even in posing the contrast between what the World War I soldiers did and what "we" didn't have to do it reiterates Simpson's awareness of continuity between the two wars:

> But men who have stepped off the ledge
> know all that there is to know:
> who survived the Bloody Angle,
> Verdun, the first day on the Somme.
>
> As it turned out, we didn't have to.
> Instead, they used Typhoons.
> They flew over our heads, firing rockets
> on the German positions.
>
> So it was easy. We just strolled
> over the embankment,
> and down the other side . . . (272–73)

The point of the story is not the choice, because they didn't have to make the choice, but the fact that years later he maintains the sense of imminent peril—a hangover from the war that sharpens his moment-by-moment sense of inhabiting a ledge, the border between life and death:

> Yet, like the man on the ledge,
> I still haven't moved . . .
> watching an ant
> climb a blade of grass and climb back down. (273)

A man on such a ledge would take a keen interest in even the smallest details of life.

Simpson again explores the consciousness of the soldier after the end of the war in "A Bower of Roses," also from the 1980 volume. Here he conveys something of the same sense as Blunden in "1916 Seen from 1921" and Shapiro in "Human Nature." The poem offers the story of a wounded soldier who forms a strong relationship with a prostitute while recovering in a hospital in Paris. After being released for duty, he catches up with his division during what has usually been called the mopping-up operation in Germany. His observation of the ongoing fighting reflects a wry judgment on one of the causes of wars:

> Now and then a shell flew over.
> For every shell Krupp fired
> General Motors sent back four. (275)

After the German surrender and an unspecified time spent in occupation duty, his unit is sent back to France, "only sixty kilometers from Paris," and he again seeks out his girl. Contrary to the reader's expectations, she welcomes him warmly with an affection that seems to have been constant. The rest of the poem shows him learning one more of life's surprising lessons and facing a quandary:

> That night, lying next to her,
> he thought about young women
> he had known back in the States
> who would not let you do anything.

And a song of the first war . . .
"How Are You Going to Keep Them Down on the Farm?
(After They've Seen Paree)."

He supposed this was what life taught you,
that words you thought were a joke,
and applied to someone else,
were real, and applied to you. (276)

It is as if the naive infantryman of "Carentan O Carentan" had lived on after his rude awakening, but even now, as a savvy, seasoned soldier, has yet another awakening, and one that promises continuing unease.

Louis Simpson's poetic voice is at once toughly realistic and personal, factual and meaning-directed. Always being surprised by experience yet always taking it in a manner that seems dogged, his has been one of the most masterful and reflective voices of twentieth-century war poetry.

In 1946, the year after World War II ended, Siegfried Sassoon asserted in his autobiographical *Siegfried's Journey* that by that time nobody needed disillusioning about war (290). The implication is that there were no illusions left, once he and his generation had awakened readers to the truth of the Great War. But his judgment on this point may not have been entirely correct. Throughout World War II, whether through misplaced patriotism or censorship, or, in Michael Sherry's words, "timidity" or "indifference," the language in which the war was reported was not clear or frank. As a result, people at home had limited access to accurate information about the conditions under which it was fought and the results of combat, and their understanding was left relatively "benign." Only in the fall of 1943 were photographs of dead American soldiers allowed to be shown, and then "only intact bodies of isolated individuals," whereas Dwight Eisenhower himself said that in France it was "literally possible to walk for hundreds of yards at a time, stepping on nothing but dead and decaying flesh" (quoted by M. Sherry 96). Americans had a clear idea neither of what their own soldiers endured nor of the impact of the war on people of other nations.[13] The poetry of fact is an important counterbalance to this conspiracy of euphemism that would otherwise muffle public realization of the stakes involved and, perhaps, public resistance to renewed wars.

8

Lament and Protest
A Poetry of Reflection

Not in our time, O Lord,
the plowshare for the sword.

—H.D., "Tribute to the Angels" (1945)

There never was a war that was
not inward.

—Marianne Moore, "In Distrust of Merits" (1943)

The hard-edged poetry of fact that emerged as the dominant mode of war poetry in the Second World War often shaded into a more reflective mode. But there is also a significant but less often recognized body of poetry of the war that eschews the hard-boiled factual mode altogether in favor of meditation, lament, or moral pronouncement. Much of this was written by women—one reason, perhaps, for Paul Fussell's dismissive reference to war poets of the period, "such as they were," in his relentlessly masculinist *Wartime* (139).[1] The distinction between the two types is far from absolute. Poets such as Louis Simpson and others writing a poetry of reportage sometimes moved to a tone of moral reflection in specific poems; much of what I have called a poetry of fact has more or less buried within it a rhetorical or meditative function. Theirs remains, however, a poetry most obviously characterized by reportage. In this chapter, I consider poems that are more obviously characterized by grieving or protesting the war, with reportage, if present at all, greatly submerged. I touch on works by Marianne Moore, Gwendolyn Brooks, Edith Sitwell, Elizabeth Bishop, Dylan Thomas, Robert Lowell, Hilda Doolittle (H.D.), and, last, T. S. Eliot and Wallace Stevens.

Marianne Moore's "In Distrust of Merits," published in 1943, is perhaps the defining example of this meditative kind of war poetry more concerned with exploring meaning than with conveying a factual sense of wartime experience. "In Distrust of Merits" was widely (though not universally) praised at the time as perhaps the consummate war poem but has been generally dismissed by subsequent critics, who find it uncharacteristic of Moore.[2] Gilbert and Gubar liken what they call its "quasi-official rhetorical posturings" to Edna St. Vincent Millay's truly quasi-official propaganda in *The Murder of Lidice* (*Letters* 108). Moore herself came to say she "wouldn't call it a poem" but "just a protest" (interview with Donald Hall, quoted by Schweik 34). It includes, of course, no battlefield details taken from direct experience, nor any arrived at (as were Willa Cather's in her much-derided World War I novel *One of Ours*) by reading and imaginative re-creation. It is not conspicuously ironic, nor is it highly visual or centered in objects or facts. Instead, it is introspective and morally purposeful—indeed, overtly religious in its moral framework, invoking such familiar emblems of Jewish and Christian religious traditions as the Star of David and the star of Bethlehem. Written during the ascendancy of modernism as interpreted by the new criticism, Moore's war poem did not fit the accepted model. It was a poem with palpable designs on its reader.

"In Distrust of Merits" moves the central conflict of the war from the outward world of events to the inner one of moral and emotional reflection, from acts to ideas. As Grace Schulman has argued, in a reading that rescues the work from charges of pious moralizing, it traces the movements of the mind itself as the mind seeks to resolve conflicting feelings toward a complex issue; it conveys "the speech of the mind" engaged in "inner argumentation" (70–75). "There never was a war that was / not inward," Moore asserts in the last stanza; that which is inward, she proclaims, is prior to the outward war, it is "what / causes war" (Moore 138). But she comes to this confident assertion through a back-and-forth process of entertaining contraries, and the statement contains its own uncertainties, including a recognition that she herself, constituted as a representative person among many, has persistently tried to evade this recognition and may not yet be able to "conquer" the causes of war lurking within her soul. Thus, despite its seeming certainty, the ending is, Schulman concludes, "an open one" (75). It is, moreover, a significant ending, given the traditional "entitlement" of men, but not women, to write war poetry. Moore implicitly claims a part in the war, by virtue of being a part of guilty humankind.

Her struggle against the inner fault that causes war is rendered in no-tably military terms as an effort to *conquer* it.[3] Making no attempt to insert herself into the position of the soldier involved in conflict, Moore also makes no pretense of writing about actions she has not experi-enced, but tacitly proposes that what she *has* experienced—her own state of mind, generalized through inference or observation to the state of mind of others as well—is at the center of what "war" means. Indeed, she insistently distances herself from the troops engaged in fighting the war by her choice of pronouns, referring to the troops six times as "they" (not counting other distancing terms) and to civilians like herself as "we." Though soldiers may equally have need of inner self-examination, their reflections, it seems, must necessarily be deferred until they have finished "fighting, fighting, fighting." Nevertheless, she insists that the two—the outer war and the inner war—cannot be wholly separated.[4] At two points in the poem the soldiers' military aim is merged with a moral one:

> they're fighting that I
> may yet recover from the disease, My
> Self . . . (136)

and

> . . . they are fighting,
> fighting, fighting
> . . . that
> hearts may feel and not be numb. (137)

Moore was writing a war poem without any of the elements usually rec-ognizable as aspects of warfare.

Curiously, however, the criticism of the poem that replaced its wide-spread praise during the war itself has not always centered on the lack of realistic and urgent details, but on the presence of "too much [of] the pressure of news" (Costello 110, applying a phrase from Wallace Stevens). Moore herself located the origin of the poem in a newspaper picture of a dead soldier. It can also be traced, by way of her notebooks, to conversations with her mother. Phrases that appear in the poem begin in her notes by July 1942.[5] In addition, as Schweik demonstrates, the poem may also have derived in part from Moore's interest in Asa Jackson's interventionist *Behold the Jew* (1943 in England, 1944 in the United States with Moore's advocacy). Ironically, then, Moore's poem has been disregarded in the same years that have seen an elevation of World War II to the status of the "good war" on precisely the grounds that Moore was arguing in the poem—that it was a necessary battle against hatred and persecution. Moore, though, located the hatred and persecution in all of "us"—ordinary citizens, civilians—whereas devotees of the "good war" generally locate the hatred and persecution solely in the Germans, whom "we" were therefore committed to conquering.[6]

Moore's challenge, as one of the major voices of literary modernism, was to reconcile the modernist mode of indirection and irony with a confessional mode of earnestness (cf. Schweik 33). It was a considerable departure from her more usual fragmented and allusive mode—though, to be sure, "In Distrust" itself utilizes breaks and sudden shifts in its rhetoric. In the end, her reconciliation of the two apparently incompatible modes was weighted toward earnestness and confession.

A perhaps more balanced reconciliation had already been effected, however, by Moore's literary mentee Elizabeth Bishop. Like "In Distrust of Merits," Bishop's poem "Roosters," written in 1940 during the national "great debate" about rearmament, was explicitly situated by its author in an impulse of war anxiety. In a letter to Moore on October 17, 1940 (cited by Schweik 343 and by Goldensohn, *Elizabeth Bishop* 153), Bishop said that she desired to "emphasize the essential baseness of militarism." Yet the poem is far from a straightforward denunciation of war. Rather, it is (in the first and by all odds the simpler of its two parts) a sly critique of the masculine aggressiveness that Bishop saw as an underlying cause of war. This critique is couched in a barnyard fable of raucously crowing roosters whose "protruding chests" are feathered in "green-gold medals" and whose red combs proclaim their "virile presence." The strutting roosters eventually fly into a "mid-air" fight inescapably reminiscent of fighter planes.

Part of the critique within the parable of the fighting roosters is aimed at war rhetoric, as the strident cries of one are readily taken up by others:

At four o'clock
in the gun-metal blue dark
we hear the first crow of the first cock

just below
the gun-metal blue window
and immediately there is an echo

off in the distance
then one from the backyard fence,
then one, with horrible insistence,

grates like a wet match
from the broccoli patch,
flares and all over town begins to catch. (38)

With Bishop's translation of the roosters' "uncontrolled, traditional cries" as proclaiming possessively "This is where I live!" the poem also becomes a critique of the very essence of the nation-state and thus of the origin of war, territoriality.

The roosters' macho belligerence does not go unchallenged. "Roosters," the speaker demands, "what are you projecting?" In effect, what are you up to? Not that her protests avail to ward off the skirmish that these "very combative" birds are stirring up. They fly into battle and, despite their braggadocio, die and are "flung / on the gray ash-heap." The parable is scarcely flattering to military officers and their prowess, let alone their willingness (or not) to listen to dissenters. The "raging heroism" shown in the poem is, after all, only a matter of barnyard cocks' self-assertion, and the urge to fight is slyly, by implication, attributed to mindlessness, with a reference to the littleness of the roosters' heads:

The crown of red
set on your little head
is charged with all your fighting blood. (39)

In the second and considerably more difficult section of the poem, however, Bishop shows us another kind of rooster and offers hope, or at

least the bare possibility of hope, for a more peaceful existence. This
rooster is the biblical cock whose cry opened Peter's eyes to his own sin
of denial and thus to the possibility of divine forgiveness. The story is
rendered in sculptural form:

> Christ stands amazed,
> Peter, two fingers raised
> to surprised lips, both as if dazed.
>
> But in between
> a little cock is seen,
> carved on a dim column in the travertine,
>
> explained by gallus canit;
> flet Petrus underneath it,
> There is inescapable hope, the pivot . . . (41)

"Travertine" is the stone of which the column is carved, and the Latin
inscription "gallus canit" means rooster sings out; "flet Petrus," Peter
flees. We see in the carving the moment when Simon Peter realizes he has
fulfilled Jesus's prophecy of betrayal. "There," Bishop says, as if pointing, right there is the turning point, at the very point of betrayal. The
cock has crowed for the third time, and Peter has denied his Lord. Now,
"heart-sick," the denying saint-to-be "still cannot guess / those cock-a-
doodles yet might bless" by calling him to self-awareness and "forgiveness." But Bishop insists that "'deny deny deny' / is not all the roosters
cry," and at once, as soon as this insistence is voiced, comes an image of
hope, as she resumes the first parable:

> In the morning
> a low light is floating
> in the backyard, and gilding
>
> from underneath
> the broccoli, leaf by leaf;
> how could the night have come to grief?

The roosters' war is like a nightmare that goes away at sunrise. Now, with dawn light magically gilding not the upper but the *under*sides of the leaves in the very broccoli patch where a rooster had crowed with "horrible insistence," a modicum of hope seems to come both from beyond and from within the earth itself. In this happy dawning, the roosters are "almost inaudible"—not gone, and as far as we know not reformed from the urge to fight, but at any rate less troublesome. It would be an ambiguous but minimally hopeful ending—but is not quite, in fact, the end, for Bishop holds out something more than hope: reconciliation. Shifting once again from her own parable of the fighting roosters back to the biblical story, or perhaps uniting the two, she continues for one last stanza:

> The sun climbs in,
> following "to see the end,"
> faithful as enemy, or friend. (42)

Just as Peter, who was both enemy (betrayer, denier) and friend (disciple, apostle), followed to see the end and was reconciled, so, she implies, may we enemies become friends now. But first we have to hear the rooster's call and wake up.

As Goldensohn comments, we can readily discern in retrospect the application of Bishop's poem to wartime posturing and violence and can easily see the roosters as "both macho and militarist," even though the application of the roosters' crowing and conflict to human warfare is "sidelong" (*Elizabeth Bishop* 156–57)—for example, in the description of the birds' gleaming breast feathers as "green-gold medals" and the even subtler characterization of the early dawn light and its reflection on the windows of houses as "gun-metal blue" (Bishop 38). In a letter to Moore in which she rejected some of Moore's rather imperious suggestions for "Roosters" and avowed its antiwar intent, Bishop singled out the repeated word "gun-metal" as a detail she particularly wanted to keep, saying that her visualization of the village where the roosters crow was derived from photographs of Scandinavian villages occupied by the Nazis (quoted by Goldensohn, *Elizabeth Bishop* 153). The letters between Moore and Bishop over "Roosters" constitute a remarkable exchange. Given Moore's intimate knowledge of the poem, one wonders whether her subsequent "dying, dying, dying" in "In Distrust of Merits" may have been a sound-alike allusion to Bishop's stanza describing the rooster's combat: "and one is flying, / with raging heroism defying / even the sensation of dying" (*Poems* 40). Both, by their own statements, began with the day's news and reached far beyond it.

⌒

Gwendolyn Brooks wrote poems given to a very different kind of moral reflection on the war. Included in her celebrated 1944 volume *A Street in Bronzeville* was "Negro Hero," a monologue revealing the injustice with which black soldiers were treated despite the devotion with which they—or in this case the black soldier in whose voice Brooks, a woman, dares to speak—fought for their fellow soldiers and for an ideal of democracy. "I had to kick their law into their teeth," the speaker begins, "in order to save them." He, the speaker, fought for white Americans —that is, both for his fellow soldiers (though the armed forces were still segregated) and for white Americans in general—despite constantly having to question his own acceptability in American society:

> Still—am I good enough to die for them, is my blood bright enough to
>   be spilled,
> Was my constant back-question—are they clear
> On this? Or do I intrude even now?
> Am I clean enough to kill for them, do they wish me to kill
> For them or is my place while death licks his lips and strides to them
> In the galley still?
>
> (In a southern city a white man said
> Indeed, I'd rather be dead;
> Indeed, I'd rather be shot in the head
> Or ridden to waste on the back of a flood
> Than saved by the drop of a black man's blood.) (Brooks 20–21)

Splitting the two voices, one black and one white, into two separate stanzas emblematizes the racial split in American society.

As Schweik has pointed out, the poem is silent on another division in

American society at the time of its writing, the inequality of women. But silence does not necessarily mean absence, nor does absence mean disregard. That division, too, is tacitly treated by virtue of the poem's attention to issues of masculinity. Like Louis Simpson in "The Heroes" or Wallace Stevens in poems written throughout his career, Brooks examines the idea of heroism—what qualifies as heroism, where military heroism comes from, what is the proper estimate of the military hero. Such questions entail the idea of war itself as well as, by implication, other aspects of the issue of gender. And she finds that even if heroism sometimes incorporates devotion ("I loved. And a man will guard when he loves"), it, or by implication war, springs more basically from masculine immaturity:

> It was a tall time. And of course my blood was
> Boiling about in my head and straining and howling and singing me on.
> Of course I was rolled on wheels of my boy itch to get at the gun.
> Of course all the delicate rehearsal shots of my childhood massed in
>   mirage before me.
> Of course I was a child
> And my first swallow of the liquor of battle bleeding black air dying
>   and demon noise
> Made me wild. (19–20)

It is a view of the fighting man comparable to Bishop's in "Roosters," where the "combative" birds whose combs are "charged with all your fighting blood" are seen aggressively cockadoodling their territorial claims. Schweik comments that Bishop's "critique extends to all forms of territoriality and aggression" and "specifically to masculine behavior and, perhaps . . . masculine nature" (218). Much the same could be said of "Negro Hero," which demonstrates one of Gwendolyn Brooks's specialties—a poem that gets more complex the more one reads it. It examines, either directly or indirectly, multiple divisions in American society and their intersections.

Brooks adopts the voices and the perspectives of both male and female, black and white, in the sonnet sequence "Gay Chaps at the Bar," a title that puns on bar for drinking / color bar. The fourth of the sonnets, "looking," is a rather conventional war poem by a woman in that it speaks seemingly from the perspective of a mother seeing her son leave for the war, pondering how best to say good-bye and knowing that nothing will "haul your little boy from harm" (24). The identification of the speaker as a woman is not explicit, however; the voice could be that of a father or even a teacher—anyone devoted to the departing soldier in a parental or quasi-parental way that might justify the phrase "your little boy." Once again, then, Brooks undermines stable identities and distinctions in the context of the war. In the seventh sonnet of "Gay Chaps at the Bar," "the white troops had their orders but the Negroes looked like men," she undermines stable distinctions and expectations of an equally pervasive though less amiable nature—the assumption by white men that they are more worthy than black men. Adopting the perspective, though not literally the voice, of white soldiers, she acknowledges the existence of entrenched prejudice—"They had supposed their formula was fixed"—and then its unsettling:

> But when the Negroes came they were perplexed.
> These Negroes looked like men. Besides, it taxed
> Time and the temper to remember those
> Congenital iniquities that cause
> Disfavor of the darkness. Such as boxed
> Their feelings properly, complete to tags—
> A box for dark men and a box for Other—
> Would often find the contents had been scrambled.
> Or even switched. (25–26)

The quietly acerbic language here, with its promenade of near-rhymes and its feigned perplexity as to how to maintain accustomed prejudices when experience keeps calling them into question, switching the boxes, is distinctively Brooksian.

In the last of the twelve sonnets, "the progress," the racial consciousness of the sequence yields to revelation of a different fault line in American, and indeed human, history—the seemingly eternal return of war:

> For even if we come out standing up
> How shall we smile, congratulate: and how

Settle in chairs? Listen, listen. The step
Of iron feet again. And again wild. (29)

Here Brooks joins her voice with the voices of other poets also deploring
the recurrence of war, but at the same time writes distinctively and from
a perspective too little expressed in American war poetry, that of race
consciousness.

∾

A more difficult poet to discuss with the brevity necessary here is
H.D., Hilda Doolittle, whose visionary trilogy of World War II positions
the twentieth century and its war-wrecked places in parallel with ancient times and the fragmentary remains of ancient civilizations. Louis
Martz observes that with the dedication of "The Walls Do Not Fall"—
"for Karnak 1923 / from London 1942"—H.D. "equates the opening of
an Egyptian tomb with the 'opening' of churches and other buildings by
the bombs" (Martz xxx). The first canto begins with images of ruin in
contrast with reassurances of Spirit's persistence:

An incident here and there,
and rails gone (for guns)
from your (and my) old town square:

in green, rose-red, lapis;
they continue to prophesy
from the stone papyrus:

there, as here, ruin opens
the tomb, the temple; enter,
there as here, there are no doors:

the shrine lies open to the sky,
the rain falls, here, there
sand drifts; eternity endures

ruin everywhere, yet as the fallen roof
leaves the sealed room
open to the air

so, through our desolation,
thoughts stir, inspiration stalks us
through gloom:

unaware, Spirit announces the Presence . . . (509–10)

Small bits of color and moisture promise a resurgence of life in spite
of devastation, even as "inspiration" reasserts itself "through gloom."
What is perhaps most remarkable about H.D.'s work here is that her
elaborate paralleling with the ancient does not drain the present of its
impact:

we pass on

to another cellar, to another sliced wall
where poor utensils show
like rare objects in a museum;

Pompeii has nothing to teach us . . . (510)

Both the destructiveness of modern total war and the resilience of
pained humanity are fully present in H.D.'s poem:

the bone-frame was made for
no such shock knit within terror,
yet the skeleton stood up to it:

the flesh? it was melted away,
the heart burnt out, dead ember,
tendons, muscles shattered, outer husk dismembered,

yet the frame held:
we passed the flame: we wonder
what saved us? what for? (510–11)

Even the burning of books (as a result of the bombing and in the bon-
fires of the Third Reich) cannot, she insists, kill the spirit. The final
canto proclaims:

Still the walls do not fall,
I do not know why;
. . . .
dust and powder fill our lungs
our bodies blunder

through doors twisted on hinges,
and the lintels slant

cross-wise;
we walk continually

on thin air . . .

we know no rule
of procedure,

we are voyagers, discoverers
of the not-known,

the unrecorded;
we have no map;

possibly we will reach haven,
heaven. (542–43)

The "cross-wise" slant of the lintels and the hope of reaching haven or
heaven are only two traces of Doolittle's macrolevel frame of reference
here and in the second and third poems of Trilogy. Schweik has discussed the elaborate "disruptive and disrupted" biblical (Christian) narrative that underlies the poem (242–58).[7] As she compellingly demonstrates, H.D.'s war writing—pointedly unrecognized at the time but more
often discussed as feminism began to revise the canon—occurred within
the context of a wartime surge of a "firmly conventionalized but still
powerfully effective rhetorical strategy" based on Christian and apocalyptic reference (Schweik 248). Indeed, Moore's "In Distrust of Merits"
and Bishop's "Roosters," with its references to the crowing of the cock
in the story of Peter's betrayal of Jesus, participate in that surge.

The hope that "we will reach haven, / heaven" voiced at the end of the first poem of H.D.'s trilogy is echoed in the epigraph to the visionary second poem, "Tribute to the Angels," which was dedicated to Osbert Sitwell, the brother of Edith Sitwell. The poem begins with more images of breakage and shattering and an invocation of Hermes Trismegistus, "patron of alchemists," to "collect the fragments of the splintered glass" and to "melt down and integrate, / re-invoke, re-create" the "shards" of ruin (547–48). In language from the Book of Revelation (in the Christian Bible), the poet's voice struggles between vision and misgiving until being answered in the words of Revelation 21:5: "I make all things new."[8] Yet she cannot entirely accept this assurance. After "He of the seven stars" announces his putatively reassuring resolve to "make all things new," she remembers that this is he (now significantly in the lower case) of the "seventy-times-seven bitter, unending wars." In the fourth canto she laments in the biblical language of peacemaking,

Not in our time, O Lord,
the plowshare for the sword,

not in our time, the knife
sated with life-blood and life,

to trim the barren vine . . . (549)

Yet hope returns toward the end with a vision of the crossing of a "charred portico" and a missing wall, images from "The Walls Do Not Fall," to find a symbol of renewal of life: "an ordinary tree / in an old garden-square" (559). Echoing but not entirely replicating Christian symbols, the mystical tree returns with added details as the "other-half" of a tree that "looked dead"—"a half-burnt-out apple-tree / blossoming" (561)—an affirmation that life renews itself.

At the time of H.D.'s writing, the world was still embroiled in war. The confidence of this assertion of its return to life is truly, then, visionary. Dated London / May 17–31, 1944, "Tribute to the Angels" looks beyond its present circumstances to an envisioned "flowering of the burnt-out-wood" and offers prophetically, as if she were even then certain of the outcome, the poet's "thanks that we rise again from death and live."

⌒

In stark contrast to H.D.'s confident hope is Edith Sitwell's despairing immersion in the present moment in "Still Falls the Rain," written during the bombing of London in 1940. In this poem—more distraught in tone even than her World War I poem "The Dancers (during a Great Battle, 1916)," with its "floors . . . slippery with blood"—Sitwell elaborates the frequently invoked Great War trope of the soldier as Christ to an apocalyptic vision of the (British, civilian) world as a suffering Christ, conjoined with a vision of the ongoingly crucified Christ suffering for the world, or more precisely, it seems, for London.[9] The "rain" of the title is first the rain of bombs, then a rain of blood from Christ's side—a revision of the scriptural account in John 19:34, where a flow of blood and water together is said to proceed from the body's side where Jesus is pierced after his death. In "Still Falls the Rain" there seems to be little prospect of survival or redemption to come; for thirty of the thirty-three lines Sitwell's vision is fixed solely on the violent sufferings of the Battle of Britain. Only the final three lines give a gesture toward the "dawn" of the poem's subtitle ("The Raids, 1940. Night and Dawn") with an assertion of ongoing love by the One who suffers with humanity and who is "still" faithful, just as the natural rain, not just the rain of bombs, "still" falls. This differs considerably, however, from H.D.'s expression of thanks, in the present tense, for the looked-for survival that was yet to come.

Sitwell's poem is written in a language so heightened, so assertively declarative of misery and horror, that it could well be called overwrought. Fussell has intemperately referred to it as "preposterous, theologically pretentious," a "theatrical farrago [full of] empty portentousness," and as "that Sitwellian disaster" (*Thank God for the Atom Bomb* 137). "Still Falls the Rain" is indeed, in my own reading, discomfiting. On the other hand, its linguistic excesses ought fairly to be estimated within the stresses of the times in which Sitwell wrote them. She was by no means alone in conceiving of the events of the war in apocalyptic terms. Many Britons daily expected death from bombing or a worse ordeal when German troops invaded, as was actually feared. Some, like Leonard and Virginia Woolf, planned their suicides in that event—a particularly urgent concern in their case because Leonard was Jewish. Moreover, we should recall that if Sitwell seems poetically out of control here, she showed very firm self-control when, on at least one occasion, she completed a public reading while bombs were falling so close by that she could scarcely be heard.[10]

The heightened language that characterizes Sitwell's "Still Falls the Rain" is equaled, perhaps, by that of the characteristically declamatory Dylan Thomas and more surprisingly by that of Robert Lowell in poems about the bombing of civilians that also employ the cadences and images of biblical Christianity. All three of these poems, then, participate in the World War II poets' broadening of the trope of the soldier as Christ to include noncombatants and therefore women, since as Susan Gubar writes, the experience of "air raids, blackouts, rationing, or even occupation end[ed] the possibility of a separate sphere for women" (230; also Schweik 249).

Thomas's "A Refusal to Mourn the Death, by Fire, of a Child in London" (1946) asserts in three sweeping sentences carried through twenty-two lines the poet's refusal to express grief on grounds that the fact of the death is itself an "elegy of innocence and youth" that exceeds in solemnity and meaning any possible prayer or lament he might utter. In elaborate hyperbole Thomas does, of course, utter that lament while declaiming his refusal to do so, and in so doing elevates the anonymous child's death by burning to the level of an absolute exemplum of mortality not to be exceeded until the end of time. Despite a rhetorical pitch that threatens to tumble over into bathetic excess, the poem is a powerful and moving recognition of the extremity of suffering produced by this war that so dramatically expanded the zone of conflict to encompass whole civilian populations—of London, Hamburg, Dresden, Tokyo, Hiroshima, Nagasaki.[11]

Like Thomas's "Refusal to Mourn," Lowell's uncharacteristically elevated and rhetorically formal "The Dead in Europe" was written shortly after the end of the war. Little anthologized or discussed, it is a tour de force of wordplay reminiscent, in its elaboration and its ultimate solemnity, of the metaphysical wit of John Donne and other seventeenth-century poets. The first stanza of "The Dead in Europe" initiates patterns of sound and idea that play through the rest of the poem:

> After the planes unloaded, we fell down
> Buried together, unmarried men and women;

Not crown of thorns, not iron, not Lombard crown
Not grilled and spindle spires pointing to heaven
Could save us. Raise us, Mother, we fell down
Here hugger-mugger in the jellied fire:
Our sacred earth in our day was our curse. (Lowell 79)

The "Mother" of the fifth line of this intensely Catholic poem is, of
course, Mary, the mother of Jesus. In the second and third (final) stanzas the words "mother" and "Mary" chime seven times, and "Mary"
gives rise to "marry" (foreshadowed, of course, in line 2, quoted above)
in a startling conceit for the intermingling of flesh in the bombing and
fires. "Our Mother," the poet prays, "shall we rise on Mary's day / In
Maryland"—a playful renaming of heaven as Mary's envisioned land
and at the same time an invocation of an earthly place that was heavenly
in that it was not bombed. In a vision of the Last Day, he hears "earth's
reverberations and the trumpet / Bleating into my shambles" and, pulling together the wordplay that has twined through the whole, prays,
"Mary, hear, / O Mary, marry earth, sea, air and fire," presumably into a
redeemed whole. At the end, the line that ended the first two stanzas,
"Our sacred earth in our day was our curse," takes on a startling immediacy that makes the torture of war real and threatening to the reader:
"Our sacred earth in our day *is* our curse" (emphasis added). Like Dylan
Thomas, Lowell could not write of the extremity of suffering in war except in terms of last things, the end of the world ("Rising-day"). It is
ironic that his vision of this extremity would in its title ("The Dead in
Europe") exclude the dead of Japan, even though the poem was written
after the "planes unloaded" there.

∼

The most celebrated of visionary, religiously based poems of the war
was T. S. Eliot's "Little Gidding," the 1942 conclusion of his four quartets. As we have seen, the war brought a powerful resurgence of biblical typology, as people despairing amid the horrors of renewed and terribly "advanced" warfare conceived of their experience in eschatological
terms in which they sought to find salvific meaning for their lives. Eliot's
own spiritual journey has been extensively discussed by others. My purpose here is to recognize the importance of "Little Gidding" in this
context.

Like the other three quartets, "Little Gidding" is a poem in five movements. Its title refers to the name of an Anglican religious community
founded in 1625. Thus, in characteristic Eliotic fashion, the poem's invocation of a Christian framework is indirect. More than any of the other
meditative poems of the war discussed here, however, except perhaps
Bishop's "Roosters," it utilizes a deep structure profoundly characteristic
of the New Testament, the structure of paradox. Paradoxes abound from
the very first words of the first movement, "midwinter spring" and continue through

> Taking any route, starting from anywhere,
> At any time or at any season,
> It would always be the same (139)

to the ending, "England and nowhere. Never and always"—to consider
the first movement alone. The central and overarching paradox is the
idea of redemption through suffering, a concept that took on new meaning for Eliot and his readers during the war years as they struggled to
find a justifying rationale for their ordeal.

In the second movement, the reference to the war becomes overt. The
scene of bombed-out London is set in the terse opening stanza's pun-
ning reference to "the place where a story ended"—the place, that is, in
what was once a house where a story or floor of the building ended,
was destroyed, and where a family's story, or family history, ended. It is
a domestic image of apocalypse. After three tight stanzas evoking the
elements of air, water, and fire, all linked to death, the poet begins a
parable in which he himself, in his actual wartime role as an air-raid
warden, is seen in the hours before dawn, after a German bomber—
"the dark dove with the flickering tongue"—has turned back toward the
Continent (140). As he walks his grim route, there, "between three dis-
tricts whence the smoke arose," he has an encounter with a "compound
ghost" comprised of the spirits of two "dead master[s]," W. B. Yeats and
Jonathan Swift (140). Both urge him to reconceive his past misdeeds and
submit himself to the "refining fire"—that is, both the fire of the bombing and the fire of purgatory, or more figuratively, spiritual fire—so that
he can be purged. A possible purpose of the devastation, then, both in a
personal and in a collective sense, is purification.

In the third movement Eliot amplifies the idea of sin and purgation by reference to the story of England's King Charles I and his two aides who were executed by the Puritans in 1649. Even in this context, and by implication in the context of the war, he can assert in the words of Dame Julian of Norwich, "All shall be well, and / All manner of thing shall be well" (142–43), because everything works together toward redemption. Redemption is asserted—in a sense, is realized, poetically—in the fifth movement, which evokes biblical cadences to state a parable of spiritual journey, again through paradox:

What we call the beginning is often the end
And to make an end is to make a beginning.
The end is where we start from . . .

We shall not cease from exploration
And the end of all our exploring
Will be to arrive where we started
And know the place for the first time. (144–45)

To do so, to reach the promised state where "all shall be well and / All manner of thing shall be well," we must experience the "in-folded" state in which "the fire and the rose are one": the fires caused by the bombing, the fires of suffering and purgation, and the rose of spiritual beatitude. It is a highly visionary ending, asserting as it does the certainty of redemption and bliss even in the days and nights when the bombing was continual and the outcome of the war, including the survival of England and her people, in question.

Before reaching this conclusion, however, Eliot offers his concise fourth movement, which unites a clearly visualized reference to the bombers with a statement of faith in redemption through one or another, historic or spiritual, fire. Here is the brief fourth movement:

The dove descending breaks the air
With flame of incandescent terror
Of which the tongues declare
The one discharge from sin and error.
The only hope, or else despair

Lies in the choice of pyre or pyre—
To be redeemed from fire by fire.

Who then devised the torment? Love.
Love is the unfamiliar Name
Behind the hands that wove
The intolerable shirt of flame
Which human power cannot remove.
        We only live, only suspire
        Consumed by either fire or fire. (143–44)

With intense metaphysical irony, the "dove descending" becomes simultaneously a dive-bomber and the emblem of the Holy Spirit. The tongues are at once the flames caused by the bombing and the tongues of flame symbolizing the presence of the Holy Spirit in the biblical story of Pentecost. The "intolerable shirt of flame" is the irremovable shirt of vengeance in Greek myth, but here Eliot asserts his faith that its "torment" was "devised" for the loving purpose of redemption. These stanzas were set to music by Igor Stravinsky as "The Dove Descending," an anthem for unaccompanied choir. Completed by Stravinsky in January 1962, it has not been considered a major work but is an emotionally powerful one.[12]

Eliot's spiritually charged meditation on the war experience demonstrates the richness and variousness of poetry that came out of World War II and also of the hope that humankind will "come out of" war in a more ultimate sense. "Little Gidding" also illustrates, when we contrast its overt spiritual aspiration to the brokenness and dry disillusionment of *The Waste Land,* the richness and variousness of Eliot's own response to war. If the answer it implies—that the flames of war were sent by God or were used by God to purify us, or at any rate can be received in that way—is not an altogether acceptable one to some readers, it nevertheless testifies to the literary and cultural urge to turn grieving toward some larger end.

∽

Wallace Stevens has often been paired with T. S. Eliot in critical claims that one or the other was the poet of the century, as if there were some sort of contest. Fortunately, we are now hearing less of this "great man" kind of criticism. Still, it seems appropriate to take up the two together. Both produced poetry of meditation and moral concern about the war. Unlike Eliot's, however, Stevens's meditations were not rooted in religious, and specifically Christian, tradition. Except perhaps at the very end of his life, his mind was of a humanistic and secular cast—though, to be sure, his probing of the imagination and its importance took on a religious value in itself. Unfortunately, it is impossible to discuss Stevens with the brevity that a book like this requires. At the same time, it is impossible *not* to discuss Stevens. In the spirit of his own title, "Asides on the Oboe," then, I offer merely an aside.

Stevens is not often thought of as a war poet, largely because his poetry is generally so abstract—despite his hearty devotion to the round "mundo," the real world. He is rarely topical. In the words of his own injunction, "The poem is the cry of its occasion, / Part of the res itself and not about it" (473). He did not so much write poems "about" subjects as provide poems whose language evokes sensations that may lead us to think about certain matters. His poems are like freshly washed windows with no streaks: they give us a clear view of the colors and shapes outside, though we may not immediately know what it is that we are looking at.

Throughout the years of his enormous productivity, Stevens wrote poetry that resounds with the "cry" of the "occasion" of war. If we look at the sweep of Stevens's work with the purpose of seeing how the world wars entered his consciousness and colored his work, we find a recurrence of both a language of war ("soldier," "captain," "hero") and expressions of hope for peace. To be sure, when Stevens wrote the word "soldier" or "hero" he was not necessarily writing about literal soldiers or literal war heroes; his ongoing interest in the idea of the hero, or "major man," was directed primarily toward the nature of the capable imagination. Yet because his mind was part of the "res" (Latin for thing or reality) and the "res" part of his mind, we might well ask whether his preoccupation with "major man" would have persisted if the idea of the hero had not been so insistently pressed on his attention by wars.

In a number of poems, though, Stevens addressed the subject of wars, or the problem of war in general, directly and clearly. I would include in this group "The Death of a Soldier" and others in the "Lettres d'un Soldat" sequence of 1917–18, "Dry Loaf," "Martial Cadenza," perhaps

"Examination of the Hero in a Time of War," "A Woman Sings a Song
for a Soldier Come Home," and "Imago." One of the more traditional
and straightforward of such poems, both in language and in sentiment,
is "The Men That Are Falling," from the volume *Ideas of Order* (1936).
The term "falling" (or even more so, "fallen") is so inescapably identified with war that we must believe its use here was informed by that intention. Assuming so, I see the poem as being at least in part a tribute to
a dead soldier of World War I, who "spoke only by doing what he did."
Essentially, it endorses the idea of sacrifice: "This death was his belief
though death is a stone. / This man loved earth, not heaven, enough to
die" (188). Buried in these lines is the familiar idea of the soldier as
Christ. At the same time, the word "fall" in its various forms rings with
echoes of the biblical fall in Eden. Are those who fall into wars, then—
but not necessarily those who fall *in* wars—morally fallen? Such a meaning is not clearly implied, let alone stated. Stevens seems to be grappling
with a concept he has not resolved, trying to find what he wants to say.

In "Gigantomachia," from *Transport to Summer* (1947), he again pays
relatively straightforward tribute to those who fought:

> They could not carry much, as soldiers
> There was no past in their forgetting,
> No self in the mass: the braver being,
> The body that could never be wounded,
> The life that never would end, no matter
> Who died, the being that was an abstraction,
> A giant's heart in the veins, all courage. (289)

One wonders if the title of Tim O'Brien's Vietnam novel *The Things
They Carried* came out of Stevens's line "They could not carry much, as
soldiers."

"Dutch Graves in Bucks County," also from *Transport to Summer*,
bears traces of a spirit more pervasively troubled by war in its imagining of "semblables," men like himself, seemingly men who have fought
in wars. These men—imagined or surviving in collective memory, or
history—are like wraiths, tapping "skeleton drums inaudibly" and "shuffling on foot in air . . . marching." Their weary "shuffling" as they march
calls to mind certain photographs of worn-down World War I troops or

World War II "dogfaces" (a common term for U.S. infantrymen, used especially by those of the other services who considered themselves superior). The poet's awareness is haunted by these "semblables" and "circles of weapons in the sun" and by a more abstract "rumble of autumnal marching"—apparently, his awareness of war itself and the twentieth century's persistent miring in war. A previous generation, the "mossy cronies" of World War I, fought with "nothing won," no lasting outcome, certainly not the idealistic outcomes that were held out as war aims; then men of a new generation, "the lewdest and the lustiest," were doomed to go again into the "incorrigible tragedy" of what amounted to mass suicide:

> Freedom is like a man who kills himself
> Each night, an incessant butcher, whose knife
> Grows sharp in blood. The armies kill themselves . . . (292)

This, Stevens says, is "the pit of torment": that the same thing should happen "year, year and year," that the end of a war (presumably he has the Versailles Treaty in mind) should prove so ineffectual, "that placid end / Should be illusion." Almost overwhelmed by the noisy voices "that will cry loudlier / Than the most metal music, loudlier, / Like an instinctive incantation," he calls for "a peace that is more than a refuge" (291)—a robust peace.

Stevens's most insistent pondering of issues relating to World War II came in his 1942 volume (revised in 1951) *Parts of a World*. In "Martial Cadenza," yearning for his contemporaries' lives to return "still young" in the way that the stars keep coming back in successive seasons, his consciousness is instead oppressed by

> . . . the silence before the armies, armies without
> Either trumpets or drums, the commanders mute, the arms
> On the ground fixed fast in a profound defeat . . . (237–38)

Perhaps he means here the defeated armies of World War I, soon to become active armies, or perhaps the disheartening end that came to the Wilsonian hope of a war to end wars. The actual star that keeps returning shines "over England, over France / And above the German camps";

Stevens has seen it again, he says, "only this evening." With his vision of
the star he notably demonstrates a vision of a reality that goes beyond
nationalism—as he also does in "Imago," from the 1950 volume *Auroras
of Autumn,* where he asks,

> Who can pick up the weight of Britain,
> Who can move the German load
> Or say to the French here is France again? (439)

It seems incongruous, in "Martial Cadenza," that as "time flashe[s]
again" (238) the return of the beautiful (the star) should be linked with
the implied return of the ugliness of war. Our instincts revolt—but
Stevens seems to be facing forthrightly the "res," that which is.

He again writes of such an unflinching encounter in "Man and Bottle."
Present in his own poem as a man "find[ing] what will suffice" (a potent
word for Stevens) by discarding the romantic trappings of poetry of the
past, he realizes that he does so explicitly "in a land of war" (239). War
is the essential and unavoidable fact of his poetry. It, poetry,

> . . . has to content the reason concerning war,
> It has to persuade that war is part of itself,
> A manner of thinking, a mode
> Of destroying, as the mind destroys,
>
> An aversion . . . (239)

The word "aversion" clearly indicates that Stevens's place is among antiwar poets.

"Examination of the Hero in a Time of War," another of the *Parts of
a World* poems, avows its concern with World War II not only in its
title but in its beginning, "Force is my lot." Place-names, references to
weapons, hints of a German presence—all speak of the war then raging
though it remains unnamed:

> The Got whome we serve is able to deliver
> Us. Good chemistry, good common man, what
> Of that angelic sword? Creature of

Ten times ten times dynamite, convulsive
Angel, convulsive shatterer, gun,
Click, click, the Got whom we serve is able . . . (273)

The poem also directly addresses the "common hero" as "soldier." All together, this is about as topical as Stevens gets. His desire, clearly, is not so much for victory as for peace: "*Gazette Guerriere.* A man might happen / To prefer *L'Observateur de la Paix*" (276).

Given the force and recurrence of these and other relatively direct references to war among Stevens's poems, we are justified, I believe, in reading his more abstract musings—on order and chaos, "red weather," the elusive nature of "major man" or "meta-man" (the hero he kept positing and trying to define), and the hope for a beatitude in which the imagined and the real are joined—as being deeply rooted in the troubling of his mind by war. In "Dry Loaf" he describes a nightmare vision that conveys his sorrow over events the world seemed doomed to repeat:

It was the battering of drums I heard
It was hunger, it was the hungry that cried
And the waves, the waves were soldiers moving,
Marching and marching in a tragic time
Below me, on the asphalt, under the trees.

It was soldiers went marching over the rocks
And still the birds came, came in watery flocks,
Because it was spring and the birds had to come.
No doubt that soldiers had to be marching
And that drums had to be rolling, rolling, rolling. (200)

In "Asides on the Oboe" he laments an unspecified year when "death and war prevented the jasmine scent / And the jasmine islands were bloody martyrdoms," after which "we" joined in lamenting "those buried in their blood" (251).

In "Extracts from Addresses to the Academy of Fine Ideas" Stevens mocks, more directly than we expect of him, those who believe it is only an "artificial world" and denounces "the laughter of evil" which is "death / That is ten thousand deaths and evil death" (253). Deaths in such numbers, characterized as "evil," would seem to be war deaths. Breaking into a paean to peace, he cannot altogether shut out an awareness of war's persistence:

> We live in a camp . . . Stanzas of final peace
> Lie in the heart's residuum . . . Amen.
> But would it be amen, in choirs, if once
> In total war we died and after death
> Returned, unable to die again, fated
> To endure thereafter every mortal wound,
> Beyond a second death, as evil's end?
> It is only that we are able to die, to escape
> The wounds. Yet to lie buried in evil earth,
> If evil never ends, is to return
> To evil after death, unable to die
> Again and fated to endure beyond
> Any mortal end. (258–59)

If we could not die, that is, we might have to endure wounding (in war?) again and again, and more terribly the mental wounding of knowing that wars still go on. He insists, "The chants of final peace / Lie in the heart's residuum." But his brave assertion is again interrupted by anxiety as he asks, "How can / We chant if we live in evil and afterward / Lie harshly buried there?" Determined to posit a vision of a better way, despite these persistent fears, he concludes by directing our attention to a vision: "Behold the men in helmets borne on steel, / Discolored, how they are going to defeat" (259). It is an ending as visionary, as little based on observed fact, as Owen's "knowing" that wars will come when men will fight for peace, not flags.

Stevens sighs for peace as persistently as he alludes to war. Sometimes the yearning is explicitly located in a context of war, as it is in "Yellow Afternoon," from the 1942 *Parts of a World:*

> He said I had this that I could love,
> As one loves visible and responsive peace
> . . . .

> A unity that is the life one loves,
> So that one lives all the lives that comprise it
> As the life of the fatal unity of war. (236)

The sigh for peace surfaces with a seeming gratuitousness, which in itself may indicate how continually present this entire concern was in Stevens's mind. It is especially significant, I think, that one of these sighs comes in the prelude to his major work "Notes toward a Supreme Fiction," addressed to his friend Henry Church. The prelude ends, "The vivid transparence that you bring is peace" (380). Another of these seemingly unconnected passing references (or sighs) comes in "The Owl in the Sarcophagus," an elegy for Church—"Peace stood with our last blood adorned" (434).[13]

Most compelling of all, perhaps, is "Puella Parvula," in which massively troubling presences yield to a call for peace:

> The elephant on the roof and its elephantine blaring,
> The blaring lion in the yard at night or ready to spring
>
> . . . .
>
> Over all these the mighty imagination triumphs
> Like a trumpet and says, in this season of memory,
> When the leaves fall like things mournful of the past,
>
> Keep quiet in the heart, O wild bitch. O mind
> Gone wild, be what he tells you to be: *Puella.*
> Write *pax* across the window pane. And then
>
> Be still . . . (456)

What would it mean for this "tiny girl," perhaps the embodiment of Stevens's inner hope, to write *pax* across the "vivid transparence" of our mental window glass? That our entire perception of the world would be *through* peace.

9

Looking Back on the "Good War"

When I was born
they had just gotten
the hang of it.

> —William Trowbridge, "War Baby" (1989)

God, have you taken cognizance of this?
> —Robert Frost, "No Holy Wars for Them" (1947)

In the American popular imaginary, World War II has become something like an action movie, a narrative of violent excitement that entailed pain and destruction, yes, but also served as a proving ground for masculinity and a demonstration of national might. In its construction as the good war, the Second World War has stood, as well, for national right or virtue.[1] Typical of this view is the insistence one meets far and wide that the United States entered the war out of indignation over German abuses and prosecuted it for the sake of fairness and decent treatment of those less powerful. But in fact the American people were overwhelmingly isolationist and wanted nothing to do with the war that broke out in Europe in September 1939. Only when attacked at Pearl Harbor by a people many Americans regarded as racial exotics and for that matter racial inferiors (or even, as the war progressed, subhumans) was the nation willing to rouse itself.[2]

If the myth of the good war is a distortion of history, it is also a demonstration of the vigorous persistence of this war in popular memory, as well as literature and the arts. Bookstore gift-book tables are still, more than half a century later, packed with volumes of photographs of Allied soldiers and sailors paying the price in wounds and hardships but winning a righteous victory. World War II movies continue to make it big at the box office. Even now, many of these cultural products are devoted to masculine heroics. On the other hand, a great many memorializations of the war in literature, the arts, and popular culture are characterized more by grieving. Some "come out of war" in the sense of expressing a vision of leaving war itself, as a social practice, behind.

Collective grieving for the spectacle of suffering and death provides, of course, the most common rationale offered for ending war. And World War II, with its enormous numbers of civilian casualties—from shelling and bombing and especially from the horror of atomic bombing—provided ample occasion for such pleas. One thinks, for example, of the Polish composer Krzystof Penderecki's piece for string orchestra "Threnody to the Victims of Hiroshima" (1960), which with its screeching, wailing, and ominously thumping sounds still makes audiences distinctly uncomfortable more than forty years later, both musically and with the evocation of pain and suffering signaled by its title.[3]

Both popular and artistic commemorations display a wide variety of motive, emphasis, and manner. Given the massive scope and complexity of the war itself, we would expect no less. Such a public memorialization as the Washington, D.C., statuary commemorating the raising of the American flag on Iwo Jima (based on the widely circulated photograph made by photojournalist Joe Rosenthal on the occasion) glorifies the muscle, determination, and cooperative effort of enlisted men, while the flag itself commands the compositional center. It is a monument to patriotism. Similarly, the recently completed World War II memorial on the Mall in Washington strikes many viewers as a glorification of national power. How different are the monuments clustered around the Mall that memorialize the Vietnam and Korean War dead—the Korean War monument so clearly paying tribute to the troops' doggedness and hardships, both the Vietnam Wall and the monument to nurses in Vietnam so expressive of grieving. In the case of the Wall, it is a mute grieving, in that only the names are offered for contemplation, without the usual embellishment of verbal or figural gestures.[4] Another public expression of grieving and memorialization, perhaps less publicized and less often critically "read" than the Vietnam Wall, is, collectively, the cemeteries for American war dead in Europe, with their associated monuments and chapels. But even these memorial structures most overtly dedicated to grieving perform other kinds of cultural work as well. Ron Robin argues that the cemeteries for World War II dead actually "divert attention from mourning individual deaths" in order to "celebrate a sophisticated and collective triumph" and "an imperial vision" of the future role of the United States as world leader (67, 70). Grieving is expressed, yes, but is subordinated to an expansionist national purpose.

Complexity of intention and style is also evident in the art music that came out of the war—from Arnold Schoenberg's horrified and protesting "A Survivor of Warsaw" (1947), for which Schoenberg wrote text as well as music; to Benjamin Britten's cry of pain "Canticle III: Still Falls the Rain" (1954), a setting of Edith Sitwell's poem by that title; to Richard Rodgers's triumphalist *Victory at Sea* (1952), in effect a vast symphony commissioned as the musical score for a much-noted TV documentary series celebrating the role of the U.S. Navy in World War II.[5]

Victory at Sea has been called a kind of monumental "musical commercial" for the navy (Beidler 82), in that one of its purposes was that of advancing the navy's prestige (and budget) at a time of bitter interservice rivalry. Telecast in a series of twenty-six half-hour segments during the 1952–53 season, it attracted such an enormous audience that it is said to have reached "more human beings than any other motion picture or TV series in history" (Bluem 148), not counting its subsequent audience through spin-offs such as videocassettes, books, and compact disks. The series not only launched a conceptual sea change in the understanding of the television medium and its genres, as Beidler observes in his analysis of the work in the context of officially sanctioned communications; it also played a significant role in mythicizing the war to its present status of the "good war," providing audiences "a welcome reaffirmation of the grand American and Allied effort" (Beidler 189).

The project was conceived by Henry Salomon, who had become aware of the huge archives of film and still photographs of the war through his work as a member of a wartime team of historians directed by Samuel Eliot Morison at Harvard, producing a fourteen-volume chronicle of the navy's role in the war (Bluem 147). Assembling a nucleus production team of writers and editors, with a newly minted sociologist as his assistant, Salomon reviewed some 60 million feet of film, some of it having to be declassified, from not only U.S. archives but those of England, France, India, Japan, Germany, and Italy, selectively reducing these to 60,000 feet for the production as telecast. Salomon and Richard Hanser developed the story line and script, with each of the twenty-six segments constituting a "thematic episode" emphasizing a particular aspect of naval operations during the war. Bluem goes on to state that "the distinction between the journalistic point of view and the artist's expression of theme was made clear" in each segment, and moreover that Salomon brought to the work "the gentleness of time remembered and an enlarged sense of humanity—a compassion for mankind and a capacity to create expressions of this compassion in terms of the pictorial records of war's brutality" (146–47). I see considerable irony and ambiguity in the text, however, particularly in the interplay of music and visual image.

Early in the three-year process of producing *Victory at Sea* Salomon conceived the idea of having a major musical score composed specifically for the production, rather than assembling existing music as background. Richard Rodgers was chosen as composer of background music for the panoramic presentation on the basis of his long and successful musical career in a variety of modes and especially his enormous audience appeal from such Broadway successes as *Oklahoma!* (with Oscar Hammerstein, in 1944), *Carousel* (1945), and the widely loved memorial of the Pacific Theater of World War II, *South Pacific* (1949). Rodgers's inspired score for *Victory at Sea* (orchestrated and arranged by Robert Russell Bennett) employs a traditional musical rhetoric of sonorous grandeur and strength, conveyed through marching rhythms and the sweeping surges that support the emphasis on the sea. It is relentlessly upbeat, to the point of providing such startling examples of ironic dissonance between music and visual image as the cheerful march being heard while flamethrowers are directed into the caves of Japanese soldiers on a South Pacific island and human torches come running out. Apparently it was not considered that viewers might feel any other emotion than gratification. Ultimately, with its infectious celebration of American military might at sea and the American people's sturdy home front efforts, Rodgers's technically fine music serves the perpetuation, not the cessation, of war as an instrument of public policy.

~

Retrospective views of the war in poetry have been equally varied. As we saw with respect to the poetry that came more immediately out of the war or soon after, it ranges from documentation to moral reflection, from expressions of personal grieving to enunciations of societal values. As with poetry of retrospection on the First World War, one rarely hears

in the range of tones employed by poets looking back on the war a traditional tribute to courage. Anger, grieving, moral disgust, satire, yes,
but rarely glorification.

Surprisingly, the often topical or occasional British poet Gavin Ewart,
most of whose writings are in a facetious or satiric (even flippant) vein,
did voice such a tribute. Yoked with self-deprecation, it appears in one
of the many poems Ewart wrote over a period of, apparently, decades as
he continued to ponder the war, usually with only terse references appearing in his verse. Amid his many humorous poems, sometimes silly,
sometimes lame or sad, mostly about sex, aging, common follies, and his
fellow poets (he was especially given to satiric or even directly critical
poems about W. H. Auden), Ewart's prolonged attention to the war, even
when it is in a humorous vein, strikes a darker note. One detects in it a
repressed anxiety, an inability to put the matter to rest. In "A Contemporary Film of Lancasters in Action," he recalls that he himself was
"never a hero." Asking himself whether his emotion on seeing the film
of bomber pilots referred to in the title is "bogus or inflationary," he answers with what seems an uncharacteristic directness of tribute mingled
with survivor's guilt:

> I say they were the patient venturing lions
> and I the mean dog that stayed alive;
> we owe them
> every valedictory mark of respect
> (bravery's facing such boring dangers)
> that we can possibly, too late, show them. (*Selected Poems* 94)

The emphatic spondees of "we owe them" are a particularly polished
touch, conveying the seriousness of his insistence on paying tribute to
the bravery of those who fought.

Ewart's exercise of irony and the stiff upper lip is evident in "When
a Beau Goes In." In a similar vein, "Incident, Second World War" commemorates an incident in which a test of the effectiveness of airborne
gunnery goes awry. The point of the exercise is to improve the ability to
make projections of casualties likely to result from certain kinds of attacks. Target figures are set up on a hillside, with observers of the ex-

periment positioned on the other side of the hill. But the pilot charged with making the attack confuses the one with the other and aims at the wrong group, at the watchers who helplessly see him coming:

> They waited. And suddenly, waiting, they saw that angel of death
> come at them over the hillside. Before they could draw breath
> he passed with all guns firing; some fell on their faces, flat,
> but the benefit was minimal that anyone had from that.
> He reckoned that *they* were the dummies, in his slap-happy lone-wolf
> > way,
> that trigger-crazy pilot. He might have been right, some say.
> But bitterness and flippancy don't compensate for men's lives
> and official notifications posted to mothers and wives.
>
> Nevertheless, there *were* results; percentages were worked out,
> how 10 per cent could be written off, the wounded would be about
> 50 per cent or so. Oh yes, they got their figures all right.
> Calculated to units. So at least that ill-omened flight
> was a part of the Allied war effort, and on the credit side—
> except for those poor buggers who just stood there and died. (*Selected
> > Poems* 60)

It is a parable of the callousness and folly of war, told with a sardonic anger that for the most part remains tacit, buried in the narration itself, but shows itself unmistakably in the sarcasm of "Oh yes, they got their figures all right" and in the last line.

In a very different retrospective, "Pian dei Giullari," Ewart takes his adult daughter with him on a trip back to his wartime post in Italy. While there during the war, he had had a transient love affair. Seeing the place again, Ewart asks himself, somewhat in Edmund Blunden's vein of recalling his service in the Great War with nostalgic regret even while recognizing its hatefulness, whether it was a "sad or happy" time:

> Our weak, nice Major died
> (I saw his obituary by accident),
> the love affair came to nothing.

In those days we were careless—
as the war was careless of us.
Nobody thought very far ahead.
Girls were like wine for the drinking.

Whether it was "sad or happy," now that he has returned he feels the tug of that period, which was so emphatically set off from the rest of his life:

The landscape that we saw from our windows
in a time of cicadas and nightingales
stood there unaltered.
I looked at it and felt the warm lightness
of khaki drill on my shoulders. (*Selected Poems* 102)

There seems to be an implication that frivolous as it was, with its "careless" embracing, the intensity of the war experience has made his postwar life empty, despite the presence of his daughter.

In another particularly notable poem, Ewart's preoccupation with his World War II experience extends to a nightmare view of World War I. This is perhaps the most serious, the least humorous, of any of Ewart's poems. It is called "The Moment":

There are even photographs of it:
the moment when, for the first time,
in that tense, expectant landscape,
the enemy troops appear.

There they are, advancing—
Germans from World War One
running with rifles.
As, from far back in time, so many others.

You are the opposing infantry—
this means you.
Your brain falters. *This
is it*, you think,

these are the ones we've heard
so much about. Like old people
when, for the first time, they confront
the unambiguous symptoms. (*Selected Poems* 101)

The hallucinated war experience, with its uncanny immediacy ("There they are," "*This is it*"), becomes emblematic for the approach of death by illness or age. But if mortal illness is like war, war is also like a sickness. The two become equivalent; they serve as metaphors for each other. With a seeming inevitability (since all "old people" will confront such an assault unless, as Ewart writes in a poem called "Exits," they have "luck" and are taken by an "instant killer") the soldiers advance on us as they have advanced on others. Again making apt use of spondaic feet (as with "we owe them" in "A Contemporary Film of Lancasters in Action"), the poet warns, "This means you." War, then, is a social plague whose symptoms, soldiers, are recurrent; or the approach of natural death is as fearful as an infantry attack—either way, a chilling message.

∽

E. E. Cummings continued to write poems protesting against the First World War long after it ended. Similarly, he continued to lament and denounce the betrayals and cruelties of the Second World War after its end and to mock the conformity that leads to mindless support for bellicose political and military leaders. Between the wars, in the mid-thirties, Cummings had begun to warn against turning a new generation of young men into killers ("blokes with ammunicions") and in his 1940 volume *50 Poems* he cried out against the return of war in Europe. In several poems in his 1944 volume *One Times One* he expressed his hatred for war in general, including an uncharacteristically clear statement of war's betrayal of all that he typically associated with "april":

armies(than hate itself and no
meanness unsmaller)armies can
immensely meet for centuries
and(except nothing)nothing's won
—but if a look should april me

for half a when,whatever is less
alive than never begins to yes (*CP* 580)

In his 1950 volume *Xiape* Cummings's language is at times more fractured and cryptic, perhaps, than at any earlier period of his writing.[6]
Among the more fractured and cryptic of the *Xiape* poems are several
that include brief or sidelong references to the "good war"—as if his
persisting thoughts on the war are stylistically linked to a sense of disorder or near-chaos in society. One of these is reminiscent of the common soldier song from World War I, "I'll Tell You Where the General
Was," with its burlesque of top-rank officers keeping themselves safe
while sending men of the lower ranks out to do battle:

where's Jack Was
General Was
the hero of the Battle of Because
        he's squatting
in the middle of remember
with his rotten old forgotten
full of why
        (rub-her-bub)
        bub?
        (bubs) (642)

The "Battle of Because" and the general's being "full of why" are sly allusions to the empty bombast commonly used in official justifications of
war or explanations of why ordinary soldiers need to rise up and do their
duty. We have repeatedly seen Cummings's disgust at such rhetoric. In
this 1950 volume he explains that "war just isn't what / we imagine," particularly in its effects on those who fight, the most obvious reason being
that people get killed: "yes it's true that was / me but that me isn't me"—

. . . christ but you
must understand
why because
i am
dead (638)

A fundamental change in identity indeed, but the statement "that me isn't me" also opens our awareness into other ways in which soldiers are changed by their experience.

Even more cryptic is the fragmented sonnet ["whose are these"] where imagery of blackened skin, "alive:chaos," and "mostful" murder indicates an ongoing horror of the "illimitable hell" inflicted by the United States on Hiroshima and Nagasaki in a "twiceuponatime wave":

> whose are these(wraith a clinging with a wraith)
> ghosts drowning in supreme thunder?ours
> (over you reels and me a moon;beneath,
>
> bombed the by ocean earth bigly shudders) (639)

I take the "ghosts drowning in supreme thunder" to be a reference to the Japanese citizens destroyed by the two atomic bombs. In the closing couplet, the "black skin" of victims of the blast (those who did not utterly vaporize) in effect takes over the role of Cummings's poetic muse: "put out your eyes,and touch the black skin / of an angel named imagination."

In contrast, one of the clearer and more direct of the poems in this postwar volume pronounces a sarcastic summation of Cummings's attitude not only toward the late war and the corruption of language that wars bring but also toward the act of public memorializing itself, which he regards as inane:

> why must itself up every of a park
>
> anus stick some quote statue unquote to
> prove that a hero equals any jerk
> who was afraid to dare to answer "no"? (636)

The explanation, perhaps, is that without such monuments people might forget "that if the quote state unquote says / 'kill' killing is an act of christian love." As if in response to this patent absurdity, he recalls, or purports to recall, that in 1944 "generalissimo e" (Eisenhower) declared that "nothing . . . can stand against the argument of mil / itary necessity"—that is, that war trumps every other value. Recognizing that this is, in effect, true, the poet exclaims in disgust, "you pays your money and / you doesn't take your choice. Ain't freedom grand."

Cummings's reference in this sonnet to the "jerk" who didn't dare answer no to his country's call reminds us of his post–World War I lament for the conscientious objector Olaf. In contrast to the soldiers memorialized in this park statue—such a debasement of art that Cummings refers to it as a statue in emphatic verbal quotation marks in the same way as he refers to the "state," "quote statue unquote"—Olaf did dare to answer no, whether he was afraid or not. That, Cummings implies, is true heroism, not the acceding to the state's directive, lacking genuine free will, that is memorialized in this debased art. It is one of his most explicit statements of antiwar principle.

An elderly Robert Frost (1874–1963) also wrote of the war in retrospect in the years soon after it ended. In several poems gathered in the "Editorials" section of his 1947 volume *Steeple Bush*, Frost treats the war with sardonic humor. It is a tone notably at odds with his popular image as a kind of benevolent elder uncle—an image serious readers of Frost have long recognized as inaccurate. In several poems commenting directly on America's possession and use of atomic weapons, Frost's clipped, satiric tone is also a far cry from that of Cummings. He makes no effort to address the suffering caused by the bombing of Hiroshima and Nagasaki but comments tersely and in seeming detachment on certain issues raised by the event. A "nuclear phenomenon" might, he observes in "The Planners," "put an end to This"—this world, this existence—and thereby "shorten . . . human history."

In "No Holy Wars for Them" Frost mockingly ponders the "Global Mission" proper to nations "strong enough to do good" or—the juxtaposition is sly—strong enough to wage great wars, while the "puny little states" can only stand around and watch:

> God, have you taken cognizance of this?
> And what on this is your divine position?
> That nations like the Cuban and the Swiss
> Can never hope to wage a Global Mission.
> No Holy Wars for them. The most the small
> Can ever give us is a nuisance brawl. (567)

The reader is likely to protest that a "nuisance brawl" is preferable to global conflagration.[7] Is the poem, then, after all, a celebration of geopolitical smallness? The condescending terms directed toward "the small" scarcely seem to sustain such a reading, though Frost is always slippery and one suspects his tone is facetious. From the perspective of the twenty-first century, the comment dates itself; with the evolution in methods of warfare (including terrorist warfare) since 1945, small states can indeed be more than a mere "nuisance."

Two other poems by Frost in the same 1947 group are more biting in their implied criticism of American military might. In "Bursting Rapture," another pondering of the "nuclear phenomenon," he pretends to have complained to "the physician" (God) about its becoming so hard to be a simple farmer, farming now being complicated by science. The divine answer, that the problem is not only individual but international,[8] is scarcely reassuring:

> What you complain of all the nations share.
> Their effort is a mounting ecstasy
> That when it gets too exquisite to bear
> Will find relief in one burst. You shall see.
> That's what a certain bomb was sent to be. (568)

Equally concerned with the development, use, and proliferation of atomic weapons, and implicitly critical of American determination to keep for itself and a few select others the right to maintain weapons of mass destruction, is the four-line "editorial" called "U.S. 1946 King's X":

> Having invented a new Holocaust,
> And been the first with it to win a war,
> How they make haste to cry with fingers crossed,
> King's X—no fairs to use it any more! (569)

The phrase "new Holocaust" is particularly pointed, applying, as it does, to America's use of the atomic bomb the term that has come to be used for Nazi Germany's enormity. Dissent of this kind was not entirely safe in the late 1940s. There is a great difference between these wry comments and Frost's retrospective on World War I, "A Soldier," where he pays tribute to an individual soldier in implicitly ennobling archaic terms. Here, he writes not so much in pity for the fallen as in distaste for the whole enterprise, expressed in a dry and tight-lipped humor.

~

Frost had, of course, witnessed both world wars. Many other poets who were only children during the early '40s or had not yet been born have sought to imagine the war's killing fields and have pondered related moral issues, especially the Holocaust and the use of the atomic bombs.

William Trowbridge, born in 1941, the year of Pearl Harbor, writes in "War Baby" of his sense of the Holocaust as a kind of violent Grimm (or grim) fairy tale populated by ogres and witches. The brave woodsmen unfortunately arrive too late to save the children from the oven. What "they" had "just gotten / the hang of" at the time of Trowbridge's birth, in the passage used as an epigraph for this chapter, was efficiency in killing Jews, but the meaning of "they" could well be broadened to include other combatants just getting "the hang of" modern efficient warfare (Stokesbury 190).

In 1985, forty years after the end of the war, Andrew Hudgins, born in 1951, published a poem called "Air View of an Industrial Scene" in which the scene referred to is Birkenau's extermination "industry." Imagining that he is looking down from an airplane and watching people arrive who are "going to die soon" (Stokesbury 210), he wishes he could have wiped it all out with a bomb—perhaps a wish, too, that he could wipe out the memory of these events. But clearly neither Hudgins nor any others of the many, many who have wished to forget can do so.

Edward Hirsch's troubling "Leningrad (1941–1943)," also published in 1985, seeks to imagine and depict the multiple sufferings of the Russian people under siege by Germany, bombed and starving. It is a poem of such appalling horror that one hesitates to quote it.

Mary Jo Salter's 1984 poem "Welcome to Hiroshima" records her disgust both with what happened there and with the memorials to the event seen by visitors to the city.

In these poems and others, the war remained a compelling and torturous preoccupation decades afterward for people too young to have witnessed the events they wrote about.

A very different retrospective on the war, Karl Shapiro's late '60s poem "Human Nature" was written from the perspective of a veteran who was there and who now has trouble pursuing his postwar life because of the dissonance between the two and his inability to find a sense of balance or meaning in that disjunction. The poem concludes, "I am homesick for war" (Shapiro, *CP* 253; Stokesbury 57)—an ending that reminds us of Edmund Blunden's "1916 Seen from 1921," except that Blunden knew why he felt nostalgic for the war: he missed the loving comradeship it occasioned. Shapiro's statement of homesickness for the war is made with a sad irony, in full knowledge that what he misses was a terrible time. He is homesick for the war for no reason he can name except that it supplied at least the semblance of a meaning for going on. The difference between his poem and Blunden's is perhaps a measure of the "progress" of the twentieth century.

Many postwar poems treat the aftereffects of the war on veterans. Wallace Stevens, notably, writes in "A Woman Sings a Song for a Soldier Come Home" (in his 1947 *Transport to Summer*) of the ex-soldier who remains in a living death. Trowbridge writes in "Sunday School Lesson from Capt. Daniel Mayhew, USAAF, Ret." of a troubled veteran who obsessively repeats stories of combat and danger to the young boys in his class until one Sunday when "his big hands / began to shake, the amazing tears welled" (Stokesbury 193). In another of Trowbridge's poems, "G.I. Joe from Kokomo," such a veteran is permanently infantilized by the war, permanently fixated in the adolescence in which he entered the army, so that forty years later he still has not become fully an adult: "Twenty-one again this June, he plans / to marry, study law, then run for office" (Stokesbury 194). Similarly, Dorothy Coffin Sussman, born in 1945, writes of her father's return from the war through exercise of the imagination, but through exercise of sympathetic understanding writes about his ruination, and the ruination of his wife's hopes, by drinking. Such characters are trapped in their war experience and are unable to go beyond it.

The anthology in which all these postwar poems are printed, Leon Stokesbury's *Articles of War,* is particularly important in that it collects a number of such works by writers who are not widely known, whose poems might otherwise be difficult to know about or locate. Turning these pages, it is striking how much powerful verse has been written by people whose childhoods were haunted by the distant war that they heard about in bits and pieces, or whose memories retain childhood scenes of the departure of loved ones. Many write, years later, poems grieving or paying tribute to lost fathers. James Tate, born in 1943, laments his inability to gain any understanding whatever of the father he never knew. Whether seeking to imagine the experience of wounded or dying fighting men or of civilian victims of bombing, such latter-day poets try to arrive at some judgment of the morality or immorality of the war. For the most part, their efforts follow the mode Wilfred Owen identified as the essence of antiwar poetry, an emphasis on "the pity of war." Sometimes they use the mode of anger and denunciation, as in Karl Shapiro's prose-poem "After the War," which sees a general returning "with the power of a god," what should be his "disgrace" being celebrated as a "triumph" (Stokesbury 57). Repeatedly, hopes are expressed that the world will learn and change.

Writing of the claim that military service makes boys into men, May Sarton calls on readers to swear that "this shall be better done in peace!" (Stokesbury 45). More disheartened, Peter Viereck envisions, in "*Vale from Carthage*," continuities between modern and ancient wars; just as the ancient Roman soldier would "see your Forum Square no more," so his brother who died in World War II

> . . . will
> Not see Times Square—he will not see—he will
> Not see Times
> change. (Stokesbury 68–69)

With his last line—"What's left but this to say of any war?"—Viereck's lament becomes not only for his brother but also for the seemingly endless repetition.

To see even this small sampling of retrospective poems about the war and thus to gain some insight into the troubled place that it still occupies in the minds of these writers is to realize, once again, how vastly larger war is than the dates and places customarily listed in the history books and how vastly more inclusive is the entitlement to speak of it. The woman who writes about being troubled by her father's postwar behaviors, or the man who writes about his last memory of his brother, who took him sledding before going away to the army, is writing about war, just as surely as a Ciardi or Simpson writing about the experience of battle.

∽

Earlier, we noted the significance of popular music in conveying a culture's needs and responses to war. I will end this chapter with a consideration of a song by Paul Simon that can also be considered (as a number of Simon's song lyrics have been) as poetry. The gently wistful "René and Georgette Magritte with Their Dog after the War" was written after the Korean War and the war in Vietnam, and some thirty-seven years after World War II. Its references to war almost certainly refer to household "wars" as well as public ones. Even so, the title phrase "the War," which recurs repeatedly throughout the song, is necessarily recognized as a reference to the Second World War, in the way that Americans of a certain age regularly use the phrase. Additionally, those who have some acquaintance with the great painter Magritte will recognize that that is the war with which he is most associated.

René Magritte (1898–1967) was indeed married to a woman named Georgette. Their marriage seems to have been one of mutual lifelong devotion. Thus, the note of companionable romance that Simon's lyrics seem to convey is biographically accurate. So too is the presence of the dog. The Magrittes owned a series of small dogs, all named Loulou (Torczyner 10)—the dog referred to in the picture caption that according to Simon himself was the source of the title phrase.[9] The Loulou of the mid-fifties, the time period referred to in the song, was a black Pomeranian. Also accurate, so far as the song's representation of Magritte himself, is the concern about war and its destructiveness, conveyed in a submerged way in the song's perhaps sad, perhaps yearning tour of what we recognize as New York. The Magrittes stroll on Christopher Street, and its commercial viability is an implicit contrast to the state of such war-ravaged cities as Paris (which they knew well) or Brussels, their home.[10]

Early in World War II, Magritte was separated from Georgette for a time when she had to stay behind in Brussels recovering from appendicitis while he took refuge from the Nazi occupation at Carcassonne. In a letter to a friend he wrote, "If it weren't for the hope of seeing Georgette again one day, I wouldn't be able to go on living" (Torczyner 30). The experience can only have intensified the repugnance the artist felt toward Belgium's invaders and toward warfare generally. Belgium had also, of course, been brutally invaded at the outset of World War I and

remained occupied by its German conquerors throughout the war. In
Harry Torczyner's words, Magritte "abhorred violence . . . hated soldiers
and detested those organized massacres, wars" (22). Nevertheless, he involved himself in the war to the extent of working, for a time, for the
resistance, an activity that must have been acutely distressing to him
since it would have meant (to paraphrase Joseph Conrad's *Lord Jim*) im-
mersing himself in the destructive element of what he hated.

Rather than responding to the war experience with an art of violence,
Magritte attempted to counter what he called the havoc wrought by the
"Nazi cretins" and his society's resultant "widespread pessimism" with
images of "pleasure" or "commonplace," if elusive, cheer (Torczyner
187). He later reflected that the war was a "turning point" in his art
in that it forced on him the necessity to "express charm" as a "counter-
offensive" against a "disagreeable world" (Schneede 107). The nature of
the charm or pleasure that Magritte counterposed to war's misery (Torczyner translates Magritte's term as "joy"—certainly a stronger word
than my "cheer") was, to be sure, usually colored by fantasy, but its com-
ponents were generally domestic and quotidian in nature. By all accounts, he was personally devoted to domesticity, even to banality (a
term that pops up in many commentaries on Magritte), and "led the life
of an unobtrusive middleclass citizen" (Schneede 115). The everyday was
an inexhaustible source of interest for Magritte and a source of emblems of comfort or well-being, perhaps even of redemption. His devotion to everydayness is well conveyed, for example, in his painting *Personal Values* (1952), which shows a room filled with ordinary objects
(though its walls are, fantastically, the sky): a bed, an oversized comb
and shaving brush, a similarly oversized goblet and match, a wardrobe,
a reflected window with curtain. Similar tributes to the value of the
everyday are the paintings *The Key to Dreams* (1930), with six compart-
ments containing ordinary (though mislabeled) objects, and the forthrightly titled *The Beautiful Realities* (1964), which shows a dining table
with tablecloth neatly in place and a large green apple.

The devotion to the quotidian that we see in Magritte's paintings of
objects and experiences from everyday life is well conveyed in Simon's
lyrics. The Magrittes, with their dog, are seen "after the war" returning
to a hotel suite, shedding their formal attire (perhaps their convention-

alism, or perhaps the association with the social elite that often goes with being a successful artist) and dancing

> by the light of the moon
> to the Penguins, the Moonglows,
> the Orioles, and the Five Satins

—"deep forbidden" popular music that they have been "longing for." These musical groups, though they are referred to as if they were relics of the prewar past, did not in fact exist until the late '40s and '50s. The Moonglows and the Five Satins were popular, and the Penguins probably lesser known, doo-wop or rhythm and blues groups in the 1950s, and the Orioles were slightly earlier, having begun recording in the late '40s.[11] The mixing of times and contexts might be said to carry out a surrealistic quality comparable to that of Magritte's paintings. One of the most literate of popular musicians, Paul Simon would certainly have been aware of this. In notes on the song in which he explains the source of the title, he does, in fact, refer to the lyrics as "a story and . . . a surreal picture, a surrealistic lyric."[12]

In the second verse, the Magrittes are seen strolling "with their dog after the war" down Christopher Street, in Greenwich Village, where they look into a men's store and are moved to tears by the clothing on display—perhaps because of its abundance, in contrast to wartime scarcity, or perhaps because its style reminds them of prewar attire. Their emotional response is left unexplained, ultimately mysterious, except that we know it is evoked by an element of ordinary life, merchandise in a shop window. Last, after a musical bridge that refers to their falling asleep, apparently in death, the Magrittes (and their dog) are again seen at some future time peeking surreptitiously into the "bedroom drawer" of dinner hosts from among the "power élite." There, surprisingly enough, they find "hidden away" the same emblems of popular culture that had cheered them at their hotel—"the Penguins, the Moonglows, / the Orioles, and the Five Satins."

The song is pervaded by a sense of loss and nostalgia—Simon's own nostalgia for the decade of the '50s and its music but also, as conveyed in the fragmentary story line with its insistent labeling of "after the

War," the Magrittes' supposed nostalgia for their European life as it was before it was ruined by war. The presence of rhythm and blues musical groups in the consciousness of the Magrittes is, of course, anachronistic—not literally so, since they did live through the decade of the fifties, but as it represents their longing for a past time. The logic seems to be something like this: just as Paul Simon looks back on the music of the '50s, so René and Georgette Magritte look back on a time when they were happier, a time that held strong emotional meaning for them. But since the phrase "after the War" is not explicitly defined as referring to World War II, and since the historic context of the song's composition included most recently the Vietnam War, its resonance becomes any war. This, it seems to say, is how these particular people felt after World War II, but this is how all sensitive people, as represented by the Magrittes, might feel after a war, when life returns to a semblance of normalcy.

Given the initial appearance of "René and Georgette Magritte" on the 1983 album *Hearts and Bones*, where Paul Simon sang of very personal matters in the wake of his first divorce and remarriage (Kingston 265; Perone 8), the phrase "after the War" may also have referred, in his own mind, to himself and his first wife and to their ongoing friendship after the divorce. The nostalgia may in part be for life as it was before this personal war. Such multilayering of meaning is well suited to the song's multilayered music. Kingston accurately notes the counterpoint of "melancholy doo-wap" to Simon's vocal, in combination with a "traditional string orchestration" (268). Such unobtrusive combining of disparate elements is an aspect of the "subtlety" that Charles Hamm praises in his *New Grove Dictionary* entry on the Simon and Garfunkel duo. True, such multilayering also adds to the abstruseness that caused critics to complain that the *Hearts and Bones* album was difficult, even while they praised its artistry. "René and Georgette Magritte" well illustrates Simon's "understated, droll approach" and the "eclecticism" that has distinguished his career (Perone 6–8). At the same time, the puzzling quality of its lyrics reflects the interspersing of vernacular language with what Simon calls "enriched language," a technique that he says was much in evidence in the *Hearts and Bones* songs and which didn't always reflect "logic or anything" (Luftig 211).

However we read the specific references in "René and Georgette Magritte with Their Dog after the War," we must recognize that the phrase "after the war" shapes our response. For this songwriter, working almost four decades after the end of the particular war to which the lyrics seem to refer, it is popular culture and everydayness (as represented by clothes in stores and by one's pet dog) that provide meaning, or at any rate consolation and hope, for people living in a war-torn time. Whether they are artists or everyday people (the eminently bourgeois Magritte was himself both) or members of the "power élite," the war lingers in the minds of postwar survivors as a break in time, a milepost. We now live, and the Magrittes are seen as they live, "after the war." World War II serves as a catalyst evoking nostalgia for a life in which one can take pleasure in ordinary, basic human activities and desires without moment-to-moment fear of annihilation: a nostalgia to which post-9/11 Americans can well relate. This has been true in the past—in the words of the song, "as it was before" ("decades gliding by like Indians"), is now, and will be "ever after."

10

Benjamin Britten's *War Requiem* and the Hope of Learning Peace

Are we doomed to repeat endlessly the mistakes we've made in the past?
—Errol Morris, Filmmaker, in a PBS Interview with
Robert McNamara, November 2003

Gazette Guerriere. A man might happen
To prefer *L'Observateur de la Paix.*
—Wallace Stevens, "Examination of the Hero in a Time of War"

The twentieth century can be summed up as a century of war. It was also, and not incidentally, a century of technological innovations in weaponry and support systems. We know the result. Robert McNamara, secretary of defense under Presidents Kennedy and Johnson and one of the chief prosecutors of the Vietnam War, calls the twentieth century "the bloodiest, by far, in human history" (*In Retrospect* 4). It is little wonder, then, that a widespread preoccupation with war, its violence, and its devastation has been evident in all forms of cultural products—comic strips, commercial media, film, drama, music, visual and plastic arts, fiction, poetry.

Long after World War I had reached a depth of misery and destruction that impelled a dramatic change in attitudes toward war on the part of thinking people, some of these cultural expressions continued, anachronistically, to glorify and heroize warfare. I think, for example, of the moment in the blockbuster movie *Saving Private Ryan* when one of the soldiers overcomes his scruples about killing: it is treated as a moment of victory. I think of *Victory at Sea.* Of "The Ballad of the Green Berets," popular during the Vietnam War. In part, the survival of a traditional language of sacrifice, bravery, and toughness rested on the fact that it served the purposes of national—and nationalistic—power structures and was either directly or indirectly fostered by them. In part, it stemmed from the understandable desire of survivors and the bereaved, and of men and women generally, to find a larger significance in the losses and suffering inflicted by war, to give them an acceptable rationale. War retained—and for some still retains—a capacity to glamorize life, to give it the illusion of larger meaning and purpose. That is, if one ignores an array of grim and brutal facts. Former war correspondent Chris Hedges insists that war retains this capacity even among people like himself, who know intimately the ugly face behind the mask. War, he writes, is an "enticing elixir" that makes its addicts feel more intensely alive (3).

As we have seen, however, an overwhelming number of texts and artworks expressing cultural responses to war in the twentieth century have resisted traditional rhetorics of glorification in order to convey, instead, various kinds of antiwar messages. These may take the form of the "merely" descriptive in which the ugliness or horror of what happens is rendered without falsifying patinas or the ennobling abstractions traditionally associated with warfare. ("Not a neat job—the revolver / Was too close," wrote Herbert Read.) In descriptive accounts of this kind, the ugliness or horror is allowed to speak for itself. To be sure, as Goldensohn writes, "representing the horror of war is not the same thing as committing oneself or others to ceasing its practice" (*Dismantling Glory* 41) Usually, however, we infer an antiwar statement.[1] Alternatively, poems and other texts may employ a more directly emotional or declarative rhetoric, overtly expressing grief or moral abhorrence. In any event, whether the protest against war is openly proclaimed, only implied, or deeply disguised by an appearance of objectification, twentieth-century poetry of war has typically conveyed an antiwar statement.

One of the most emotionally powerful and influential of such statements remains Wilfred Owen's sequence of poems written in late 1917 and 1918, in the months leading up to his death in combat. More than forty years later, Benjamin Britten set nine of these poems to music in *War Requiem* (1962). In the resulting song cycle interspersed among the sections of the Latin mass for the dead, the persuasive impact of Owen's poems is compounded by the emotional power of Britten's music, a score that is intellectually challenging but at the same time accessible and emotionally intense.[2] The result is a singularly compelling whole incorporating music, poetry, and pageantry in an expression of grieving and of hope. Both in its breadth of historical relevance and in its eloquence and multidimensionality as an exhortation to seek peace, Britten's *War Requiem* serves as a culminating expression of twentieth-century artistic revulsion against war.

The *Requiem* memorializes both world wars—the First, because of the interweaving of Owen's poems; the Second, because it was commissioned for the reconsecration of Coventry Cathedral in England (or to give its formal name, the Cathedral Church of Saint Michael), which was redesigned and rebuilt after its destruction by incendiary bombing during World War II.[3] In its combining of the two, it goes further, becoming, as Michael Oliver writes, a "threnody for the dead of all wars" (174), a dirge for war itself.[4]

Like Owen's poetry, the *War Requiem* makes its antiwar argument primarily through appeal to emotions of grief and pity. As Owen famously proclaimed, "The poetry is in the pity," and Britten seems to have agreed. Only once in the poems set to music by Britten do we hear an explicit call for an end to war. This single instance is the declaration at the end of "Sonnet, on Seeing a Piece of Our Artillery Brought into Action" (beginning "Be slowly lifted up, thou long black arm") where, after calling on the "long black arm" itself to finish off the present fighting, the speaker/singer then calls on God to blast such weaponry from our souls. Metonymically, it is a call for the spirit of war-making to be eradicated. Even here, both the original poem and Britten's musical setting work through the emotions rather than through argumentation (granted, it is hard to imagine a reasoned argument against war that could avoid heightened emotion); the wish to rid humankind of the impulse to make war, as represented in weapons of mass destruction, is expressed as an imprecation: "May God curse thee, and cut thee from our soul!" In the musical setting, in the tonality of A minor, this phrase comes as a moment of great intensity, with the word "soul" sung on a high D-sharp, thereby invoking the uneasy, traditionally significant interval of the tritone, or the *diabolus in musica*. As sung in the premiere performance of the *War Requiem*, this call for a final use of the "long black arm" took on added resonance, with a German baritone, Dietrich Fischer-Dieskau, singing words written by the English poet. In Owen's poem, "that Arrogance" which the "long black arm" is called on to strike is presumably the arrogance of Germany. There is an implication, then, that when a German sings the words they may refer to arrogance on the part of England. Thus, by setting the poem for the baritone, rather than the tenor—intending the baritone part specifically for Fischer-Dieskau—Britten implied an acknowledgment of guilt on both sides, an essential acknowledgment if a stable peace is to be achieved.

But the call for an end to war does not have to be explicit in order to be effective. Britten included among the poems he chose for the *War Requiem* Owen's vision of a time when humankind will war "on Death, for lives," and in the others of the poems he included, pity and grieving are a statement in themselves—an especially powerful one in that they are for the most part dramatized, rather than declared. In any event, the emotions expressed and evoked (in the listener) through both words and music—as well as through the visual dramatization of the work's staging, especially in its premiere performance at Coventry Cathedral—are so strong and clear that their intention is unmistakable.[5] The *War Requiem* becomes a clearly pacifist work lamenting the cruelties of war and offering a hopeful vision of redemption. It is a "cry for peace" (Greene 91).

Britten himself was a longtime pacifist. He had been a member of the Peace Pledge Union and had composed works of antiwar import in the 1930s, when he was only in his twenties. His later opera *Owen Wingrave* (1971) was also "explicitly pacifist."[6] Here, in the *Requiem,* he not only proclaims his pacifism "on the largest scale and in a way such as would strike home to the largest possible number of listeners" (Palmer 8), but by drawing on Wilfred Owen for the English-language portion of the text he joins his own convictions to those developed by Owen in the final year or two of the poet's life. As Christopher Palmer points out, Britten, like Owen, wanted to warn as well as to remember.[7] But the retrospective linkage extends further. Because the *War Requiem* embraces not only Owen's twentieth-century words but also the Latin words of the mass for the dead, Britten links his pacifism to a religious tradition that, however often it has been invoked to sanction war, claims as its roots the teachings of an itinerant holy man who preached a message of forgiveness, reconciliation, and peace.[8] Moreover, the *Requiem* was composed for an occasion that, so one would suppose, could scarcely *not* convey antiwar messages—the restoration of a religious edifice destroyed by war.

James Herbert questions this last supposition, arguing persuasively that the physical setting of the first performance of the *Requiem,* the cathedral for whose consecration it had been commissioned, was in fact an ironic one that did not fully convey the message of reconciliation and peace that pervades Britten's work. Although the avowed purpose of the church leaders who marshaled the reconstruction effort was, in the words of R. T. Howard, the provost of Coventry from 1933 to 1958, to heal "the long breach between Britain and Germany," various of its architectural features (as Herbert reads them) betray the purpose of reconciliation and peace and enact, instead, a refusal to forgive (Herbert 543). One of these features is the incorporation of the facade of the destroyed cathedral into the new structure—an architectural indication that German aggression would not be forgotten, even if it were (nominally) forgiven. Another is a massive sculpture of the angel Michael, the cathedral's namesake, trampling Satan. As Herbert reminds us, Michael is "a warrior, not a maker of peace." (In Revelation 12:7, "Michael and his angels fought against the dragon," or as the New English Bible has it, "waged war upon the dragon.") In context, the sculptural "personification of evil [being] vanquished" by the angel would seem to refer to Germany (548). As Herbert argues, in these and other highly symbolic features the rebuilt structure maintained reminders of German militarism and the suffering and destruction it caused. The words of seeming reconciliation carved into the wall of the old structure, "Father Forgive," carry, in his reading, an implicit judgment of German war guilt and a "connotation that someone else's greater sins required first pardon" (555–56)—that is, that God needs to forgive the Germans and that the British are willing to petition for that forgiveness but do not themselves stand in need of it. Thus, he continues, the cathedral "relegate[s] reconciliation . . . to the realm of the divine" and says, in effect, "Meanwhile, let us remember and rehearse, over and again, the injustices inflicted upon us. Let us dispense our own partial forgiveness, but only from a position of self-righteous moral authority borrowed from God and earned through our suffering, suffering wreaked on us by others."

I have quoted and summarized Herbert's argument at some length because of what I see as its importance in exploring the interactive elements of the *Requiem* as a total experience, a work of experiential art, in its original performance. His argument is weighty and painstaking in its

detail. Even so, not all who contemplate the symbolism of the structure see it this way. Some have experienced the Cathedral Chapel of
Christ in Gethsemane, in particular—a space not discussed in Herbert's
article—as positioning all visitors alike (German, French, American,
Russian, British: all) in the shadow of fallibility by its lighting design.
Figures representing the sleeping disciples in the garden inhabit a dim-
ness shared by visitors, in contrast to a brilliantly lighted figure of the
praying Christ. Or some may see the sculpture of Michael trampling
Satan as implying humanity, as a whole, trampling the dragon of war. In
any event, the ironies perceived by Herbert do not color the meaning of
Britten's work itself, except as they complicated the symbolism of its
performance at Coventry. Herbert himself insists that the *War Requiem*
"warrants no such righteous us—and likewise permits no personification of evil in them" as he sees in the cathedral (555).

Even though the *Requiem* was composed for the consecration of a cathedral and was first performed in that cathedral, it does not entirely
endorse either the physical or the institutional structure within which it
comes into being. It is to the Christian tradition in its ineffability, not its
flawed history, that the *Requiem* pays obeisance—though only partial
obeisance at that. The work also affirms the suffering twentieth-century
voices, embroiled in war, of the tenor and baritone who sing Owen's
English-language words, and these at times contest the chorus's singing
of the church's traditional message. Britten's composition links poetry,
music, visible enactment, and the words of the Latin mass in a generally,
but not entirely, harmonious whole haunted by the complex instabilities
of war.

Neither my purpose here nor my qualifications allow commentary on
the music itself, but by examining it to the extent that an amateur can,
we can more fully understand the nature of the work as a whole and its
participation in the twentieth century's culture of grieving.

Recorded many times since its first performance on May 30, 1962, and
thus readily available, the *War Requiem* is nevertheless not often performed. Largely this is because its technical demands and its requirements of personnel and space are so extreme. The score calls for both a
full chorus and a boys' choir, stationed separately in the performance
space, as well as two separate orchestras—a full symphony orchestra
that accompanies the chorus, joined by a soprano soloist, primarily in

passages devoted to the mass, and a chamber orchestra with its own conductor that accompanies the two male soloists. In addition, the score requires a harmonium, or field organ, such as might play for religious services on a battlefield. Yet this distinctive, reedy-sounding instrument is played, not along with the two soloists who sing Owen's words (and who thus serve to represent the voices of soldiers), but with the boys' choir, which in the divine drama that develops in the course of the work represents the realm of the ineffable, "innocence unstained by war" (Oliver 174).

The *Requiem*, then, is an intense and complex work in the interplay among its various textual and performing entities—soloists, choruses, and orchestras. It is equally complex in its harmonic structure, which is built on a recurrence of the tritone, the interval of, for example, C to F-sharp—an inherently unstable and traditionally ominous interval mediating between major and minor keys but resolving to neither. Despite moments of harmonious concord and sections of peaceful beatitude, the music continually returns to the tritone and its expression of uneasiness and uncertainty—perhaps uncertainty that the redemption promised by the choirs can prove efficacious for those caught up in the brutal immediacy of war, perhaps uncertainty that war itself can ever be truly ended, despite the hopeful vision of the final duet between tenor and baritone (the setting of Owen's "Strange Meeting") and the concluding measures that follow. Moreover, since the three separate groupings of performers are identified with differing perspectives or understandings, and since various structural interactions, either of seeming contradiction or seeming agreement, occur as one section (in either the mass or the poetry) succeeds another, the various voicings readily take on the status of dramatis personae in a vast play.[9]

These qualities of dramatization in the *War Requiem* were accentuated in its original performance. The physical setting itself played a role in the pageant of human and divine debate over how and when war may be ended, in that the huge spaces available in the cathedral, by allowing spatial separation of the orchestras and singers, emphasized the distinctions among their dramatic roles. Obviously, the mere fact that the performance took place in a cathedral destroyed in war and rebuilt in the hope of peace contributed its own dramatic value, adding to the power of words and music its symbols of eternal conflict and ultimate resolution, with the looming presence of the bombed-out ruins nearby.[10] Moreover, in this first performance the three soloists served to represent allegorically three of the great powers that had fought both World War I and World War II: the tenor soloist, Peter Pears, Britten's life companion, representing England; the baritone, the celebrated Dietrich Fischer-Dieskau, Germany; and the soprano, Galina Vishnevskaya, Russia. This "casting" has been criticized as being so melodramatic as to verge on the "ham-handed" (Herbert 560, reporting a view that is not, in fact, his own final judgment). Yet most listeners who are aware of the identity of the singers find it genuinely moving, as representing a momentary reconciliation of enemies that may prefigure a world of nations reconciled, a world in which war is no more. Fischer-Dieskau was reportedly so moved by the experience of singing the final movement with Pears that he wept and had to be helped from the platform at the end.

One can understand such a response. A German singing about war in England, he took, in the final poem, "Strange Meeting," the role of a dead German soldier joining in mutual forgiveness with the English soldier who had bayoneted him. "Strange Meeting" dramatizes the encounter of these two soldiers in an undefined netherworld lying underneath the battlefield amid the ribs of the earth. Recognizing each other from their fatal encounter the previous day, the two soldiers share their regret at having lost the joy in life they might have had were it not for the war. They share, as well, their even greater regret that death prevents them from pressing a message of peace on the living. But so it is, and they conclude with a resigned, "Let us sleep now." It is an ending of reconciliation for the two soldiers, but an indeterminate one for the future of humankind, since the likelihood that nations will adopt their peaceful posture remains uncertain, not even guessed at.

In Britten's setting, "Strange Meeting" forms part of the final movement, the Libera Me, which begins quietly but quickly moves to a confession by the chorus and the soprano soloist of their fear and trembling at the thought of the Lord's coming to judge the earth with fire. This confession and their contemplation of the flames of hell drive the music to greater and greater agitation as drum and trumpet figures enter in announcement of the judgment. In direct response to the chorus's closing cry "Libera me, Domine" (Deliver me, O Lord), the tenor enters narrating the vision of reconciliation between enemies. Is human reconciliation, then, offered as the means of deliverance? So it seems. In contrast to much of their role in the *Requiem,* the two male soloists are here accompanied by subdued strings, woodwinds, and harp in what might easily—but in my view does not—become an overly obvious, excessively sweet vision of beatitude. That it does not, is primarily due to the indeterminate tonality of the music, which continues to convey uncertainty. At the line "the pity of war, the pity war distilled," in the baritone's long narrative of what both have lost, we hear muted trumpet echoes of the figure played at "knowing that better men would come, / And greater wars" in the setting of "The Next War," heard earlier and also sung by tenor and baritone together (the poem beginning "Out there, we walked quite friendly up to Death"). Similarly, when the baritone sings about missing "the march of this retreating world," the music echoes that of "We whistled while he shaved us with his scythe," also from "The Next War." These references both resummon the misery of battle and allude to the visionary hope of future wars "on Death, for lives; not men, for flags."

At the final half-line of "Strange Meeting," "Let us sleep now," the tenor joins, echoing the baritone's proposal that they together enter a sleep of forgetfulness. At that point the boys' choir enters, asking angels to lead them to paradise, then the chorus and soprano, while the two "soldiers" continue to repeat the phrase "let us sleep now," their voices alternating and twining together to the end. A chime sounds, recalling the tolling of "What passing bells for these who die as cattle," of the first movement. The last word sung before the quiet "Amen" is the Latin *pace,* peace. Perhaps a "saccharine denouement" (Herbert 360)? The music is indeed of ineffable sweetness. Even so, it is an ending of some uncertainty, expressing only "tentative accord." The sweetness, then, may be self-ironizing—the tritone returns—or it may convey recognition that the hope of reconciliation and peace is truly postulated only as a vision, not yet a realistic present expectation.

～

One might almost think that so beautiful and emotionally powerful a piece of music, built on poems of like beauty and power, would lead hearers to become emissaries for a society free of war. Of course, many thousands have heard the *War Requiem* either in concert or from recordings, and that has not happened. Thousands of others have read the poetry of E. E. Cummings, Marianne Moore, John Ciardi, Siegfried Sassoon, and others discussed here, and the social practice of making war has not ceased. Why, after the outpouring of antiwar sentiment in the persuasive forms we have touched on—literature, art, architecture, music—have people not risen up in great numbers to put an end to war? Why have all these poets failed? Obviously, I am asking rhetorical questions I cannot hope to answer. Nor have philosophers and war theorists far more deeply versed than I in the political and historical roots of twentieth-century (and now twenty-first-century) conflicts been able to provide answers. Even so, the question of why war still goes on must be addressed, along with the hope voiced by Maxine Hong Kingston in the epigraph to this book, alluded to in its title and the title of this chapter—the hope of learning peace.

Why have all these poets failed to bring about the massive public outcry that might put an end to war? First, because not many people read poetry—far fewer, certainly, than did in the nineteenth century and the first decade or two of the twentieth. Poetry held its own during the nineteenth century as literacy greatly expanded both in England and in the United States and even as novel-reading expanded along with literacy rates and cheap printing. A tradition of reading aloud, in families, helped maintain the place of poetry in the reading lives of many, even those of only modest education. In the twentieth century, however, as broadcast media began to replace home performance of poetry and other literature, readers increasingly favored novels, and favored reading them in silence—a custom that further shrinks the audience for poetry. Too, modernist poetry became experimental, difficult, and indirect, cutting itself off from a wide readership.[11] The antiwar message in twentieth-century poetry has indeed been eloquent, and that message has often been conveyed in relatively unvarnished revelations of battlefield maiming and suffering which we might expect to be compelling. But it reached, and reaches, only a small segment of the general public.

Then, too, there is a problem of authority. Despite Shelley's confidence that poets can serve as the "unacknowledged legislators of the world," they rarely have even the slightest political power. Unacknowledged, yes; legislators, no.

Those media that did reach a wide public during the twentieth century—especially, toward midcentury, movies and popular music, along with journalism as practiced by war correspondents—tended to be aligned with statist powers leading the various war efforts, and tended to view their role as one of morale boosting. With few exceptions, harsh truth-telling was not much favored.

But if we are to make even some tentative conjectures as to why war continues despite a flood of cautionary statements and expressions of grief over its devastation and losses, we have to look beyond the issues that lie within poetry and the arts themselves, to conditions in the larger society. First, even if the popular media had more widely embraced critical analysis and had been prepared to endure the charges of unpatriotism that it inevitably attracts, readers are understandably resistant to unpleasant messages. If the newly brutal war poetry of World War I and the factual poetry of World War II were well calculated to awaken readers—the relatively few who read poetry—to the evils of modern technological warfare, it still could not awaken those who chose not to hear. In E. E. Cummings's words from his 1926 volume *is 5*:

> . . . a god damned lot of
> people don't and never
> never
> will know
> they don't want
> to
> no (*CP* 271)

Or again, from his 1944 volume *One Times One*:

> plato told
>
> him:he couldn't
> believe it(jesus
>
> told him;he
> wouldn't believe
> it)lao

tsze
certainly told
him,and general
(yes

mam)
sherman;
and even
(believe it
or

not)you
told him:i told
him;we told him
(he didn't believe it,no

sir) . . . (553)

That is, messages may be sent, but not necessarily received. We are like the people Theodore Roethke speaks of in "Lull (November, 1939)," a poem explicitly addressing the renewal of war: "Fools who will never learn."

The unpleasant fact is, people find wars interesting. Look at the abundance of illustrated volumes about war on gift-suggestion tables in bookstores. Look at the frequency of "documentaries" about war on television, especially on outlets like the Discovery Channel and the History Channel. War is exciting. It's suspenseful. It has a plot that looms bigger, more momentous, than our own little individual lives—indeed, a plot that distracts us from daily irritations and quandaries. Laurence Bergreen, the biographer of Irving Berlin, writes that at the beginning of World War II "the prospect of war sent a shudder of dread through the American people, but it also created a thrill of excitement." More recently, war correspondent Chris Hedges has similarly written that war, like drugs, is addictive. (It is interesting to note that audiences tend to shout him down.)

We might think the dimensions of the devastation caused by a succession of twentieth-century conflicts would in themselves lead to widespread resistance to the perpetuation of warfare. Hedges claims that some 62 million *civilians* were killed in the various wars of the twentieth century, with an additional 43 million dead among military personnel (13). Robert McNamara places the total higher, at some 160 million people killed in wars around the globe (*In Retrospect* 4; also *Wilson's Ghost* xv). Such enormous losses produce ever more grieving among bereaved family members and friends. Why, given such vast losses and such widespread mourning, have citizens not risen up against the practice of war? It would seem to be a natural reaction. In 2003, for example, there was widespread speculation as to just how high a rate of daily death in Iraq it would take (that is, daily death of U.S. soldiers; Iraqi deaths in the war were for the most part being disregarded) for the American people to demand an end to U.S. involvement there. Whatever that rate might be, it seems not to have been reached. And of course no such demand came in the wake of the enormously greater American losses mourned in World War I and II, and in Korea, and only in conjunction with other powerful factors in the case of Vietnam—to mention only the most extensive U.S. military involvements.

Instead, we see again and again that when the bereaved mourn their spouses, offspring, or brothers and sisters killed in wars, they choose to do so within long-established conventions of military glory. Listen to a radio broadcast or watch a TV news report of ceremonies honoring the dead in Iraq or any other recent military involvement. You will hear parents, even, saying that they comfort themselves with the belief that their son or daughter died while serving his or her country or while bringing freedom to whoever is the stated beneficiary of U.S. military attention. Whether or not it is actually true that soldiers died in the century's various wars for noble causes or causes they served willingly, it is easier for the bereaved to reconcile themselves to the death (or maiming) if they can adopt that interpretation. The need to find a rationale for death or suffering is familiar, whether in connection with war or in cases of disease or accident. We seek a structure within which we can accept the pain of loss. Unfortunately, such structures for rationalizing deaths in combat tend to perpetuate nationalistic sentiments and war, in large part through a long-established rhetoric validating the idea of sacrifice.

In Hedges's words, "ceremonies . . . of remembering and honoring the fallen" serve as means of "sanctify[ing] the cause" (145).

The vastly multiplied experience of grieving for the loss of lives and the losses of homes, personal mementoes, and whole communities caused by twentieth-century war, then, is not sufficient to teach us peace. Even the huge cemeteries for those "fallen" in war—"fallen" being an example of the kind of euphemism that gives token recognition to the cruelty of war while in fact veiling our eyes to it—are not sufficient to bring us to the point of saying "hold, enough!" As Ron Robin demonstrates in his study of the American war cemeteries in Western Europe, even those monuments explicitly devoted to grieving may well convey other messages than the message of sorrow—messages of lofty serenity (in their quiet expanses and neat vegetation), of discipline (in the orderly ranks and files in which grave markers are arranged), and of national pride and power, messages of determination not to forget, not to let go the resentment and the desire for revenge. So long as political power structures are constituted according to notions of nationalistic aggrandizement, it is not in their best interest to allow antiwar sentiments to propagate.

We might note, too—and this is one of the yet uglier faces of the twentieth-century rush from war to war—that it is not in the interest of corporations that build and sell weapons and other necessary goods to the armed forces through government contracts. If antiwar sentiment became an effective force, it would hurt business. When Dwight D. Eisenhower left the office of president, he delivered a televised warning to Americans to "guard against the acquisition of unwarranted influence, whether sought or unsought, by the military-industrial complex" (quoted by M. Sherry 234). Louis Simpson tersely evokes the role of that very military-industrial complex when he writes in "A Bower of Roses," "For every shell Krupp fired / General Motors sent back four." Humankind has been held hostage to such corporate entities, with their direct interest in perpetuating war. How can we even imagine that mere poets and composers, artists and songwriters, singers and filmmakers could stand up against such powerful forces?

"All poets can do is warn," Wilfred Owen said, but his own practice showed that poets could do more. In Genevieve Taggard's words, poets can and must "Lay what is most exact / For the door-sill of [their] home" (24). Poets can help us realize what goes on that does not (with rare exceptions such as the widely printed photograph of the fleeing child on fire with napalm in Vietnam) get reported. As Robert McNamara writes, "poets, novelists, memoirists, playwrights, painters, photographers, and filmmakers . . . convey . . . the *human* tragedy as it has occurred, human being by human being" (*Wilson's Ghost* 23). That is, such artists can help us feel the pity of it all. Pity may not seem like a very potent force, in comparison with the Krupps and the General Motors and the secretaries of "defense" of the world. I remember once, while in graduate school, chatting with one of my professors about the movie *M*A*S*H;* I was startled when he said that showing the suffering isn't a strong argument against war. Maybe not, but I can't think of a stronger. Pity does educate the heart. Michael Ignatieff writes in *The Warrior's Honor* that it is in "the mourning of the dead" that "the desire for peace must vanquish the longing for revenge" (Ignatieff 189–90, quoted by McNamara and Blight 151). Poets and artists compel us to mourn.

In the wake of World War II, of course, not only was our mourning multiplied but an entirely different argument against war was added. In David Cannadine's succinct formulation, "Increasingly, the key to world peace has lain in the recognition that, if global conflict comes again, there will be no winners" (236).

Denise Levertov, who produced a major body of poetry about Vietnam, uses pity for the cruelty of war as her primary antiwar argument, along with exposure of the corruption of language that invariably accompanies wars. To convey both these ideas, she employs a technique combining heightened emotion with a blunt immediacy that brings the war before our eyes more vividly than we probably wish. This is one reason poets are so important to the antiwar culture of grieving; they can make war real for us, as it needs to be. They can compel us to share, empathetically, the experience of those who suffered, so that we *can* mourn the dead, all the dead—an essential step, as Ignatieff argues, if we are to "vanquish" the desire for revenge that fuels wars. Poets such as Levertov and many of the world war poets discussed here can impress the realities of war on our memories, as the photographer did whose picture of the burning child in Vietnam impressed itself on the memories of a generation. They can help ward off the massing of powers (powers of entertainment and the quasi-entertainment news media, powers of war matériel manufacturers and sellers, most of all powers of national governments) that employ a language that clouds or meliorates reality in an effort to keep us uninformed about the real ugliness of war. A true poet lives by language; honest language is the poet's reason for being, "the door-sill of [the poet's] home." And honest language is what we need if we are to understand the abhorrent nature of war and the certainty of mass destruction in nuclear war clearly enough to find ways of avoiding it.

The importance of language that gives a blunt account even of facts readers would prefer to evade is stated by Adam Gopnik: In resistance to the "grand, indifferent language of Hegelian mega-history," we need to "recall that what happened was not an entry on a tally sheet but the violent death of a human being, loved and cared for by a mother and father, and full of hope and possibility, torn apart by lead balls or shreds of sharp metal, his intestines hanging open, or his mouth coughing blood, in a last paroxysm of pain and fear. And then to recall that any justification for a war has to be a justification for this reality" (84).

We can hope, then, that poets like Edward Hirsch will go on writing about things we want to avoid seeing, about episodes like the siege of Saint Petersburg and the starvation it entailed, with such lines as

> We saw a soldier cradling a kneecap in his palms
> And children watching the soft red fluids
> Of their intestines flowing through their fingers

or even, as he continues,

> I have lanced the boils on every finger
> And sucked the warm pus; I have eaten
> A thin jelly made of leather straps (Stokesbury 207–9)

As Wilfred Owen wrote in his visionary poem "At a Calvary Near the Ancre," we don't need any more "scribes" who "bawl allegiance to the state," but rather writers who make it their mission to utter the most truthful words they can, even if that means the ugliest words they can, in allegiance to humankind. We need to be made to recognize and to remember, even if we don't wish to. We need poets to go on demanding, with Elizabeth Bishop, "Roosters, what are you projecting?" Or in the words of Chris Hedges, an observer and journalist of wars half a century and more after Owen's, we need writers and news reporters and artists who will puncture the "myth of war" and call it what it is: organized murder.[12]

In 1939, as he witnessed the approach of World War II, W. H. Auden, recognizing the importance of honest language and the need for poets willing to speak the truth as they saw it, wrote in "September 1, 1939":

> All I have is a voice
> To undo the folded lie,
> The romantic lie in the brain
> Of the sensual man-in-the-street
> And the lie of Authority
> Whose buildings grope the sky . . .

An ominous foreshadowing of the World Trade Center.[13] And continuing:

> Defenceless under the night
> Our world in stupor lies;
> Yet, dotted everywhere,
> Ironic points of light
> Flash out wherever the Just
> Exchange their messages . . . (*Collected Poetry* 59)

Even though Auden later rejected his own words as romantic sentiment, many readers continue to find hope in them. Earlier that same year, 1939, in his poem "In Memory of W. B. Yeats," Auden had written a perhaps even stronger call for the poet to persist in a time of the approach of war:

> In the nightmare of the dark
> All the dogs of Europe bark,
> And the living nations wait,
> Each sequestered in its hate;

Intellectual disgrace
Stares from every human face,
And the seas of pity lie
Locked and frozen in each eye.

Follow, poet, follow right
To the bottom of the night,
With your unconstraining voice
Still persuade us to rejoice;

With the farming of a verse
Make a vineyard of the curse,
Sing of human unsuccess
In a rapture of distress . . . (*Collected Poetry* 51)

Neither poets nor pacifist composers like Benjamin Britten will ever be able to reform this most horrendous of all "human unsuccess," but their honest messages are a prerequisite to any hope of our doing so. They are, in the mathematical sense, a necessary if not sufficient condition for the ending of war. We may not read them aright and we may not persevere in the political and social (and economic) challenges that a serious and sustained antiwar effort must entail, but we can hope that if such teachers are persistent in spelling out the lesson of peace, we can learn it.

Notes

Preface

1. Cannadine also discusses the surge of interest in spiritualism that followed World War I in England, as the bereaved struggled to retain a sense that those they had lost lived on in another dimension and, moreover, remained present in their own lives (227–31). The modes of remembrance of the war and those who died varied, of course, from country to country and must be studied in culture-specific ways. In Germany, such remembrances continued to be observed with great solemnity into the last years of the twentieth century. To be present at Cologne Cathedral on Germany's Memorial Day and to hear the solemn tolling of the cathedral bells and see the procession and the quietly mournful presence of citizens—as I did in 1983—is a deeply moving experience.

2. Lorrie Goldensohn notes that approximately ten times as many German and Austrian civilians as British civilians were killed in bombing during World War II (*Dismantling Glory* 27).

3. Beaumont adds that such information is elusive because the "side effects and 'collateral damage'" of warfare such as "wanton destruction, atrocity, pillage, and rape" are usually not included in the official or historical "description of combat and supporting statistics" (97).

4. Fussell, *Wartime* 135–39. See also Fussell's anthology *Norton Book of Modern War* 313.

Chapter 1

1. Vincent Sherry argues in *The Great War and the Language of Modernism* that it has usually been made *only* as a commonplace, without searching examination of its

meaning. I regret that Sherry's book became available so late in my work that I was able to gain only cursory benefit from it; however, its emphasis is more on the nature and theory of modernism, and on the work of a handful of high modernists, than on the war itself and a wide diversity of poets. He sees World War I as the chief, though not the only, social trauma that caused the "breakage" of "liberal rationalism" (216).

2. The vorticists, led by Ezra Pound and Wyndham Lewis, produced the first issue of the journal *Blast* in June 1914. Its list of things "blasted" included pacifism, while those "blessed" included violence (Harrison 111). Lewis even opined that "killing somebody must be the greatest pleasure in existence" (quoted by Hynes 9). Meanwhile, the leader of the at least equally "belligerent" Italian vorticists, F. T. Marinetti, announced a wish to "glorify War" as the "only health-giver of the world." Both the futurists and the vorticists promoted "contempt for women" (Hynes 7, also 8–10). Milton Cohen views the avant-garde movement in the arts throughout Europe during the years 1909 to 1914 differently than Hynes, pointing to the prevalence of metaphors of combat in the writings, paintings, and music of avant-garde artists, as well as the "mock-battles" that surrounded the appearance of such works as Stravinsky's *Le Sacre du Printemps,* to demonstrate, rather than refute, the linkage between aesthetic modernism and the war. See Cohen's "Fatal Symbiosis"; also Hynes 8–10.

3. Home was fairly readily accessible to British officers, at least, by way of medical leaves as well as in letters, albeit with enforced brevity and understatement. I am not arguing that warfare had not been filthy, miserable, and impersonal before, but that in the trenches of World War I these aspects of the soldier's experience sank to new depths and were communicated to civilians with comparatively greater readiness. With awareness of the nature of trench conditions, public perception of the nature of war changed in an absolute sense. Only with determined effort could significant numbers of people go on regarding warfare in heroic or knightly terms.

4. Numbers of deaths in the influenza pandemic are given by Fogel (7–12), citing W. I. B. Beveridge, *Influenza, the Last Great Plague.* We might also ask how many of those who died because of the ravages of rampant colonialism in the nineteenth century, such as the 10 million dead in the largely forgotten holocaust of the Congo between 1880 and 1920, should be linked with the war's dead as parts of the same vast historic process of imperialism and colonialism. On the ravages wrought in the Congo by Belgian colonialism, for example, see Adam Hochschild's controversial *King Leopold's Ghost: A Story of Greed, Terror, and Heroism in Colonial Africa.*

5. David D. Perlmutter implicity challenges Norris's argument by observing dishearteningly that "there is little evidence that any antiwar image [or poem?] has ever stopped a war" (207).

6. Note, for example, Cork's chapter titles: for art of 1915–16 "Disillusion," and for that of 1916 "The Great Carnage."

7. There had been exceptions to be sure; for example, the innovative Civil War verse of Herman Melville and Walt Whitman.

8. See Cecil D. Eby, *The Road to Armageddon.* Eby especially examines rhetoric of

sport and the mentality on which it was based in relation to the institution of the public school and fiction about public school life (86–127 and 248–50).

9. Mark Twain mocked this kind of thinking in his 1905 "War Prayer," in which a minister in church prays, "O Lord, our God, help us to tear their soldiers to bloody shreds with our shells; help us to cover their smiling fields with the pale forms of their patriot dead; help us to drown the thunder of the guns with the shrieks of their wounded, writhing in pain; help us to lay waste their humble homes with a hurricane of fire; help us to wring the hearts of their unoffending widows with unavailing grief" (Anderson 88–91).

10. The effectiveness of such musical calls to duty is noted by Niall Ferguson, who cites several primary sources to the effect that "the stirring sound of military bands playing outside recruitment offices in the very early stages of the war was more effective" in stimulating recruitment "than any number of speeches by local dignitaries" (205).

11. According to its own estimates. the *Times* received about a hundred poems a day during August 1914, "the vast majority" being, as Ferguson notes, "in the patriotic/ romantic vein" (229). See also Hynes 25. In New Zealand, Gallipoli produced a similar outpouring of verse, to the point that it had its own label: "Dardanelles verse" (Pugsley 155).

12. See Adrian Caesar, *Taking It Like a Man* 4–7, discussing Christianity as the "central pillar supporting the dominant imperialist ideology of the Victorian and Edwardian era" and a religion centering on an image of sacrificial pain "said to be an image which represents 'love.'" On Benjamin Britten's rejection of the idea of sacrifice in his *War Requiem*, see chapter 10.

13. Sandra M. Gilbert, in a return to the argument of her earlier book *Sexchanges* (vol. 2 of *No Man's Land*), links the deeply ironic cast that emerged in the war, especially in attitudes toward elegy and mourning for death, with Eliot, Wallace Stevens (specifically, in "The Owl in the Sarcophagus" and "Lettres d'un Soldat"), and other modernist poets who testified to "the war's inescapable factuality" and the turn from an emphasis on "rebirth" to "dissolution"; "'Rats' Alley'" 185, 188.

14. Two informative studies of such monumental and widely social forms of memorializing war are Ron Robin's "'A Foothold in Europe,'" and the first two chapters of Steven Trout's *Memorial Fictions*.

15. Spear quotes an approving verbal echo of Kipling's "Who dies if England live?" from a newspaper of October 1916 but an explicit rejection of its fatuousness in February 1917; see Spear 29.

16. "A Song in Storm" first appeared around November 30, 1915, in several newspapers in England and the United States, under varying titles and with varying numbers of stanzas; Harbord 5444.

17. First published in a pamphlet issued in the United States in 1916, under the title "The Neutral," the poem appeared in Kipling's *Sea Warfare* (1916) again as "The Neutral" but was changed in 1919 to the title used here; Harbord 5447.

18. The three stanzas that include this reference to Kipling's views are included in

the poem "In Memory of W. B. Yeats" in the 1945 *Collected Poetry* but were later deleted by Auden himself and therefore do not appear in the 1976 *Collected Poems* edited by Edward Mendelson.

19. Eby reports that some seventy-three thousand copies of the *Georgian Poetry* anthologies were sold between 1911 and 1922 and that Brooke was "the most celebrated" of the group (208). James Hannah comments that one can "gauge the changing attitudes toward the war by the erosion of Georgian and Edwardian sensibilities" (357).

20. Leed quotes many examples of statements by participants who felt the mobilization in August 1914 as a release from a life of "indecision, aimlessness, and loneliness" or the "constraints of bourgeois life" into a flow-state "replete with palpable meanings, clear precise goals, and nonconflicting demands." A recurrent emotion expressed at the time and in retrospect was a joyful release from divisions of social class; see Leed 54–55, 17, 56. Questioning the prevalence of this euphoria, Niall Ferguson argues that even Brooke felt "ambivalence" toward the war in that, as he wrote on August 3, he regarded England's ally Russia as a "despotic and insane" regime that he hoped Germany would "smash," even while he labeled Prussia itself "a devil"; quoted by Ferguson 184–85. Alliance with Russia was a sticking point for many in England.

21. The image of young swimmers diving into war as if into a cleansing pool is slyly parodied in Willa Cather's novel *One of Ours* when her hero and his friends dive into a pool of standing water only to release gases from submerged bodies at the bottom. We can feel fairly confident that she was acquainted with the image because two poems by Cather were published in a wartime volume that also included Brooke's sonnet with the leaping swimmers: *The New Poetry: An Anthology* (1917), edited by Harriet Monroe and Alice Corbin Henderson.

22. By the end of 1915 many in England already felt a sense of the war's being interminable. Such a sense is keenly established in Rose Macaulay's satiric, ultimately pacifist novel *Non-Combatants*. The following passage (71–72) conveys the depression of the heroine, Alix, but is not limited to her point of view:

> June went by, and the war went on, and the Russians were driven back in Galicia, and the Germans took Lemberg, and trenches were lost and won in France, and there was fighting round Ypres, and Basil Doye had the middle finger of his right hand cut off, and there was some glorious weather, and Zeppelin raids in the eastern counties, and it was warm and stuffy in London, and Mrs. Sandomir wrote to Alix from the United States that more than ever now, since their darling Paul was added to the toll of wasted lives, war must not occur again.
>
> July went by, and the war went on, and trenches were lost and won, and there was fighting round Ypres, and a German success at Hooge, and the Russians were driven back in Galicia, and Basil Doye left hospital and went with his mother to Devonshire, and there were Zeppelin raids in the eastern counties, and the summer term at the art school ended, and Alix went away from Clapton to Wood End, and her mother wrote that American women were

splendid to work with, and that it was supremely important that the States should remain neutral, and that there were many hitches in the way of arbitration, but some hope.

August went by, and the war went on, and Warsaw was taken, and the National Register, and trenches were lost and won, and there was fighting round Ypres, and a British success at Hooge and in Gallipoli, and Zeppelin raids on the eastern counties, and Nicholas and Alix went away together for a holiday to a village in Munster where the only newspaper which appeared with regularity was the *Ballydehob Weekly Despatch,* and Violette was shut up, and Mrs. Frampton stayed with Aunt Nellie and Kate and Evie with friends, and Mrs. Sandomir wrote from Sweden that the Swedes were promising but apathetic, and their government shy.

September went by, and the war went on, and the Russians rallied and retreated and rallied in Galicia, and a great allied advance in France began and ended, and the hospitals filled up, and there were Zeppelin raids on the eastern counties, and Mrs. Frampton and Kate and Evie came back to Violette, and the art school opened, and Alix came back to Violette, and the Doyes came back to town, and Mrs. Sandomir wrote from Sermaize-le-Bains, where she was staying a little while again with the Friends and helping to reconstruct, that it was striking how amenable to reason neutral and even belligerent governments were, if one talked to them reasonably. Even Ferdinand, though he had his faults. . . . [*sic*]

October began, and the war went on, and Bulgaria massed on the Serbian frontier, and Russia sent her an ultimatum, and the Germans retook the Hohenzollern Redoubt, and the hospitals got fuller, and the curious affair of Salonika began, and Terry Orme came home on leave, and Basil Doye interviewed the Medical board, was told he could not rejoin yet, visited Cox's, and, coming out of it, met Alix going up to the Strand.

23. Throughout this section I draw, in abbreviated form, on an article coauthored by Alan Houtchens and myself, " 'Scarce Heard amidst the Guns Below.' "

24. "In Flanders Fields" was only one of a series of three war songs Ives composed that same year, the other two being the more overtly patriotic "He Is There!" (completed on May 30, 1917, according to its dating in Ives's 1922 volume *114 Songs,* but revised at the outset of World War II to rather different effect) and the melancholy "Tom Sails Away," dated 1917 in *114 Songs* but given the more specific dating of September 1917 on the autograph manuscript (Kirkpatrick 200–201). All three were written before American troops went into combat, when the public was not yet stunned by casualty lists. After the war, Ives revised "In Flanders Fields," resulting in its 1919 dating in the published volume, and added a song variously titled "Nov. 2, 1920" or "An Election" (in *114 Songs* 50–55 and *Nineteen Songs* 26–31, respectively), which reflects a postwar perspective on the Treaty of Versailles and the defeat of Woodrow Wilson's avowed ideals.

Interestingly, in "Tom Sails Away" the words "But today! In freedom's cause Tom sailed away for over there, over there, over there!" are set to a plaintive echo of George M. Cohan's phenomenally popular song by the same name. The song ends in a dissonance as inconclusive and enigmatic as the final bichord of "In Flanders Fields." "He Is There!" in a sprightly march time throughout, is the least ambiguous of the three songs, but so much so that one suspects parody. Snatches of echoed melodies link the Great War with the Civil War, while the text links the present effort to the German revolutionary struggles of 1848. In the third verse the "yankee boy" who is "there" "Does his bit that we may live, / In a world where all may have a 'say.'" Yet the fact that this "yankee boy" mindlessly shouts "Hip Hip Hooray!" while marching to the front in Flanders, which by 1917 was well established as a killing field, is enough to give us pause. The song ends with an echo of the melancholy Civil War song "Tenting Tonight on the Old Camp Ground" with the words revised to "a new camp ground"—perhaps a campground in the new war against war itself?

25. Irving Berlin's biographer Laurence Bergreen states that "like everyone else at Camp Upton," where he was sent for training in 1918, Berlin had been "beguiled by Cohan's 'Over There'" (151), but the statement seems hyperbolic since Berlin, at least, had not enlisted but been drafted. Berlin himself, like George M. Cohan, produced a big hit song late in the war, "Oh, How I Hate to Get Up in the Morning," which he performed himself in his revue *Yip! Yip! Yaphank,* written under army auspices and performed entirely by soldiers. Yaphank, New York (on Long Island) was the location of Camp Upton, where the revue was conceived and first performed. "Oh, How I Hate to Get Up in the Morning" sold a million and a half copies in sheet music (Bergreen 153) and was revived in Berlin's World War II revue *This Is the Army,* in which he again performed it himself.

26. The three poems discussed here were reprinted in Binyon's *The Winnowing Fan: Poems on the Great War* in 1915, then in *The Cause: Poems of the War* in 1917, and in *The Four Years: War Poems* in 1919. In *The Cause,* cited here, they appear on pages 23–24, 38–39, and 40–41.

27. Wilfred Owen, who received from his mother a copy of the *Times* war poems supplement, collecting verse published there during the twelve months beginning August 1914, wrote to a friend three days later that Binyon's poem was "all right!" (*Collected Letters* 355). The language Owen used bears the mark of the efforts toward understatement that he was making in his poetry at the time.

28. Throughout this section I draw on my article coauthored with Alan Houtchens, "'That dreadful winnowing fan.'"

29. In the next year, 1915, Binyon himself would spend several weeks in France working in a military hospital as a Red Cross volunteer *ambulancier* and orderly.

30. See Robert L. Ivie regarding war rhetoric.

31. Other examples (among many) of the trope of the soldier as Christ, with its corollary of the war as a Gethsemane or a Golgotha, are seen in Kipling's "Gethsemane"; in Alice Meynell's "Summer in England, 1915," with its appropriation of "No man hath greater love than this, / To die for his friend"; in Siegfried Sassoon's "Reconciliation," "The Redeemer," and "The Prince of Wounds" ("I say that he was Christ"); and in

Wilfred Owen's "At a Calvary near the Ancre," which was set to music by Benjamin Britten in *War Requiem.*

32. In a letter to the critic Ernest Newman dated April 15, 1916, Elgar pointed out that the three movements of *The Spirit of England* were connected by the recurrence of themes, particularly whenever lines in the other two poems warranted the recall of "the theme associated with the courage and hope of the first poem"; quoted by J. Moore 296.

33. Miriam Cooke questions whether there ever was a place of removal from warfare for women. "Postmodern inquiry into the nature of the front and combatants," she observes, "calls into question the authenticity" of that distinction. Tracing the breakdown of "the distinction between battlefield and civilian space" to medieval wars, she nevertheless concedes that "to an unprecedentedly vast extent the total wars of 1914–18 and 1939–45 involved those who should have had nothing to do with bloodshed" (116).

34. Michael Kennedy, in his important essay arguing that Elgar was not really an Edwardian at all but rather a Victorian out of tune with his times, emphasizes that Elgar and Alfred, Lord Tennyson (1809–92) were kindred spirits, even calling Tennyson "the Elgar of poetry" (109).

CHAPTER 2

1. Jonathan Goldberg makes the point that some critics, however, have believed that Owen, Sassoon, and certain other soldier poets might have thanked God for matching them with that hour in that their war experience allowed them either to transcend (in Fussell's view of Owen) or to "work out" the "conflict" of their homosexuality (106–7).

2. Though I frequently differ with J. H. Johnston's views of World War I poetry, my conception of the response to the Somme as a swerve, rather than part of a steady progression, parallels his. "For a few dramatic weeks in the spring and early summer of 1916," as preparations for the Somme Offensive were under way, Johnston writes, "the doubts and suspicions which had troubled the mind of the volunteer were forgotten" as the "sheer magnitude of that attack, which promised to end the war within weeks, brought a final resurgence of the enthusiasms of 1914." It was by contrast with this renewal of an "idealistic attitude" (which he demonstrates with examples of verse written during that brief period) that the failure and brutality of the offensive evoked such a "shock of disillusion"; see Johnston 71–78.

3. Quinn and Trout, editors of *The Literature of the Great War Reconsidered,* make essentially the same point: "Today . . . the designation 'war literature' has moved beyond the battlefield to include the creative expressions (whatever their rhetorical context or ideological orientation) of anyone, soldier or civilian, man or woman, who struggled to interpret the unthinkable" (1).

4. For biographical information about Edward Thomas and many other poets of the war, I am indebted to the notes provided by a number of earlier scholars and an-

thologists, primarily Giddings, in *The War Poets;* James Bentley, in *Some Corner of a Foreign Field;* Nosheen Khan, in *Women's Poetry of the First World War;* and Claire Tylee, in *The Great War and Women's Consciousness.*

5. A similar priority held sway, of course, in poetry—one reason for the privileging of the male poet over the female. When war was narrowly defined as being synonymous with "battle" or "battlefield," few women could be eyewitnesses.

6. During the early years of World War II, Paul Nash returned to the subject of war, painting airplanes and monster submarines in his *Totes Meer* (1940–41), a sea of wrecked German planes (see fig. 9).

7. Richard Cork notes several examples of such works in *A Bitter Truth.* A drawing by Albert Forestier published in the *Illustrated London News* on July 15, 1916, which purported to show the "big push" on the Somme, had soldiers walking erectly and confidently forward with "hardly any casualties . . . visible" and "[no] sign of the barbed-wire entanglements which made the advance across No Man's Land so treacherous" (Cork 125). "Virulent" anti-German propaganda was produced by Charles Butler in large and heavily theatrical paintings, such as one in which a brightly haloed Christ succors wounded British soldiers being ignored by Kaiser Wilhelm. In 1917 Lucy Kemp-Welch produced "a monumental painting with the gung-ho title *Forward the Guns!*" which ignored "the horrors of machine-age destruction" in order to show clean-cut and hearty British artillerymen driving teams of horses pulling cannon across the supposed fields of France (Cork 128).

8. Read's poem "Kneeshaw Goes to War" refers both to "Polygonveld" and "Polygonbeke." Both words seem to have been, in a sense, coinages; at any rate, neither "veld" nor "beke" is to be found in my 1958 *Cassell's German-English Dictionary.* Both, however, are very close to words that *Cassell's* recognizes: "welt," world, and "bach," brook or stream. The Polygonwald was a park of planted trees roughly pentagonal in shape, as shown on a visitor information sign at its entrance. By September 1917, when it was taken from the Germans in the Battle of Polygon Wood, it had been reduced to a devastation of stripped and broken dead trees.

9. Poppies, the characteristic wildflower of Flanders, are seen in numerous paintings and have been remembered in the paper poppies that for many years were customarily worn on Memorial Day in the United States as well as in England.

10. Such a view is not unanimous, however. Patrick Quinn writes that Sassoon "had spoken more effectively than any of his contemporaries about the horrors facing the ordinary soldier in this war" ("Siegfried Sassoon" 230).

11. Hibberd explains a code that Owen had worked out with his mother before he was sent to France, by which he was able to let her know where he was in spite of censorship that would have eliminated any place-names (206, 209, 225).

12. According to Harold Owen and John Bell's dating in the *Collected Letters* (13), "Exposure" was written in February 1917, but Stallworthy's dating (*Complete Poems* 186) places its composition as December 1917 to early 1918. Despite the harrowing immediacy of the description, stanzaic artifice and a certain decorativeness of language seem to speak of the earlier period, before Owen's major blossoming of late 1917.

13. Owen's self-diagnosis while he was in the casualty clearing station was that he supposed he had had "a 'breakdown'" and might be "a little mad" (*Collected Letters* 453–54, written May 2 and May 4, 1917). It is perhaps not incidental that on May 14, while he was still awaiting transport back to England, he wrote his younger brother, Colin, a long and senseless parody of jumbled biblical stories (*Collected Letters* 458–60). Like Sassoon, he was finding established notions of the sacred bitterly laughable in light of what he had experienced.

14. Although it is generally supposed that Owen wrote "Dulce et decorum est" in response to Pope's "The Call," published in the *Daily Mail* on November 26, 1914, Khan conjectures that he may more likely have been recalling later encounters with her books at the front, as they were "very popular with the troops" (19).

15. Norgate points out that "prior to Owen, more than one piece of Soldier Poetry retailed this same Latin tag [dulce et decorum est pro patria mori] entirely unironically" (520). Owen himself had rather incredibly drafted a poem early in the war in which he opined, "But sweeter still and far more meet / To die in war for brothers"—the "sweet and meet" of *dulce et decorum* (Stallworthy 104).

16. Mary McLean observes that the seemingly awkward repetition of the rhyme-word "drowning" enacts the implied "again" of the returning nightmare; personal communication with the author.

17. With the possible exception of "The End," which was probably begun in late 1916 but not completed until November 1917 or January 1918, all nine of the poems set by Britten were written between August 1917 and July 1918; see Jon Stallworthy's notes in Owen, *Complete Poems and Fragments* 1:159. This is not to say, however, that he did not draw on material written earlier in bringing these poems to fulfillment.

18. We know that Owen possessed a copy of Binyon's poem. On August 12, 1915, he received from his mother a copy of a *Times* poetry supplement called *War Poems from the Times,* published on August 10, which contained both Binyon's "For the Fallen" and Kipling's "For All We Have and Are," among others. We know, too, from a comment in a letter, that Owen read the collection. See Stallworthy 124–25.

19. Although "Sonnet (On Seeing a Piece of Our Artillery Brought into Action)" is powerfully effective in Britten's musical setting (which uses only six of the fourteen lines), its ponderous tone and archaic diction ("yea," "thy," "thee") make it somewhat uncharacteristic of Owen's newfound mature style and therefore, in my judgment, less satisfying than others.

20. The passage arguing that death is simply death and there is no more to be hoped is one of many that Owen had drafted earlier—in this case, before the war. Hibberd, who gives several examples of Owen's revising earlier passages and incorporating them into his war poems, comments, "Wilfred was not driven to that conclusion by the Somme, as is sometimes assumed." See Hibberd 195–96, 270, 277, 318.

21. The strolling priests of "At a Calvary near the Ancre" may indicate an acquaintance with William Blake's "Garden of Love," where the "garden" has tombstones in place of flowers and "Priests in black gowns were walking their rounds, / And binding with briars my joys and desires."

22. For example, Gilbert, "'Rats' Alley'" 192; Norgate, "Wilfred Owen and the Soldier Poets" 520; Bäckman, *Tradition Transformed* 96–117.

23. Hibberd indicates that Owen was engaged in an intensive study of the elegy as a form between December 1917 and June 1918, and that he developed the form in ways "both radical and comfortless" (291).

CHAPTER 3

1. The lack of recognition of women war poets was an intensified form of the more general neglect of women writers that was prevalent until the efforts at feminist canon revision of the 1970s and after. Of the sixteen poets I touch on here—Mary Borden, May Wedderburn Cannan, Margaret Postgate Cole, Elizabeth Daryush, Elizabeth Chandler Forman, Hilda Doolittle (H.D.), Diana Gurney, Helen Hamilton, Mary Henderson, Teresa Hooley, Amy Lowell, Rose Macauley, Alice Meynell, Margaret Sackville, May Sinclair, Edith Sitwell—only four are even acknowledged in passing in David Perkins's otherwise wide-ranging *History of Modern Poetry*, and there is no indication whatever that any of them ever addressed the subject of the war. A different explanation of the narrowing of recognition of war poetry to the effusions of those who fought is given by Margot Norris, who conjectures that it may have been "concern with fiction's inability to match the 'truth value' of historical facticity" that tended to "privilege writing that has testimonial power" (22).

2. Giddings also selected "Field Ambulance in Retreat" as the one example of Sinclair's verse in his anthology *The War Poets*. It is recognized as an exceptionally well-achieved poem and also as an example of the metrical freeness of much of the new poetry in the early decades of the twentieth century.

3. Henderson's lines provide a particularly clear illustration of the contrast drawn by Gilbert and Gubar between women's unaccustomed freedom of movement at the front and men's immobility.

4. It is not clear to me why "mourning" should be regarded as "inevitably . . . secondary" to death in the experience of loss in war, as Margaret Higonnet and her coeditors write in their introduction to *Behind the Lines* (14).

5. Claire Tylee points out (252) that it was difficult for writers to avoid the martial tone since "all criticism . . . which implied that the war was anything other than a holy crusade against the bestial hun, was ruthlessly suppressed." Tylee cites as an example the burning of a pacifist children's book *The Last Weapon; A Vision* by Theodora Wilson.

6. Chandler Forman's poem was presumably written while the war still continued; it appeared in a 1919 volume called *War Verse*, edited by Frank Foxcroft, published in New York by Crowell.

7. Khan accurately observes, in reference to this poem, that "Owen is not justified in alleging that those at home were 'dullards whom no cannon stuns'. Macaulay's poem shows that war was an ever-present reality which had to be striven with—thus the attempts at indifference—if people at home were to retain their hold on sanity. Owen, pre-

occupied perhaps with conveying the truth of the soldiers' war, overlooked the fact that civilians, too, like combatants, could subscribe to the belief: 'Dullness best solves / The tease and doubt of shelling'" (95).

8. She later worked at the Ministry of Information and drew on her experience there for a satire on government bureaucracy and censorship that was itself censored under the Defence of the Realm Act and withheld from publication until after the end of the war; see Tylee 120–21.

Chapter 4

1. In the Middle East, in particular, they were more than haunted, as the collapse of the Ottoman Empire led to conflicts resulting in the establishment of the nation of Turkey, as well as power struggles in the mandates accorded to Britain and France in other formerly Ottoman territories, including the area now known as Iraq. In the ensuing unrest, Baghdad would be bombed. At the root of these outside interests and their imposed order were, of course, the oil resources of the region.

2. Among the World War I songs used in *Oh What a Lovely War* are "Long Long Trail," "Pack Up Your Troubles in Your Old Kit Bag," "Belgium Put the Kibosh on the Kaiser," "We're 'ere Because We're 'ere" (an expression of the doubt of any purpose to the war, which became popular among the troops), and a number of parodies that were sung in the trenches.

3. Readers who wish to hear this obscure composition may be able to locate a compact disk recording by Thomas Hampson, baritone, with the London Symphony Orchestra, called *Night and Day: Thomas Hampson Sings Cole Porter*, EMI Classics recording CDC 7 54203 2.

4. "My Dream of the Big Parade" was recorded with a studio orchestra on June 30, 1926, in New York, and was originally issued on Victor 20098. It can be heard on *Praise the Lord and Pass the Ammunition: Songs of World Wars I and II*, Recorded Anthology of American Music, New World Records NW 222 (1977).

5. See Perkins 423–24. Surprisingly, John H. Johnston names Graves and Blunden specifically in stating that "among the soldier-poets who survived the war . . . not one returned to his battle experiences as the source of further poetic inspiration" (250). Johnston then goes on, however, to discuss Herbert Read's 1933 "The End of a War," praising the long (four-hundred-line) poem as a "remarkable" work that addresses "the higher level of motive and belief" rather than the limited sensuous impressions of the soldier (279). He also devotes a full chapter to David Jones's allusive 1937 masterwork *In Parenthesis*. Clearly, both these works return to the authors' war experiences.

6. The accuracy of Larkin's depiction of the hopefulness in the rush to enlist is underscored by Leed, who, however, does not locate it in the men's having been sold a bill of goods: "War was greeted as a liberation because it was felt to signify the destruction of an economic order. . . . Many hurried to the recruiting offices fearing that the war would be over before they could engage the enemy" (61).

7. As Pat Barker has the psychologist W. H. R. Rivers (who treated both Sassoon and Owen at Craiglockhart) say in her novel *The Eye in the Door,* "In war there's this enormous glorification of love between men" (156).

8. The two quoted lines are usually printed "I will not kiss your f.ing flag" and "there is some s. I will not eat." The 1991 *Complete Poems,* which I use here, follows Cummings's manuscripts in spelling out the words.

9. Cummings's last line is echoed in a retrospective poem on World War II by Donald W. Baker, "Delinquent Elegy," which praises his "long-dead" friend killed in World War II as having been "as smart as most, as brave as any" (Stokesbury 125).

10. The four unspaced ellipses are Cummings's.

11. The 369th Infantry, from Harlem, was assigned to the 161st Division of the French army and fought in the front lines. More than 150 of its men were awarded the Croix de Guerre (J. Anderson 103–8).

12. See Adam Gussow, *Seems Like Murder Here.*

13. Hynes points out in *A War Remembered* (340) that Pound wrote "sometimes elegiacally, sometimes angrily" at least as much about what the war had done to the literary life in London in which he had "made a significant place for himself" as about the war itself. He adds that "no one got the retrospective sense of the war . . . better than Pound did" in the two sections of "Mauberley" explicitly devoted to the war and its effects.

14. *The Fourth Canto* was published in 1919 and *A Draft of XVI Cantos* in 1925, compared to publication of "Hugh Selwyn Mauberley" in 1920.

15. Contrary to what is sometimes, as in Larkin, its presentation as a time of cheer and innocence, Richard A. Kaye has discerned the presence of a "spiritual despair hanging over Europe before the start of World War I," of which Eliot's "The Love Song of St. Sebastian," unpublished until 1988, was "one of the earliest poetic documents" (128).

16. Gilbert, "'Rats' Alley'" 194. Also reading *The Waste Land* in connection with the Great War, Michael Levenson calls it "an engagement with the civilization of violence" (3).

17. Gilbert, "'Rats' Alley'" 193, citing Peter, "A New Interpretation of the *Waste Land*." In a parallel discussed by Gilbert, Wallace Stevens's "Death of a Soldier" (1918) and the other poems in Stevens's 1917–18 sequence "Lettres d'un Soldat" were written in grief for French painter Eugene Emmanuel Lermercier, killed in combat in 1915 (Gilbert 180).

CHAPTER 5

1. Sven Lindquist writes in *A History of Bombing,* as translated by Linda Haverty Rugg:

> When did the Second World War actually begin? Was it on September 18, 1931, when the Japanese attacked China and turned the northeastern Chinese province into the Japanese vassal state Manchukuo? Or was it in March of 1932, when the Japanese air force suddenly bombed Shanghai and caused sev-

eral thousand civilian deaths? Or perhaps in January of 1933, when the Japanese occupied northern China all the way down to Beijing and Tientsin?

The Japanese called the war "the China incident." From the European perspective, all of that happened much too far away to be considered a world war. The world was in Europe. But when the Japanese attacked the railway station in Natao on August 26, 1937, and not only killed hundreds of civilian Chinese, but also wounded the British ambassador, Sir Hugh Knatchball-Huggesson, it did make an impression. (42)

2. American poet Edwin Rolfe, among others, wrote passionate laments for Spain, including "First Love" (1943) and "Elegia" (1948).

3. Auden was a notorious reviser. In his 1945 *Collected Poetry* these lines are virtually the same as they appear in the 1976 *Collected Poems*, which I follow here, but we must go back to the 1944 volume for "September 1, 1939." The twelfth of the "Sonnets from China," which I quote below, appears in the 1945 *Collected Poetry* as number sixteen in a sequence called "In Time of War." The later text, quoted here, varies somewhat but not essentially from the earlier.

4. See the Web site http//www.kz-gedenkstaette-dachau.de/english/.

5. American poet Louise Bogan had similarly lamented, in a tersely powerful poem published in 1937 and addressed to her brother killed in World War I, that everything remains as it was before except "peace alone." Bogan's "To My Brother Killed: Haumont Wood: October, 1918" may have been written as early as 1925. Susan Schweik discusses the composition history as well as the poem itself, which she calls "in one sense the quintessential Second World War poem," in *A Gulf So Deeply Cut* 7–11. It is interesting and significant that the perhaps quintessential poem of World War II is a poem of retrospect about World War I.

6. Once again I am drawing on Houtchens and Stout, "'Scarce Heard amidst the Guns Below.'"

7. Ives recorded "They Are There" on April 24, 1943. The best of three takes were spliced together and included in *Charles Ives: The 100th Anniversary*, CBS M4 32504, issued in 1974.

CHAPTER 6

1. Paul Fussell rightly cites the Chinese Exclusion Act of 1882 in making this point; see *Wartime* 161–62.

2. Blum insists that Roosevelt himself was "mindful of the calculated hysteria embedded in the propaganda of fear and hate" conducted by the Wilson administration during World War I and "shunned another public adventure in hyperbole" but was persuaded to launch a domestic propaganda campaign by "pressure from advisers" (21). Roosevelt himself identified Germany as the greater of the two threats, but Americans "despised Japanese far more than Germans," and the "racial hatred" in which, Michael Sherry asserts, they were "united" then "erupted in the Pacific war" (M. Sherry 81, 91–92).

3. Quoted by Blum 25, from *Communique,* Hollywood Writers Mobilization for Defense, March 6, 1942, and by Fussell, *Wartime* 152, from a magazine ad placed by the American Motion Picture Industry in 1942.

4. The armed services insisted on reviewing screenplays in advance, in order to decide whether they were acceptable, before agreeing to cooperate by making available tanks, bombers, and the like; Fussell, *Wartime* 191–92.

5. Michael Sherry points out that one reason radio news delivery was more closely allied with government policies in the years before World War II than the print media had ever been was that radio "depended on the federal government for various kinds of licensing and oversight" (40).

6. A useful source of information on the wartime literary scene in England is Robert Hewison's *Under Siege: Literary Life in London, 1939–1945.*

7. Frith 141; see citation by Ray Pratt 5. The volume in which Frith's essay "Towards an Aesthetic of Popular Music" appears provides extensive and multidimensional discussion of the definitional issues underlying the terms "popular" and "serious" music. Primarily these are related to the assumption that "serious" music is "autonomous," that it "transcends the social, the political and the everyday" and can be analyzed and evaluated solely on technical bases, according to its own traditions and internal rules (Wolff 1; also Leppert and McClary xviii). My consideration here assumes that *both* "serious," or high-art, and "popular" music have *both* rhetorical (sociological or instrumental) qualities *and* autonomous or technical qualities.

8. There seems to have been a larger number of songs with topical reference in England. See Huggett, especially chapter 10, "Shine on Victory Moon."

9. Charles Hamm cites this fact as one piece of evidence, among many, of Berlin's "continuity of musical style" over the years (*Yesterdays* 338).

10. The staying power of "God Bless America" is demonstrated by the fact that in the 1970s it was brought back to rally a professional hockey team, the Philadelphia Flyers, to victory in the Stanley Cup playoffs. Kate Smith herself came out on the ice to sing it, and the team won. In the context of post-9/11 tensions and the disputed war on Iraq, the song was again frequently heard during the 2003 baseball season, especially during the playoffs and the World Series.

11. Bergreen writes that in its first decade "White Christmas" sold 3 million copies of sheet music and 14 million records, and that though it plays as "essentially timeless" the song "owed its initial success to the war" (409–10).

12. Curiously, notes by Cynthia Lindsay in the *Frank Loesser Song Book* (Loesser 47) imply that "Praise the Lord," though written earlier, was not "release[d]" by Loesser until 1945.

13. "I'll Be Seeing You," written in 1938 for an unsuccessful Broadway musical, became a hit song in 1944 in a recording by Frank Sinatra with the Tommy Dorsey orchestra because its mood captured the loneliness that afflicted so many couples separated by the war.

14. These last two are conveniently grouped with other songs of the war on a Rosemary Clooney disk called *For the Duration,* Concord Records CCD-4444.

15. Popular songs of the day also reached the troops via the Armed Forces Radio Service, which had oversized "v-disks" of records that were never released to any other outlet, in order to broadcast long segments of music without interruption.

16. At the age of seventeen Aaron Copland had composed a tribute to the Allied effort in World War I called *After Antwerp*. His commitment to socially purposive music is demonstrated by his 1934 composition of a song for voice and piano called "Into the Streets May First," which was published in the *New Masses.*

17. Regarding isolationist sentiment in the U.S. in the late thirties, see Chatfield, *For Peace and Justice,* and Duroselle, *From Wilson to Roosevelt.*

18. Schweik makes the linkage between MacLeish and Millay and traces both the composition of the text and its reception in *A Gulf So Deeply Cut* 59–70 and 77–82.

19. See Schweik's full and illuminating discussion of the poem, 140–70.

20. This foundational genre for Rukeyser's poem is also discussed by Schweik in a full chapter.

21. The privileging of the male voice on grounds of direct experience would, of course, be increasingly eroded in the course of World War II, in which more casualties were sustained by civilians than by soldiers. Civilians were female as well as male—indeed, female even more likely than male, since many males were away in the military. Another important but little-known body of poetry that emerged from direct experience of the war in a very different way was the poetry of the concentration camps, such as the poetry that came out of the internment of Japanese Americans. Schweik appropriately refers to this material as "a *civilian* 'war poetry of experience'" (174).

22. See Foulkes, *Literature and Propaganda,* in full for a more searching discussion of these issues.

CHAPTER 7

1. "Naming of Parts," dated 1942, appears in Reed's *Collected Poems* in a series of poems called "Lessons of the War."

2. See Goldensohn, *Dismantling Glory* 22 and 112. I am indebted to Philip Beidler for the information that during the Vietnam War such behind-the-lines soldiers were generally called REMFs—rear-echelon motherfuckers; personal communication with the author. Here and in brief biographical references relating to other poets I draw on the "Notes on the Poets" section of Leon Stokesbury's important and useful anthology, *Articles of War,* unfortunately now out of print. Ewart and Eberhart also wrote on the basis of their own wartime experience, Eberhart having served as an aerial gunnery officer in the U.S. Navy (Stokesbury 220).

3. Jarrell's appropriation of the voice of the bomber pilot here is not to be read as a false claim about his own wartime experience, but as a legitimate act of the imagination deriving, in part, from his close work with pilots of military aircraft as an instructor in navigation.

4. Dickey's inflation and falsification of his own wartime service in the South Pacific detracts from his personal standing but not from the achievement of the poetry

itself. Regarding the biographical issue of Dickey's false claims, see Henry Hart, "James Dickey: Journey to War."

5. Shapiro writes autobiographically about his travels on a troop train in *The Younger Son* 269–73.

6. The first collection in which "Human Nature" appeared was the 1968 volume *Selected Poems*. It is retained in *Collected Poems*.

7. The poem is shown in Stokesbury's *Articles of War* and elsewhere as "Elegy for a Cove Full of Bones," but a note in Ciardi's *Collected Poems* explains that it was supposed to be "cave" and became "cove" through a misprint in the posthumous 1989 volume *Echoes*. I am following the *Collected Poems* usage even though in some places in the poem "cove" seems better suited.

8. "Return" was not included in the *Collected Poems* volume, which reprints, according to the foreword, some 62 percent of Ciardi's verse excluding children's verse. The poem can be found in the Stokesbury anthology and in *Saipan: The War Diary of John Ciardi* (Fayetteville: U of Arkansas P, 1988)—a volume, interestingly enough, not listed in the table of contents of the Ciardi *Collected Poems*. The editorial history of Ciardi's work is complex; he sometimes revised poems years after their publication.

9. The incident of Lowell's (very courteous) protest against Johnson's foreign policy as manifest in the escalation of the U.S. involvement in Vietnam is summarized by Wai Chee Dimock in "Non-Newtonian Time" 925–27. Simpson and nineteen others that Dimock calls "the nation's most prominent intellectuals" signed a telegram published in the *New York Times* on June 4, 1965, a day after Lowell's open letter to the president had appeared on the front page of the newspaper.

10. Two of the poems, "Carentan O Carentan" and "Arm in Arm," are in fourteeners—the alternating eight-syllable, six-syllable lines found in many hymns. But there is considerable variation in form, even if the individual forms themselves are rather rigidly unvaried.

11. Moran seems to believe the ambushers are literally wearing leopard skins (35).

12. Two recent articles in *Psychiatric Annals* address the history of psychological casualties in twentieth-century wars. According to Thomas A. Hicklin, "During World War I, the intensity of battle reached levels previously unknown due to advanced weaponry. . . . Enemy shelling, gas attacks, and the smells of the battlefield led to the term 'shell shock.'" Hicklin continues that in World War II psychoneuroses severe enough to require medical discharges "result[ed] in a serious loss of manpower on the battlefield" (722). Likewise, John H. Shale, Christopher M. Shale, and Jayne D. Shale write that by World War I, "with the increasing destructiveness and precision of modern weapons, the proportion of psychiatric casualties constituted a significant military medical problem," which steadily increased in subsequent conflicts. According to the Shales' figures, 15 percent of disability discharges from the British army in World War I were from psychiatric disabilities, and 30 to 40 percent of combat casualties in World War II were psychiatric, though the rate could go "much higher" in "particularly intense and protracted fighting" (726).

13. For the discussion of wartime euphemism summarized in this paragraph, see

M. Sherry 96–98. Some entire sectors of the war, Sherry writes—such as the experiences of "gays and Gypsies in Nazi camps, Japanese civilians in torched cities, Chinese murdered or starved in countless numbers"—"almost never crossed the screen of wartime imagination."

CHAPTER 8

1. Similarly, Fussell asked in 1984, in *Thank God for the Atom Bomb* (137), a question transparently based on self-confirming assumptions: "Why haven't more women written good 'war poems'?" I am grateful to Susan Schweik for calling attention (in *A Gulf So Deeply Cut* 293) to this passage from one of Fussell's less-familiar publications.

2. Regarding the history of the poem's critical reception, see Schweik 31–35.

3. I am puzzled by Gilbert and Gubar's statement that in using military terminology for her resistance to war and the moral causes of war, Moore "identifies completely with the forces of militarism" (*Letters* 109).

4. Similarly, Jane Cooper, who, as a young woman in the late 1940s, worked on "a book of war poems from a civilian's, a woman's, point of view," sees the definition of war spilling over into a great complex of issues: not only combat and bombings and deaths, both of combatants and of civilians, but treaties, shortages, sicknesses, aftereffects on the landscape, refugees, and feelings of guilt. Despite her youth, she writes, "I felt guilty because I had not participated in any direct way." See Cooper 36.

5. See Laurence Stapleton's study of the evolution of Moore's poetry out of her notebooks, *Marianne Moore: The Poet's Advance* (1978).

6. E. E. Cummings similarly but more cryptically announced in one of the poems of his 1935 manuscript *No Thanks*, "this mind made war / being generous / this heart could dare)" but as the poem develops the meaning seems to shift toward the idea that he "made war" by resisting war:

> (this poet made war
> whose naught and all
> sun are and moon
> come fair come foul
> he goes alone
> daring to dare
> for joy of joy)
> what stink is here
> unpoets do cry (*CP* 440–41)

Cummings, like Moore, is locating the most intense conflicts of war in the mind, not in external demands or actions of "unfools unfree" external to the self. The self is involved; poets are involved.

7. Schweik points out that H.D.'s Trilogy begins with an imaginative siting of bombed-out London as Golgotha—the place of the skull, the place of the crucifixion—

but rejects that siting, possibly because of its insistent positioning of women as passive witnesses to suffering, and moves from Golgotha to the Christmas story, thus reversing the biblical plot line. As Schweik recognizes, the biblical framework is also disrupted by mythology from other systems.

8. This verse from Revelation is the source of the sarcastic title of Paul Nash's painting *We Are Making a New World.*

9. Sitwell's assumption that Allied suffering evoked Christ's sympathetic blood is so characteristic of English-language poetry of the time that it seems self-evident. It is a continuation, of course, of the traditional rhetorical premise that God is on our side in a war—whichever side that happens to be. Rare indeed is the poem like John Betjeman's satiric "In Westminster Abbey" (written in 1940, the same year as "Still Falls the Rain") that calls attention to a larger view. The essence of Betjeman's poem, a supposed prayer uttered by a British woman making a hasty visit to church, can be clearly seen in this stanza:

> Gracious Lord, oh bomb the Germans.
>   Spare their women for Thy Sake,
> And if that is not too easy
>   We will pardon Thy Mistake.
> But, gracious Lord, whate'er shall be,
> Don't let anyone bomb me.

10. "Still Falls the Rain" would be set to music by Benjamin Britten in 1954 as Canticle III, in what Michael Oliver calls an "austerely eloquent" work and a "restatement of Britten's pacifism" (157).

11. A single B-29 raid in March 1945 killed some eighty-five thousand people in Tokyo. Michael Sherry comments, "No clear moral line . . . separated the firebombing of Japanese cities from their atomic incineration" (114). Civilian deaths in the Allied bombing of Germany and Austria came to some six hundred thousand, about ten times the number killed in England (Goldensohn, *Dismantling Glory* 27). Robert Lowell expressed outrage over the civilian deaths in the firebombing of Japan, as well as in the atomic bombing of Hiroshima and Nagasaki (Goldensohn, *Dismantling Glory* 227, quoting Lowell's correspondence).

12. Stravinsky set the word "terror," referring to the bombing of London, to the interval commonly called the *diabolus in musica,* the augmented fourth. On the use of this interval by Benjamin Britten in *War Requiem,* see chapter 10. Stravinsky composed "The Dove Descending" at the request of the compilers of *The Cambridge Hymnal,* but the anthem was not included in the published hymnal because of its difficulty. See Dickinson, "Connections between T. S. Eliot and Major Composers" 93–94. A recording of the anthem is available on *Stravinsky,* Columbia Chamber Ensemble, LP CBS SBRG 72808 (1966).

13. See Gilbert, "'Rats' Alley'" 179.

CHAPTER 9

1. The reluctance of Americans to give up the myth of the good war is demonstrated by the public outcry that arose late in the century when the Smithsonian Museum proposed to mount an exhibit about the *Enola Gay* and the atomic bombing of Japanese cities that did not guarantee to validate the action once again.

2. See Blum 6–7. Michael Sherry gives a more nuanced view but also recognizes, "The administration remained at pains to designate Germany as the greater enemy but rightly worried that many Americans, attuned to the war's racial dimensions, had different preferences" (66).

3. I am grateful to my colleague Alan Houtchens for pointing out that the threnody was not originally composed as a piece of program music—that is, with the identifier "to the Victims of Hiroshima"—but as an abstract piece. Even so, even if Penderecki's intentions were not originally directed toward commemoration of the victims of the atomic bomb, his later decision to make that linkage is itself an act of creative memorializing, in that he recognized what listeners have also recognized, that the music is peculiarly well suited to being thought of as a cry of pain and protest against that final act of the war.

4. A great deal has been written about the Vietnam Wall and the eloquence of its minimalist form. The fact that it continues to evoke outpourings of grief, often in the form of mementos left at the base of the wall or wreaths placed nearby, demonstrates the depth of cultural preoccupation with Vietnam but also with twentieth-century wars generally. The respectful silence of most visitors to the wall is itself an emblem of solemn commemoration.

5. Peter Dickinson (96) points out that the texts of two of Britten's other canticles, including T. S. Eliot's "Journey of the Magi" (set to music in 1971), were printed in the wartime volume *The Triumph of Life: Poems of Consolation for the English-Speaking World* (1943), the source where Britten actually found one of them. Sitwell's "Still Falls the Rain" was not the only one of Britten's canticles that had a connection with World War II.

6. At the same time, some poems in Cummings's *Xiape* are surprisingly direct—for example, his tribute to "geoffrey" and the *Canterbury Tales* ["honour corruption villainy holiness"].

7. The concept of the "holy war" is, of course, troublesome in itself and has been roundly condemned in the West in connection with the Muslim fatwa. It was partly because of the widespread discomfort with the concept, and also because of the historical insensitivity it displayed, that George W. Bush was so widely criticized for referring to his post-9/11 "war on terrorism" as a crusade.

8. Mark Richardson points out that the "physician's" reply that "all the nations share" a supposedly personal complaint creates a "confusion of the personal and the national": "Is [Frost] speaking for America, even speaking *as* America, in, let us say, a befuddled agrarian guise?" (60). Not only here, Richardson continues, but in other public

statements as well, Frost's "remarks about The Bomb were often provocatively whimsical, and they struck some readers as exhibiting very poor taste" (72). Richardson also makes the point that the context of militarized science within which Frost was working at this stage in his career can be seen in a number of his late poems, several of which also look back on the war and its aftermath, though not in such explicit terms as the three sonnets and "U.S. 1946 King's X."

9. Simon has stated in interviews that the song's title, which has the ring of a photo caption or the name of a painting, was taken from the caption of a photo of the Magrittes (with their dog) that he happened to see and that stayed in his mind.

10. I am indebted to Beth Alvarez for the suggestion that Simon's allusions to Christopher Street (the site of the Stonewall riots that led to gay pride and lesbian pride movements) and to black musical groups invoke indirectly the "wars" for civil rights for African Americans and gays; personal communication, April 29, 2003.

11. Another '50s R&B group, the Harptones, revitalized during the '70s, perform the background vocals in the recording. The Orioles, like their namesake baseball team, were based in Baltimore, raising the possibility that Simon may have singled out this group for reference in his song not only because they were particularly significant, as the first black performing group to record specifically for a black audience but with arrangements designed to appeal to a broader audience as well, but also because of his lifelong devotion to baseball. See http://www.artistdirect.com/music/artist/card/0;s4;s7;s5635,00.html. Naming them here generalizes, then, the reference to popular culture as a redemptive or at least comforting presence.

12. Paul Simon, notes written with Paul Zollo for the collection *Paul Simon, 1964/1993*, Warner Brothers 45354, released 1993.

CHAPTER 10

1. Not always; Hemingway, for example was not opposed to war.

2. Not all listeners agree. David Greene writes, "Owen's work is so complete that there is little for the music to add to it" (89). Owen's work is indeed complete in itself, but Britten's settings of the poems make—as artistically done settings of literary works do—a new whole.

3. The bombing of Coventry Cathedral was even more symbolically significant than my simple statement indicates. The church building was destroyed in the first heavy bombing of England in the war, on November 14, 1940 (Herbert 536). Herbert allows the importance of this first-ness to pass tacitly, but points out that even though the Luftwaffe bombers were not targeting the church, but rather nearby factories, the "desecration of this holy building" became a rallying point for determination to conquer the power that "once again threatened all that was good about Western civilization." That is, it flamed anti-German sentiment of the kind expressed in such terms as "barbaric Hun" (a phrase used by Herbert to illustrate the level of national hatred evoked). The local clergy's resolve to rebuild the cathedral, he says, "came to carry great symbolic

import for all of the nation" (537). Thus the occasion of the *Requiem*'s composition carried both religious and patriotic import.

4. Allen J. Frantzen sees the central thrust of the *Requiem* somewhat more ab-
stractly, as a rejection of the idea of sacrificial suffering that underlies justifications of
war (447).

5. I do not intend to imply, by saying the antiwar message is clear and unmistakable, that the *War Requiem* is a simple or obvious work. Far from it. For an analysis that
explores complexities and possible contradictions within the work itself as well as, more
emphatically, contradictions inherent in the rebuilt cathedral, see James D. Herbert's
"Bad Faith at Coventry." Herbert's analysis of the concluding alternation between the
tritone and a reassuringly simple but finally "self'-ironizing" F-major chord carries his
readers into coils of subtlety (560). Even Herbert, however, acknowledges that with the
first entry of the boys' choir, the juxtaposition of the choir and full orchestra, on the one
hand, to the boys' choir and harmonium, on the other, "offers all the clarity of a po-
lemic" (541).

6. Ellis 281; see also Oliver 55–58 and 157.

7. See liner notes by Christopher Palmer accompanying the recording of the *Requiem*
by the London Symphony Orchestra, CD 414384-2 and 414385-2. Owen's principles can
scarcely be defined as pacifist, since he continued to fight despite his abhorrence of the
suffering and of the very idea of pitting of one national group against another. His
poem "Sonnet (On Seeing a Piece of Our Artillery Brought into Action)" explicitly
urges that the fight against Germany be continued, apparently from a belief that there
was no other way of ending the present war, let alone any future war. It seems clear,
however, that his opposition to the war in which he was engaged and his desperate hope
to contribute to the prevention of future wars were intensifying during his final months.
On the distinction between Owen's and Britten's views, see Greene 100.

8. The linkages forged by Britten's joining his pacifism to that of Owen and of
Christianity, in its most radical sense, would also reach into the future. Derek Jarmon,
a filmmaker who made a dramatized film of the *Requiem* in 1989, was a committed
pacifist. Besides adding story line, Harmon incorporated segments of film from wars in
Africa and Cambodia that occurred between 1962 and the time he was working, or as he
stated himself, "all the wars that [had by then] erupted since Britten composed this music" (Frantzen 467, quoting Jarmon's 1989 book on his filming of the *War Requiem*).

9. An example of such an interaction, musically, is the brass fanfare motifs that
open the Dies Irae and occur as bridges during that movement (and others), especially
as the chorus sings *Tuba mirum spargens sonum*, or "the trumpet, scattering its awful
sound," quickly followed by "Bugles sang, saddening the evening air; / And bugles answered sorrowful to hear." The "bugles" have been singing, saddening the air, and an-
swering, but it is not clear which will prevail, the human bugles of war or the trumpets
announcing God's purposes. A more ironic interaction occurs in the Offertorium when
the chorus's "Sed signifer sanctus Michael repraesentet eas in lucem sanctam: Quam
olim Abrahae promisisti, et semini eius" (but let the holy standard-bearer Michael lead

them into the holy light, as Thou didst promise Abraham and his seed) is immediately followed by Owen's words "So Abram arose, and clave the wood." But in Owen's version the biblical story of divine mercy is surprisingly and bitterly interrupted by a statement that even after the angel's instructions to sacrifice the ram instead, "the old man would not so, but slew his son, / And half the seed of Europe, one by one." Yet the boys' choir blissfully follows, offering praise and prayers for the dead "as Thou didst promise Abraham and his seed." Here, the informed voices of twentieth-century soldiers and observers of war seem to prevail over the supposed voices of the eternal.

10. In a performance of the *War Requiem* in Atlanta in the late 1980s, the entrance of the boys' choir, which had been singing at the rear of the hall, also contributed its own note of drama and beauty. At the Libera Me, the children filed up the two side aisles of the hall in deep red robes with white collars that seemed almost to spotlight their faces: faces of a beautiful racial diversity. The idea of reconciliation and peacemaking promoted in the work itself was accentuated visually.

11. This is not to say that earlier generations had not found their own new poetry difficult. Difficulty is a relative matter. Still, the fractured surface of poetic language in the experimental practice of modernist poets—like the fractured planes of paintings by Cézanne and experimental modernist painters who followed—did step up the level of innovation and the challenge to ordinary readers and viewers.

12. Hedges—whose *New York Times* press credentials were stripped from him during the First Gulf War because he tried to evade U.S. military control and censorship—does not shrink from applying his call for recognition to our own time and our own righteous cause: "We mourn the victims of the World Trade Center attack. Their pictures cover subway walls. We mourn the firefighters, as well we should. But we are blind to those whom we and our allies in the Middle East have crushed or whose rights have been ignored for decades. They seem not to count." Before wars begin, he points out, the "first people silenced" are those who "question the state's lust and need for war" (15). The first victim is language.

13. Auden deleted the stanza beginning "All I have is a voice" from "September 1, 1939" before he finally deleted the poem in its entirety from his collected works, but the lines are still printed in many anthologies.

Bibliography

Anderson, Frederick, ed. *A Pen Warmed-Up in Hell: Mark Twain in Protest.* New York: Harper and Row, 1972.

Anderson, Jervis. *This Was Harlem: A Cultural Portrait, 1900–1950.* New York: Farrar Straus Giroux, 1981.

Andrews, Maxene, and Bill Gilbert. *Over Here, Over There: The Andrews Sisters and the USO Stars in World War II.* New York: Kensington, 1993.

Auden, W. H. *Collected Poems.* Ed. Edward Mendelson. London: Faber and Faber, 1976.

———. *Collected Poetry.* New York: Random House, 1945.

Bäckman, Sven. *Tradition Transformed: Studies in the Poetry of Wilfred Owen.* Lund: LiberLääromedel/Gleerup, 1979.

Barker, Pat. *The Eye in the Door.* New York: Penguin, 1995.

Beaumont, Roger. *War, Chaos, and History.* Westport, Ct.: Praeger, 1994.

Beidler, Philip. *The Good War's Greatest Hits: World War II and American Remembering.* Athens: U of Georgia P, 1998.

Bennett, Betty T., ed. *British War Poetry in the Age of Romanticism, 1793–1815.* New York: Garland, 1976.

Bentley, James, ed. *Some Corner of a Foreign Field: Poetry of the Great War.* London: Little, Brown, 1992.

Bergreen, Laurence. *As Thousands Cheer: The Life of Irving Berlin.* New York: Viking, 1990.

Binyon, Laurence. *The Cause: Poems of the War.* Boston: Houghton Mifflin, 1917.

Bishop, Elizabeth. *Poems. North and South—A Cold Spring.* Boston: Houghton Mifflin, 1955.

Bluem, A. William. *Documentary in American Television: Form, Function, Method.* New York: Hastings House, 1965.

Blum, John Morton. *V Was for Victory: Politics and American Culture during World War II.* New York: Harcourt Brace, 1976.

Blunden, Edmund. *Selected Poems.* Ed. Robyn Marsack. Manchester: Carcanet New Press, 1982.

Bly, Robert. "The Work of Louis Simpson." *Fifties* 1 (1958): 22–25.

Booth, Allyson. *Postcards from the Trenches: Negotiating the Space between Modernism and the First World War.* New York: Oxford UP, 1996.

Boxwell, D. A. "The (M)Other Battle of World War One: The Maternal Politics of Pacifism in Rose Macaulay's *Non-Combatants and Others.*" *Tulsa Studies in Women's Literature* 12 (1993): 85–101.

Brittain, Vera. *Poems of the War and After.* New York: Macmillan, 1934.

——. *Verses of a V.A.D.* Foreword by Marie Connor Leighton. London: Erskine Mac-Donald, 1918.

Britten, Benjamin. *War Requiem.* London: Boosey and Hawkes, 1962.

——. *War Requiem,* Opus 66. Benjamin Britten Conducting the Bach Choir, London Symphony Orchestra Chorus, Highgate School Choir, Melos Ensemble, and London Symphony Orchestra. With Dietrich Fischer-Dieskau (baritone), Peter Pears (tenor), Simon Preston (organist), and Galina Vishnevskaya (soprano). CD1 414384-2, CD2 414385-2, 1963, remastered 1985.

Brooke, Rupert. *The Collected Poems.* 1918. 4th ed., rev. With memoir by Edward Marsh and introduction by Gavin Ewart. London: Sidgwick and Jackson, 1987.

Brooks, Gwendolyn. *Selected Poems.* New York: Harper and Row, 1963.

Brown, Sterling A. *Collected Poems.* Ed. Michael S. Harper. Evanston: Triquarterly Books/Northwestern UP, 1996.

Brown, Terence. *Louis MacNeice: Sceptical Vision.* Dublin: Gill and MacMillan, 1975.

Bryant, Marsha. *Auden and Documentary in the 1930s.* Charlottesville: UP of Virginia, 1997.

Butterworth, Neil. *The Music of Aaron Copland.* Preface by André Previn. London: Toccata, 1985.

Caesar, Adrian. *Taking It Like a Man: Suffering, Sexuality, and the War Poets Brooke, Sassoon, Owen, Graves.* Manchester: Manchester UP, 1993.

Callan, Edward. *Auden: A Carnival of Intellect.* New York: Oxford UP, 1983.

Campbell, James. "Combat Gnosticism: The Ideology of First World War Poetry Criticism." *New Literary History* 30.1 (1999): 203–15.

Cannadine, David. "War and Death, Grief and Mourning in Modern Britain." In *Mirrors of Mortality: Studies in the Social History of Death.* Ed. T. Joachim Whaley. London: Europa, 1981. 187–242.

Causey, Andrew. *Paul Nash.* Oxford: Oxford UP, 1980.

Chatfield, Charles. *For Peace and Justice: Pacifism in America, 1914–1941.* Knoxville: U of Tennessee P, 1971.

Ciardi, John. *Collected Poems.* Ed. Edward M. Cifelli. Fayetteville: U of Arkansas P, 1997.

Cohen, Milton A. "Fatal Symbiosis: Modernism and the First World War." In Quinn and Trout, *The Literature of the Great War Reconsidered.* 159–71.

Cooke, Miriam. *Women and the War Story.* Berkeley: U of California P, 1996.

Cooper, Jane. *Maps and Windows: Poems.* New York: Macmillan, 1974.

Cork, Richard. *A Bitter Truth: Avant-Garde Art and the Great War.* New Haven: Yale UP, 1994.

Costello, Bonnie. *Marianne Moore: Imaginary Possessions.* Cambridge: Harvard UP, 1981.

Cowell, Henry, and Sidney Cowell. *Charles Ives and His Music.* New York: Oxford UP, 1955.

Cox, C. B. "The Poetry of Louis Simpson." In Lazer, *On Louis Simpson.* 193–208.

Cummings, E. E. *Complete Poems, 1904–1962.* Ed. George J. Firmage. New York: Liveright, 1991.

Desmond, E. S. Maxwell. "Louis MacNeice and the 'Low Dishonest Decade.'" *Modernist Studies* 1 (1974): 55–69.

DeVoto, Mark. "'Wozzeck' in Context." In *Wozzeck,* Opera Guide Series No. 42. Series editor Nicholas John. New York: Riverrun, 1990.

Dickey, James. *The Whole Motion. Collected Poems, 1945–1992.* Hanover, N.H.: UP of New England, Wesleyan UP, 1992.

Dickinson, Peter. "Connections between T. S. Eliot and Major Composers: Igor Stravinsky and Benjamin Britten." In *T. S. Eliot and Our Turning World.* Ed. Jewel Spears Brooker. New York: St. Martin's, 2001. 91–99.

Dimock, Wai Chee. "Non-Newtonian Time: Robert Lowell, Roman History, Vietnam War." *American Literature* 74 (2002): 911–31.

Doolittle, Hilda [H.D.]. *Collected Poems, 1912–1944.* Ed. Louis L. Martz. New York: New Directions, 1983.

Duroselle, Jean-Baptiste. *From Wilson to Roosevelt: Foreign Policy of the United States, 1913–1945.* Trans. Nancy Lyman Roelker. New York: Harper and Row, 1963.

Eberhart, Richard. *Collected Poems, 1930–1976.* New York: Oxford UP, 1976.

Eby, Cecil D. *The Road to Armageddon: The Martial Spirit in English Popular Literature, 1870–1914.* Durham: Duke UP, 1987.

Eksteins, Modris. *Rites of Spring: The Great War and the Birth of the Modern Age.* Boston: Houghton Mifflin, 1989.

Eliot, T. S. *The Complete Poems and Plays, 1909–1950.* New York: Harcourt, Brace and World, 1962.

Ellis, Jim. "Strange Meeting: Wilfred Owen, Benjamin Britten, Derek Jarmon, and the *War Requiem.*" In *The Work of Opera: Genre, Nationhood, and Sexual Difference.* Ed. I. Richard Dellamora and Daniel Fischlin. New York: Columbia UP, 1997. 277–96.

Ewart, Gavin. Introduction to Rupert Brooke, *The Collected Poems.* 4th ed., rev. London: Sidgwick and Jackson, 1987.

———. *Selected Poems, 1933–1993.* London: Hutchinson, 1996.

Feder, Stuart. *Charles Ives, "My Father's Song": A Psychoanalytic Biography.* New Haven: Yale UP, 1992.

Ferguson, Niall. *The Pity of War.* New York: Basic Books, 1999.

Fogel, Daniel Mark. *Covert Relations: James Joyce, Virginia Woolf, and Henry James.* Charlottesville: UP of Virginia, 1990.

Foulkes, A. P. *Literature and Propaganda.* London: Methuen, 1983.

Frantzen, Allen J. "Tears for Abraham: The Chester Play of Abraham and Isaac and

Antisacrifice in Works by Wilfred Owen, Benjamin Britten, and Derek Jarman." *Journal of Medieval and Early Modern Studies* 31 (2001): 445–76.

Freeman, John. *Collected Poems.* London: Macmillan, 1928.

Frith, Simon. "Towards an Aesthetic of Popular Music." In Leppert and McClary, *Music and Society.* 133–50.

Frost, Robert. *Complete Poems of Robert Frost.* New York: Holt, Rinehart and Winston, 1949.

Fussell, Paul. *The Great War and Modern Memory.* London: Oxford UP, 1975.

———. *Thank God for the Atom Bomb and Other Essays.* New York: Summit Books, 1988.

———. *Wartime: Understanding and Behavior in the Second World War.* New York: Oxford UP, 1989.

———, ed. *The Norton Book of Modern War.* New York: W. W. Norton, 1991.

Giddings, Robert. *The War Poets.* New York: Orion Books, 1988.

Gilbert, Sandra M. "'Rats' Alley': The Great War, Modernism, and the (Anti)Pastoral Elegy." *New Literary History* 30 (1999): 179–201.

———. "Soldier's Heart: Literary Men, Literary Women, and the Great War." In Higonnet et al., *Behind the Lines.* 197–226.

Gilbert, Sandra M., and Susan Gubar. *Letters from the Front.* Vol. 3 of *No Man's Land: The Place of the Woman Writer in the Twentieth Century.* New Haven: Yale UP, 1994.

———. *Sexchanges.* Vol. 2 of *No Man's Land: The Place of the Woman Writer in the Twentieth Century.* New Haven: Yale UP, 1989.

Goldberg, Jonathan. *Willa Cather and Others.* Durham: Duke UP, 2001.

Goldensohn, Lorrie. *Dismantling Glory: Twentieth-Century Soldier Poetry.* New York: Columbia UP, 2003.

———. *Elizabeth Bishop: The Biography of a Poetry.* New York: Columbia UP, 1992.

Goldman, Dorothy, ed. *Women and World War I: The Written Response.* New York: St. Martin's, 1993.

Gopnik, Adam. "The Big One: Historians Rethink the War to End All Wars." *New Yorker,* August 23, 2004, 78–85.

Graves, Robert. *Good-bye to All That.* 1929. 2nd ed., rev. New York: Doubleday , 1957.

Gray, Yohma. "The Poetry of Louis Simpson." In Lazer, *On Louis Simpson.* 173–92.

Greene, David B. "Britten's *War Requiem:* The End of Religious Music." *Soundings* 83.1 (spring 2000): 89–100.

Gubar, Susan. "'This Is My Rifle, This Is My Gun': World War II and the Blitz on Women." In Higonnet et al., *Behind the Lines.* 227–59.

Gussow, Adam. *Seems Like Murder Here: Southern Violence and the Blues Tradition.* Chicago: U of Chicago P, 2002.

Hamm, Charles. "Simon and Garfunkel." *New Grove Dictionary of American Music.* London: Macmillan, 1986.

———. *Yesterdays: Popular Song in America.* New York: W. W. Norton, 1979.

Hannah, James, ed. *The Great War Reader.* College Station: Texas A&M UP, 2000.

Harbord, R. E., ed. *The Readers' Guide to Rudyard Kipling's Work.* Vol. 2. Canterbury, Eng.: Elvy and Gibbs, 1969.

Harder, Worth Travis. *A Certain Order: The Development of Herbert Read's Theory of Poetry.* The Hague: Mouton, 1971.

Hardy, Thomas. *Complete Poems.* Ed. James Gibson. London: Macmillan, 1976.

Harrison, Charles. *English Art and Modernism, 1900–1939.* 2nd ed. New Haven: Yale UP, 1994.

Hart, Henry. "James Dickey: Journey to War." *Southern Review* 36.2 (spring 2000): 348–77.

Hatcher, John. *Laurence Binyon: Poet, Scholar of East and West.* Oxford: Clarendon Press, 1995.

Hedges, Chris. *War Is a Force That Gives Us Meaning.* New York: Public Affairs, 2002.

Hemingway, Ernest. *A Farewell to Arms.* 1929. New York: Collier Books, 1986.

Henderson, Mary H. J. *In War and Peace: Songs of a Scotswoman.* London: Erskine Mac-Donald, 1918.

Herbert, James D. "Bad Faith at Coventry: Spence's Cathedral and Britten's *War Requiem.*" *Critical Inquiry* 25 (spring 1999): 535–65.

Hewison, Robert. *Under Siege: Literary Life in London, 1939–1945.* London: Weidenfeld and Nicolson, 1977.

Hibberd, Dominic. *Wilfred Owen: A New Biography.* Chicago: Ivan R. Dee, 2003.

Hicklin, Thomas A. "Methods for Controlling Combat Stress Evolving over Time." *Psychiatric Annals* 33.11 (November 2003): 720–24.

Higonnet, Margaret R., ed. *Lines of Fire: Women Writers of World War I.* New York: Penguin, 1999.

———. *Nurses at the Front: Writing the Wounds of the Great War.* With excerpts from Ellen N. La Motte, *The Backwash of War,* 1916, and Mary Borden, *The Forbidden Zone,* 1929. Boston: Northeastern UP, 2001.

Higonnet, Margaret R., Jane Jenson, Sonya Michel, and Margaret Collins Weitz, eds. *Behind the Lines: Gender and the Two World Wars.* New Haven and London: Yale UP, 1987.

Hochschild, Adam. *King Leopold's Ghost: A Story of Greed, Terror, and Heroism in Colonial Africa.* Boston: Houghton Mifflin, 1998.

Houtchens, Alan, and Janis P. Stout. "'The dreadful winnowing-fan': Rhetoric of War in Edward Elgar's *The Spirit of England.*" *Choral Journal* 44 (April 2004): 9–19.

———. "'Scarce Heard amidst the Guns Below': Intertextuality and Meaning in Charles Ives's War Songs." *Journal of Musicology* 15 (1997): 64–95.

Huggett, Frank E. *Goodnight Sweetheart: Songs and Memories of the Second World War.* London: W. H. Allen, 1979.

Hummer, T. R. "Revising the Poetry Wars: Louis Simpson's Assault on the Poetic." In Lazer, *On Louis Simpson.* 334–46.

Hynes, Samuel. *A War Imagined: The First World War and English Culture.* New York: Atheneum, 1991.

Ignatieff, Michael. *The Warrior's Honor: Ethnic War and the Modern Conscience.* New York: Metropolitan Books, 1997.

Ives, Charles E. *Essays before a Sonata, The Majority, and Other Writings.* Ed. Howard Boatwright. New York: W. W. Norton, 1962.

———. *Memos.* Ed. John Kirkpatrick. New York: W. W. Norton, 1972.

———. *Nine Songs.* New York: Peer International, 1956.

———. *114 Songs.* Redding, Conn.: [the composer], 1922.

Ivie, Robert L. "Cold War Motives and the Rhetorical Metaphor." In *Cold War Rhetoric: Strategy, Metaphor, and Ideology.* Ed. Martin J. Medhurst, Robert L. Ivie, Philip Wander, and Robert L. Scott. Rev. ed. East Lansing: Michigan State UP, 1997. 71–79.

———. "Images of Savagery in American Justifications for War." *Communication Monographs* 47 (1980): 279–94.

Jackson, Ada. *Behold the Jew.* New York: Macmillan, 1944.

Jarrell, Randall. *The Complete Poems.* New York: Farrar, Straus, and Giroux, 1969.

Jason, Philip K. *Fourteen Landing Zones: Approaches to Vietnam War Literature.* Iowa City: U of Iowa P, 1991.

Johnston, John H. *English Poetry of the First World War: A Study in the Evolution of Lyric and Narrative Form.* Princeton: Princeton UP, 1964.

Kaye, Richard A. "'A Splendid Readiness for Death': T. S. Eliot, the Homosexual Cult of St. Sebastian, and World War I." *Modernism/Modernity* 6.2 (1999): 107–34.

Kennedy, Michael. "Elgar the Edwardian." In *Elgar Studies.* Ed. Raymond Monk. Brookfield, Vt.: Scolar Press, 1990. 107–17.

Khan, Nosheen. *Women's Poetry of the First World War.* Lexington: UP of Kentucky, 1988.

Kingston, Victoria. *Simon and Garfunkel: The Definitive Biography.* London: Sidgwick and Jackson, 1996.

Kipling, Rudyard. *Rudyard Kipling's Verse.* Definitive ed. Garden City: Doubleday, 1940.

Kirkpatrick, John. *A Temporary Mimeographed Catalogue of the Music Manuscripts and Related Materials of Charles Edward Ives.* New Haven: Library of the Yale School of Music, 1960.

Larkin, Philip. *The Whitsun Weddings.* London: Faber and Faber, 1964.

Layton, Lynne. "Vera Brittain's Testament(s)." In Higonnet et al., *Behind the Lines.* 70–83.

Lazer, Hank, ed. *On Louis Simpson: Depths beyond Happiness.* Ann Arbor: U of Michigan P, 1988.

Leed, Eric J. *No Man's Land: Combat and Identity in World War I.* Cambridge: Cambridge UP, 1979.

Leppert, Richard, and Susan McClary, eds. *Music and Society.* New York: Cambridge UP, 1987.

Levenson, Michael. "Does *The Waste Land* Have a Politics?" *Modernism/Modernity* 6.3 (1999): 1–14.

Lindquist, Sven. *A History of Bombing.* Trans. Linda Haverty Rugg. New York: New Press, 2001.

Loesser, Frank. *The Frank Loesser Songbook,* with preface by Richard Rodgers and text by Cynthia Lindsay. New York: Simon and Schuster, 1971.

Lowell, Amy. *Complete Poetical Works.* Boston: Houghton Mifflin, 1955.

Lowell, Robert. *Poems, 1938–1949.* London: Faber and Faber, 1950.

Luftig, Stacey, ed. *The Paul Simon Companion: Four Decades of Commentary.* New York: Schirmer Books/Simon and Schuster, 1997.

Macaulay, Rose. *Non-Combatants and Others.* 1916; rpt. London, Methuen, 1986.

———. *Three Days.* New York: E. P. Dutton, 1919.

MacNeice, Louis. *Collected Poems, 1925–1948.* New York: Oxford UP, 1949.

MacPhail, Sir Andrew. "John McCrae: An Essay in Character." In McCrae, *In Flanders Fields.* 58–83.

Martin, W. R. "Bugles, Trumpets, and Drums: English Poetry and the Wars." *Mosaic* 13 (1979): 31–48.

Martz, Louis L. Introduction to H.D., *Collected Poems, 1912–1944.* New York: New Directions, 1983.

McCrae, John. *In Flanders Fields and Other Poems.* New York and Toronto: Hodder and Stoughton, 1919.

McKinnon, William T. *Apollo's Blended Dream: A Study of the Poetry of Louis MacNeice.* London: Oxford UP, 1971.

McNamara, Robert S., with Brian VanDeMark. *In Retrospect: The Tragedy and Lessons of Vietnam.* New York: Public Affairs, 1995.

McNamara, Robert S., and James G. Blight. *Wilson's Ghost: Reducing the Risk of Conflict, Killing, and Catastrophe in the Twenty-first Century.* New York: Public Affairs, 2001.

Medina, Joyce. *Cézanne and Modernism: The Poetics of Painting.* Albany: State U of New York P, 1995.

Meynell, Alice. *The Poems of Alice Meynell.* Complete ed. London: Oxford UP, 1940.

Millay, Edna St. Vincent. *Collected Poems.* Ed. Norma Millay. New York: HarperCollins, 1956.

———. *The Murder of Lidice.* New York: Harper and Brothers, 1942.

Miller, Alice Duer. *The White Cliffs.* New York: Coward-McCann, 1940.

Moeyes, Paul. "Georgian Poetry's False Dawn (A Reassessment of Rupert Brooke: His Poetry and Personality)." *Neophilologus* 75 (1991): 456–69.

Monroe, Harriet, and Alice Corbin Henderson, eds. *The New Poetry: An Anthology.* New York: Macmillan, 1917.

Moore, Jerrold Northrop, ed. *Edward Elgar: Letters of a Lifetime.* Oxford: Clarendon Press, 1990.

Moore, Marianne. *The Complete Poems of Marianne Moore.* New York: Macmillan, 1967.

Moran, Robert. *Louis Simpson.* New York: Twayne, 1972.

Murdoch, Brian. *Fighting Songs and Warring Words: Popular Lyrics of Two World Wars.* New York: Routledge, 1990.

Norgate, Paul. "Wilfred Owen and the Soldier Poets." *Review of English Studies* 40 (1989): 516–30.

Norris, Margot. *Writing War in the Twentieth Century.* Charlottesville: UP of Virginia, 2000.

Oliver, Michael. *Benjamin Britten.* London: Phaidon, 1996.

O'Neill, Michael, and Gareth Reeves. *Auden, MacNeice, Spender: The Thirties Poetry.* New York: St. Martin's, 1992.

Owen, Wilfred. *Collected Letters.* Ed. Harold Owen and John Bell. London: Oxford UP, 1967.

———. *The Complete Poems and Fragments.* Vol. 1: *The Poems.* Ed. Jon Stallworthy. London: Chatto and Windus; Oxford: Oxford UP, 1983.

Palmer, Christopher. Liner notes for Benjamin Britten, *War Requiem,* recorded by the

London Symphony Orchestra, the Bach Choir, London Symphony Orchestra Chorus, Highgate School Choir, the Melos Ensemble, and Simon Preston, organ, with soloists Galina Vishnevskaya, Peter Pears, and Dietrich Fischer-Dieskau. Benjamin Britten conducting. CD 414383-2 and 414385-2.

Perkins, David. *A History of Modern Poetry: From the 1890s to Pound, Eliot, and Yeats.* Cambridge: Harvard UP, 1976.

Perlmutter, David D. *Visions of War: Picturing Warfare from the Stone Age to the Cyber Age.* New York: St. Martin's, 1999.

Perone, James E. *Paul Simon: A Bio-Bibliography.* Westport, Conn.: Greenwood, 2000.

Peter, John. "A New Interpretation of the *Waste Land.*" *Essays in Criticism* 2 (1952): 242–67.

Phillips, Terry. "The Self in Conflict: May Sinclair and the Great War." In Quinn and Trout, *The Literature of the Great War Reconsidered.* 55–66.

Pope, Jessie. *War Poems.* London: Grant Richards, 1915.

Porter, Katherine Anne. *The Collected Essays and Occasional Writings.* Boston: Houghton Mifflin/Seymour Lawrence, 1970.

Postgate, Margaret. *Poems.* London: George Allen and Unwin, 1918.

Pound, Ezra. *The Cantos.* London: Faber and Faber, 1981.

———. *Personae: The Collected Poems.* New York: New Directions, 1926.

Pratt, Ray. *Rhythm and Resistance: The Political Uses of American Popular Music.* 2nd ed. Washington, D.C.: Smithsonian Institution Press, 1994.

Prescott, John F. *In Flanders Fields: The Story of John McCrae.* Erin, Ontario: Boston Mills Press, 1985.

Pugsley, Christopher. *Gallipoli: The New Zealand Story.* Birkenhead, Aukland: Reed Books, 1998.

Quinn, Patrick J. "Siegfried Sassoon: The Legacy of the Great War." In Quinn and Trout, *The Literature of the Great War Reconsidered.* 230–38.

Quinn, Patrick J., and Steven Trout, eds. *The Literature of the Great War Reconsidered: Beyond Modern Memory.* New York: Palgrave, 2001.

Read, Herbert. *Annals of Innocence and Experience.* 1940. Rev. ed., London: Faber and Faber, 1946.

———. *Collected Poems.* London: Faber and Faber, 1966.

———. *The Innocent Eye.* New York: Henry Holt, 1947.

Reed, Henry. *Collected Poems.* Ed. Jon Stallworthy. Oxford: Oxford UP, 1991.

Reilly, Catherine, ed. *Scars upon My Heart: Women's Poetry and Verse of the First World War.* Preface by Judith Kazantzis. London: Virago, 1981.

Richardson, Mark. "Frost and the Cold War: A Look at the Later Poetry." In *Roads Not Taken: Rereading Robert Frost.* Ed. Earl J. Wilcox and Jonathan N. Barron. Columbia: U of Missouri P, 2000. 55–77.

Robin, Ron. "'A Foothold in Europe': The Aesthetics and Politics of American War Cemeteries in Western Europe." *Journal of American Studies* 29 (April 1995): 55–72.

Roethke, Theodore. *Collected Poems.* New York: Anchor/Doubleday, 1975.

Rolfe, Edwin. *Collected Poems.* Ed. Cary Nelson and Jefferson Hendricks. Urbana: U of Illinois P, 1993.

Rukeyser, Muriel. *Beast in View.* Garden City, N.Y.: Doubleday, Doran, 1946.

Sackville, Margaret. *Collected Poems of Lady Margaret Sackville.* London: Martin Secker, 1939.

Sassoon, Siegfried. *Diaries, 1920–1922.* Ed. Rupert Hart-Davis. London: Faber and Faber, 1981.

———. *Siegfried's Journey.* New York: Viking, 1946.

———. *The War Poems of Siegfried Sassoon.* Ed. Rupert Hart-Davis. London: Faber and Faber, 1983.

Schneede, Uwe M. *René Magritte: Life and Work.* 1973. Trans. W. Walter Jaffe. Woodbury, N.Y.: Barron's, 1982.

Schulman, Grace. *Marianne Moore: The Poetry of Engagement.* Urbana: U of Illinois P, 1986.

Schweik, Susan. *A Gulf So Deeply Cut: American Women Poets and the Second World War.* Madison: U of Wisconsin P, 1991.

Shale, John H., Christopher M. Shale, and Jayne D. Shale. "Denial Often Key in Psychological Adaptation to Combat Situations." *Psychiatric Annals* 33.11 (November 2003): 725–29.

Shapiro, Karl. *Collected Poems, 1940–1978.* New York: Random House, 1978.

———. *The Younger Son.* Chapel Hill: Algonquin Books, 1988.

Sherry, Michael S. *In the Shadow of War: The United States since the 1930s.* New Haven: Yale UP, 1995.

Sherry, Vincent. *The Great War and the Language of Modernism.* Oxford: Oxford UP, 2003.

Silkin, Jon, ed. *The Penguin Book of First World War Poetry.* 2nd ed. London: Penguin, 1981.

Simpson, Louis. *Collected Poems.* New York: Paragon House, 1988.

Spear, Hilda D. *Remembering, We Forget: A Background Study to the Poetry of the First World War.* London: Davis-Poynter, 1979.

Stallworthy, Jon. *Wilfred Owen.* Oxford: Oxford UP, 1974.

Stapleton, Laurence. *Marianne Moore: The Poet's Advance.* Princeton: Princeton UP, 1978.

Stevens, Wallace. *Collected Poems.* New York: Knopf, 1969.

Stitt, Peter. "Louis Simpson: In Search of the American Self." In Lazer, *On Louis Simpson.* 347–87.

Stokesbury, Leon, ed. *Articles of War: A Collection of American Poetry about World War II.* Introduction by Paul Fussell. Fayetteville: U of Arkansas P, 1990.

Stout, Janis P., ed. *A Calendar of the Letters of Willa Cather.* Lincoln: U of Nebraska P, 2002.

Taggard, Genevieve. *Calling Western Union.* New York: Harper and Brothers, 1936.

Tate, Trudi. *Modernism, History, and the First World War.* Manchester: Manchester UP, 1998.

Taylor, Edmond. *The Fall of the Dynasties: The Collapse of the Old Order, 1905–1922.* Garden City, N.Y.: Doubleday, 1963.

Theatre Workshop, Charles Chilton, and the Members of the Original Cast. *Oh What a Lovely War.* London: Methuen, 1965.

Torczyner, Harry. *Magritte: Ideas and Images.* Trans. Richard Miller. New York: Harry N. Abrams, 1977.

Traupman, John C. *The New College Latin and English Dictionary.* Rev. and enl. ed., New York: Bantam Books, 1995.

Trout, Steven. *Memorial Fictions: Willa Cather and the First World War.* Lincoln: U of Nebraska P, 2002.

Tuchman, Barbara. *The Guns of August.* New York: Macmillan, 1962.

Tylee, Claire M. *The Great War and Women's Consciousness: Images of Militarism and Womanhood in Women's Writings, 1914–64.* Iowa City: U of Iowa P, 1990.

Vandiver, Frank E. Foreword to Hannah, *The Great War Reader.* xvii–xxii.

Walsh, Jeffrey. *American War Literature: 1914 to Vietnam.* New York: St. Martin's, 1982.

Wilkinson, Glenn R. "Literary Images of Vicarious Warfare: British Newspapers and the Origin of the First World War, 1899–1914." In Quinn and Trout, *The Literature of the Great War Reconsidered.* 24–34.

Williams, Michael. "Wilfred Owen: A Poet Re-Institutionalised." *Critical Survey* 2 (1990): 194–202.

Wolff, Janet. "The Ideology of Autonomous Art." In Leppert and McClary, *Music and Society.* 1–12.

Index